3 1235 00245 8474

S0-ATD-270

CHILTON'S *New* Repair and Tune-Up Guide

Bultaco
Montesa
OSSA

ILLUSTRATED

629.28775
BuL
1965-1972

6.2SP

WASHOE COUNTY LIBRARY
RENO, NEVADA

Prepared by the

Automotive Editorial Department

Chilton Book Company

Chilton Way
Radnor, Pa. 19089
215—687-8200

editor-in-chief **JOHN D. KELLY;** managing editor **JOHN H. WEISE, S.A.E.;** assistant managing editor **PETER J. MEYER;** senior editor, motorcycles **MICHAEL S. YAMPOLSKY;** editor **JOSEPH F. PELLICCIOTTI;** author **JAMES H. JOHNSON**

Member

Motorcycle
Industry
Council

CHILTON BOOK COMPANY   RADNOR, PENNSYLVANIA

629.827
C437

Copyright © 1974 by Chilton Book Company
First Edition
All rights reserved
Published in Radnor, Pa. by Chilton Book Company
and simultaneously in Ontario, Canada,
by Thomas Nelson & Sons, Ltd.
Manufactured in the United States of America

Library of Congress Cataloging in Publication Data

Chilton Book Company. Automotive Editorial Dept.
  Chilton's new repair and tune-up guide: Bultaco,
Montesa, Ossa.

  1. Bultaco motorcycle.   2. Montesa motorcycle.
3. Ossa motorcycle.   I. Title.   II. Title: Bultaco,
Montesa, Ossa.
TL448.B8C46   1974   629.28'7'75   74-4029
ISBN 0-8019-5817-2
ISBN 0-8019-5888-1 (pbk.)

ACKNOWLEDGMENTS

Devon Honda
Devon, Pa.

Motorfix
Mountain Top, Pa.

Mark Skiro
Mountain Top, Pa.

Montesa Motors, Inc.
Los Angeles, Calif.

Cemoto East
Schenectady, New York

Yankee Motor Corporation
Schenectady, New York

Although the information in this guide is based on industry sources and is complete as possible at the time of
publication, the possibility exists that the manufacturer
made later changes which could not be included here.
While striving for total accuracy, Chilton Book Company
cannot assume responsibility for any errors, changes, or
omissions that may occur in the compilation of this data.

Contents

1 · Introduction

Responding to the need for reliable, inexpensive transportation in their country, the three major Spanish factories, Bultaco, Montesa, and Ossa, committed themselves to the production of two-stroke, single-cylinder motorcycles which would provide their owners with a maximum of performance and handling at a minimum cost.

Gradually refining the original designs, these companies fielded competition machines in road races and motocross events throughout Europe, scoring many significant successes.

While motorcycle factories in other parts

Ginger Malloy straightens out the corners during the 1967 Belgian Grand Prix on his works Bultaco 250 cc racer

F. X. Bulto, father of the Bultaco, puts one of his babies through its paces

1

of the world were turning out highly complex designs, the Spanish factories retained the relative simplicity of the two-stroke single, and further refined the chassis to set new standards of handling.

For the past several years, all of the factories have concentrated upon dirt machines, especially Trials bikes. Because of their light weight, broad power bands, and excellent steering geometry, these Spanish motorcycles have dominated the international trials scene and also have won great favor with the casual trail rider who requires a high quality, low maintenance motorcycle.

This Chilton guide is constructed so that descriptions, procedures, and specifications can be easily located, thus allowing experienced mechanics to isolate only the information they will find useful, and yet provide the inexperienced mechanic with background data to further expand his understanding of his machine. Detailed operational descriptions are given whenever possible.

To use this Guide properly, each operation must be approached logically and the recommended procedures read thoroughly before actually beginning the work. Cleanliness is an item that cannot be overstressed and will be emphasized repeatedly throughout the text.

Undoubtedly, many readers will find it necessary or desirable to perform much of the repair work needed on their machines themselves. An important point to remember is that patience and a careful approach are just as important as basic mechanical aptitude. These machines are very simple in design and chances are that if you can understand how they work, you can fix them when something goes wrong.

Bultaco Model Listing

STREET LEGAL MODELS

Mercurio	Campera
125	Mk 1 (4-speed)
175	Mk 2 (5-speed)
200	Matador
El Tigre	Mk 1, 200 (4-speed)
200	Mk 2, 250 (4-speed)
250	Mk 3, 250 (5-speed)

Mk 4, 250 (5-speed)	El Montadero
Mk 5, 250	Mk 1
"SD" 250	Mk 2
Metralla	Sherpa T
Mk 1, 200	Mk 1
Mk 2, 200	Mk 2
Mk 3, 250	Mk 3
Lobito	Mk 4
Mk 1	Alpina
Mk 2, 100/125	125
Mk 3, 100/125	175
Mk 4, 125/175	250
Mk 5, 125/175	350

RACING MODELS

Lobito	Mk 3, 250
AK 100	Mk 4, 250 "A"
Sherpa S	and "E"
Mk 1	Mk 5, 125/250/350
Mk 2	Astro, 250
Mk 3, S100	El Bandito
Mk 3, 125	Mk 1, 350
Mk 3, 175	Mk 2, 350
Mk 3, 200	Mk 3, 360
Pursang	TSS
Mk 1, 250	Mk 1, 125/250
Mk 2, 250	Mk 2, 125/250/350

Montesa Model Listing

Impala Sport	Cota 247
Impala	LaCross 66/67 250
Commando 175	Scorpion 250
Kenya	Sport 250
Cota 25	Cota 123
250 Trial	Cappra 250 MX
Texas	King Scorpion 250
Impala-Cross 175	Cappra 360 GP
Impala-Cross 250	Cappra 250 Five
Enduro 175	Cappra 360 GP
Sport 250	Cappra 360 DS
Cappra 250 MX	Cappra 250 GP

Ossa Model Listing

Pioneer	Plonker
Stiletto	Wildfire

2 · Maintenance

Proper maintenance always pays off in increased reliability and performance, but an extra dividend can be had if you approach the machine's needs with the proper attitude. It's very easy to merely lube the chain, adjust the brakes and ride off. But, if you stay aware and actually take notice of what you are doing, you can gain a sensitivity toward the machine and know *beforehand* when something is wearing out or needs attention.

When you encounter a frustrated rider with a seized engine, nine times out of ten he'll tell you that the engine suddenly froze up—just like that! He doesn't mention that the combustion chamber is stuffed with carbon because he probably isn't aware of it; he may swear to have adjusted the carburetor and set the plugs, points and timing right on schedule, and probably did, but he certainly never took notice of the engine's subtle changes that would have told him something was going awry.

Here in America, manufacturers of mechanical devices (especially the automobile companies) advertise their products to be practically maintenance free. While it is true that the number of maintenance operations have been reduced and maintenance intervals have been lengthened, it becomes all the more important that necessary services be carried out with great care. Unfortunately, exactly the opposite is true in most cases, and a drive-it-till-it-breaks attitude prevails.

However unfortunate this may be to the automobile driver's bank balance, one who approaches motorcycle maintenance in the same manner is risking a great deal more than money. With a car, unless a wheel falls off, a mechanical failure does not affect basic vehicular stability. Motorcycles, however, tend to fall down when a component fails under stress and the result can be quite painful.

Men who are involved with other types of machines which are unpleasant to be around when a mechanical failure occurs, take their jobs very seriously. Aircraft maintenance crews and professional racing mechanics use maintenance checklists and logbooks to make certain that no operations are overlooked and that no component is stressed beyond its maximum working life. They do not view maintenance as corrective action, but as an ordered procedure of cleaning, inspection, adjustment, lubrication, and replacement of critical items at regular intervals, as *preventive* action.

Motorcycle maintenance, especially competition machines, should be approached in basically the same manner. Keeping a machine properly serviced need not be excessively time-consuming, but services should be performed regularly and in a professional manner. This means that the owner/mechanic must have:

1. An adequate supply of good quality tools;

2. A clean place to work;

3. Enough time to do the job properly;

4. Necessary working procedures and specifications.

Again it should be noted that, just as in breaking in a new bike and getting acquainted with it, a feel should be developed for the maintenance needs of various components. The conditions under which the machine is used will have a great bearing on when a service is necessary and it may be beneficial to modify the maintenance schedule after a few thousand miles have been covered and the bike's peculiarities have become known. If yours is a competition bike, you will have to develop your own long-range and short-range maintenance schedules to fit the needs of the type of racing you do.

What it boils down to is this: preventive maintenance with observation; keep to a regular service interval and observe what you are working on. Most likely you'll notice when the drive chain is wearing or the clutch cable is becoming frayed and then be able to replace them before they break.

Periodic Inspection

DAILY

Daily inspection does not have to involve more than a quick confirmation of the bike and should take no more than a few seconds. Items to be checked before each ride should include:

1. Tire pressures;
2. Chain free-play and lubrication;
3. Cable operation;
4. Brake operation;
5. Clutch operation;
6. Headlight and stoplight

(if applicable).

WEEKLY

In addition to those items that should be checked daily, you should check the battery fluid level (on models so equipped). This is especially important in warm weather when the water can evaporate very quickly.

Lubrication

GEARBOX

The oil in the transmission should be changed at least twice a year. Drain the oil into a clean container when the engine is hot, then slowly pour it out of the container and look for foreign matter. The proper type and amount of oil to use in the transmission can be found in the "Engine and Transmission" sections.

GREASE FITTINGS

Use a hand gun filled with a medium grade of general-purpose grease. This type of gun gives complete control over how much grease is fed through the nipple and will ensure a safe pressure. Lubricate every grease fitting on the bike and don't forget the often overlooked swing arm fitting.

FINAL DRIVE CHAIN

It is extremely important to keep the drive chain well-lubricated at all times. It is recommended that you use a special-purpose motorcycle chain lubricant, as regular oil does not penetrate or cling adequately. Depending upon riding speed, mileage, weather, and chain and sprocket condition, it may be necessary to lubricate the chain one or more times daily. Don't fail to service the chain after riding through puddles, mud, sand, or a rain storm. To avoid excessive oil fling-off after the chain has been lubricated, allow the machine to sit for at lesat ten or fifteen minutes before riding it. Most special chain lubricants contain a thin compound to aid accurate delivery and complete penetration that will evaporate in this time, leaving behind a thick lubricating compound that will not be thrown off.

A dry chain can cause a noticeable drop in performance and as much as a 25% increase in fuel consumption. And, of course, the risk of chain breakage is increased, which is never pleasant. To prevent this, it is wise to replace the chain when it begins to give indications of becoming tired; i.e., stretching quickly after adjustment, tight and loose spots along the run, and being worn to a point where a link can be lifted more than $1/4$ in. off the rear sprocket after adjustment.

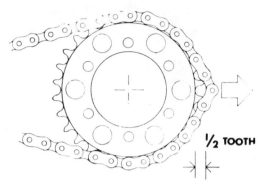

Checking drive chain wear

In addition to regular service at least every two or three hundred miles, the chain should be removed periodically and thoroughly cleaned. The most effective procedure is given below:

1. Remove the chain and clean it thoroughly in solvent.

2. Rinse the chain in clean solvent, then blow it dry with compressed air or hang it on a nail to allow it to dry completely.

3. To lubricate the chain before installation, it is recommended that it be immersed in a mixture of ½ qt. of oil and 5 oz. of petroleum jelly, heated to approximately 150–200° F. for ten minutes. If this is not possible, the chain should be soaked overnight in light engine oil and then wiped off and liberally coated with commercial chain lubricant.

CAUTION: *Do not heat oil directly over a stove or fire. Instead, place the container of oil in a pan of boiling water. After the chain has been immersed for ten minutes, carefully agitate it with a screwdriver and remove the pan from the heat source to allow it to cool before handling the chain. Wipe off any excess oil before installation.*

FRONT FORKS

The oil in the front forks should be changed regularly to ensure proper fork operation and extend seal life. Change the oil twice a year on street machines, once a month on competition bikes. The oil can also be changed to achieve stiffer or weaker damping characteristics. Refer to the "Chassis" sections.

It is best to use a special purpose motorcycle fork oil, but plain motor oil, anywhere from SAE 5W to 40W can be used, depending on the damping desired. To stiffen fork action use a heavier oil and to weaken it use a lighter oil.

CABLES

Lubricate the clutch and brake cable ends with engine oil and smear a small amount of light grease on the speedometer and throttle cable ends. It may be a good idea to invest in a cable oiler, which allows the cable to be thoroughly lubricated along its entire length.

Cleaning

WASHING AND WAXING

Unfortunately, many riders tend to ignore an accumulation of dirt and grime on their machines. This is especially true of dirt bikes, which are often run hub-deep in mud and sand. True, the brakes are sealed and the machine is built to take it, but if you leave the bike sitting in last month's mud, you'll eventually pay the piper. *Nothing* wears out wheel bearings, chains, and seals faster than dirt. If you want the bike to last, you must keep it clean.

The best way to wash the machine is with hot, soapy water and a soft bristled brush. In some instances you may need something stronger, such as a commercial grease cutter, to clean the engine area. Don't wash the machine at a high-pressure detergent car wash. The high-pressure water and detergent will cut not only through the dirt, but your wheel bearing packings as well.

After the bike is cleaned up and the chain has been lubricated, start it and ride for about ten minutes. This will warm the engine enough to evaporate any water that has accumulated in vital areas.

Protect painted finishes with wax and use chrome polish and preservative on all plated surfaces. A good, heavy application of these two will not only brighten appearance, but will also help prevent corrosion.

AIR CLEANER

Wash the air cleaner at least once every thousand miles (foam type), or blow it out with compressed air (paper type); more often if you ride in dusty areas.

If you have the foam rubber, Filtrontype cleaner element, wash it in gasoline and dry it completely, then place it in a container of oil. After it is saturated, squeeze out as much oil as possible and then reinstall it. This oil/foam type of cleaner is the most effective available, *if* it is kept clean. Remember that clean air is essential for the engine's breathing and that without it, the bike will never reach its performance potential.

Removing carbon from the cylinder head

Decarbonization

Normally, heat is dissipated throughout the cylinder head and piston top. If a heavy layer of carbon is present, however, it acts like an insulation blanket and causes all the heat to be concentrated on the rings, plugs, etc. The carbon layer also effectively reduces the combustion chamber displacement and causes significantly higher pressure on the piston and rings. As a result of this increased pressure, and consequent temperature, the rings are more apt to allow blow-by and/or freeze in their grooves, which transfers the heat to the side of the piston. The piston, in turn, expands and burns up its lubrication film, creating more heat. In addition to all this, any blow-by gases contaminating the crankcase and incoming mixture radically upset the fuel balance, leading to pre-ignition and even greater heat.

The decarbonization process to keep this from happening is very easy to perform and requires little more time than a four-stroke valve adjustment.

1. Remove the cylinder head, cylinder, exhaust pipe, and muffler baffle (if applicable).

2. Scrape carbon deposits off the cylinder head and piston top, and out of the exhaust port, ring grooves (if rings are to be replaced), and exhaust pipe. Use a blunt blade so that you don't damage any aluminum alloy surfaces. Note that it is not necessary to clean the piston crown and cylinder head surfaces down to bare metal. In fact, attempting to do so risks scoring the surfaces, which in turn will lead to uneven heat distribution in the combustion chamber and the risk of overheating.

Cleaning out the piston ring grooves. The piston does not have to be removed from the connecting rod for this operation

Scraping carbon build-up out of the exhaust port

Remove the crusted carbon deposits as directed above, but leave a light black film on the piston crown and cylinder head surfaces. The easiest method of cleaning out the exhaust pipe is with a length of old drive chain. Pull it back and forth in the pipe, then tap the pipe lightly to remove the carbon. The piston ring grooves can be cleaned out with a piece of old broken ring.

CAUTION: *Be extremely careful when performing the following operation.*

Burning baffle carbon deposits with a torch

3. Place the muffler baffle in a vise and burn off the carbon deposits with a propane torch.

4. Lightly tap the baffle against a wooden block or bench to remove the deposits. Do not use undue force when doing this.

After everything is cleaned up, put the bike back together (with new rings if the grooves were cleaned out—see the "Engine and Transmission" section) and you'll be surprised how much better it runs. Decarbonize when build-up warrants it, rather than by service intervals. Each machine will vary in its need, but the carbon should be removed at least every four or five thousand miles (excepting the piston ring grooves, which can usually go a little longer between services).

Service Checks and Adjustments

SPARK PLUGS

Spark plugs should be cleaned and gapped every 1,000 miles or sooner depending on how the machine is being used. Correct plug heat range is critical for proper performance. Refer to the plug chart at the end of this chapter for the correct plug for your machine. Note that most of the machines covered in this book use a spark plug gap of 0.016–0.020 in. (0.4–0.5 mm).

BATTERY

Regularly check the electrolyte level and add distilled water as necessary to keep the level between the minimum and maximum marks on the battery case (just enough to cover the plates). Do not overfill.

CAUTION: *Exercise extreme care when handling the battery. Electrolyte can remove paint and chrome in seconds, as well as cause uncomfortable skin burns. Baking soda can be used, if necessary, as a neutralizer.*

Check the condition of the breather tube. It must extend to a point below the frame where relatively little damage can be done should the battery boil or spill over. Make sure the tube is not pinched or closed off, or the battery may build up enough pressure to explode.

Battery charge should be checked periodically with a hydrometer. If the specific gravity reading in any one cell is below 1.22 (at 68° F.), the battery should be recharged. Do not use a high output charger unless absolutely necessary. If the battery must be charged quickly, observe the following precautions:

1. Do not exceed a 4 amp charging rate.

2. Never allow electrolyte temperature to exceed 110° F. while charging.

3. Do not quick-charge a fully discharged battery (specific gravity less than 1.15).

4. Do not quick-charge a battery more than once or twice.

5. Do not quick-charge a battery in which one or more cells has a specific gravity noticeably lower than the others.

6. Disconnect the cables if the battery is to be charged on the machine.

7. Do not charge the battery in a confined room or anywhere near a heat source, as hydrogen gas (which is highly volatile) is released during charging.

8. Never charge the battery for more than thirty minutes at the maximum charging rate.

A more desirable alternative to quick-charging is using a low-output charger, which is available at most automotive supply houses. These units usually cost around ten dollars. A battery that is charged at a low rate will take and retain a fuller charge and plate damage due to high-input current is much less likely to occur. When charging a battery at a low rate, disconnect it from the machine's wiring harness cables and observe the following:

1. Do not charge the battery for an extended period of time at a rate of charge

greater than $\frac{1}{10}$ of its ampere hour (AH) rating.

2. Electrolyte level may drop during charging. This is normal, so fill it with water as necessary.

3. When checking specific gravity after charging, allow sufficient time for the gas bubbles to disperse or a false (low) reading will be obtained.

A good battery will have a specific gravity of 1.26–1.28 (at 68° F.) in all cells. If one or more cells is low after charging, the battery should be replaced. If the battery seems to lose its charge quickly, the charging circuit of the electrical system may be at fault and should be checked before condemning the battery to the trash pile.

Don't neglect to keep the battery case and terminals clean. A solution of baking soda and water works well to remove corrosion, but make sure it doesn't seep down into the battery cells or the electrolyte will be neutralized. Petroleum jelly should be smeared over the terminals after they have been cleaned and connected to act as a corrosion preventative.

With the clear "see-through" batteries, check the bottom of the battery and the lower portions of the plates for white deposits which indicate sulfating. These deposits will become more evident in an older battery and are a symptom of aging.

If the deposits are heavy and the battery will not hold a charge, it must be replaced.

NUTS AND BOLTS

Whenever you are working on the machine, keep an eye out for loose nuts and bolts. Check critical areas (listed below) regularly and tighten up the nuts and bolts as a habit. Use the proper metric wrenches; they provide the correct angle and amount of leverage. Don't overtighten, but make sure everything is snug. Focus special attention on the following critical areas:

1. Front and rear axle nuts;
2. Swing arm shaft nuts;
3. Footrests and brake pedal;
4. Center and side stands;
5. Muffler mounting bolts;
6. Engine mounting bolts;
7. Wheel spokes;
8. Any other points subject to engine vibration or road shock.

WHEELS

Check the wheels for broken or loose spokes and damaged rims. Unless a spoke is obviously loose, don't attempt to tighten it or the wheel may become distorted. Tighten a loose spoke until it is approximately as taut as the neighboring spokes. If any of the spokes are broken, or a large number of them are loose, the wheel should be removed for complete servicing and truing.

Check the runout of the rim with a dial indicator if tire wear is uneven, or if a wobble that increases in intensity as speed is increased, is apparent. If runout exceeds 2.0 mm (0.08 in.) the wheel must be trued or, if bent, replaced. Also check the wheel bearings for condition and make sure the axles are not bent.

TIRES

Examine the tires for casing damage (splits, bubbles, etc.) and for any objects lodged in the tread.

Often overlooked, but very important, is tire pressure which is one of the main factors affecting handling and safety. The factory recommended pressures are fine to start with, but you may find it necessary to adjust them to your weight and the type of riding you do. Keep in mind that the pressure will rise as the temperature of the tire increases; therefore you should check pressure when the tire is cold.

NOTE: *It's a good idea to invest in an accurate tire pressure gauge, as gas station air pump gauges are very often inaccurate.*

SPROCKETS

Drive chain sprockets should be examined for wear whenever the chain is serviced. If the rear wheel is out of alignment, the sprocket teeth will show wear on their sides; if the sprocket is worn due to age or a worn chain, the teeth will be slightly hooked, with the hook facing away from the direction of chain rotation. If either sprocket is noticeably worn, BOTH sprockets AND the chain should be replaced. A worn sprocket can quickly ruin a good chain and vice versa.

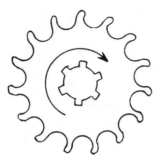

Sprocket with wear spots

Unworn sprocket

BRAKES

Remove the wheels periodically and check the shoes and drums for excessive wear or glazing. Grease or oil on the linings will cause poor stopping power; dirt or uneven wear will cause squealing. Remove any surface glaze with fine sandpaper; then clean the linings, or replace them if they are worn down near the rivets or show signs of oil penetration.

The front brake can be adjusted at either end of the brake cable. Adjust the cable so that actuation occurs after about 1 in. of free-play, measured at the arm on the brake plate, is taken up.

The rear brake is adjusted by turning the adjusting nut on the brake cam actuating lever. Pedal free-play should be about 1 in. If your machine is equipped with lights, make sure that the stoplight switch is adjusted so that the stoplight comes on when the brakes begin to bite.

CLUTCH

Always maintain clutch lever free-play at approximately ⅛ in. Cable play can be adjusted by turning the screw at the handlebar end of the cable.

FINAL DRIVE CHAIN

To check chain adujstment, put the bike on its stand and move the chain up and down at the midway point of the run. If total movement exceeds about 1 in., the chain is too loose and must be readjusted.

Loosen the rear axle nut and the brake anchor nut and turn the two adjusting cams at each swing arm end an equal amount until the chain has about ½–¾ in. of free-play. Retighten the axle nut and the brake anchor nut, and check play again. If you suspect that the rear wheel

Adjusting the rear brake

Increasing chain slack with the cam adjuster

is out of alignment with the front, this can be checked by placing two boards or two lengths of string along the length of the bike so that they touch the side of each tire at the front and rear. Place the strings or boards as high as possible without interfering with the frame or other pieces sticking out. Sight down the boards and you will be able to see any misalignment easily.

STEERING HEAD

Precise steering and stable handling are very much dependent on the steering head bearings. To check their condition, put the bike on its center stand or place blocks under the frame to lift the front wheel and swing the forks slowly through their full steering travel. Movement should be smooth, light, and free from any binding. Check for play in the bearings by grasping the bottom of the fork legs and trying to rock them back and forth in line with the motorcycle. Play can be removed by tightening the steering head main nut beneath the fork crown. TIGHTEN NO MORE THAN NECESSARY TO REMOVE PLAY. If steering movement remains unsatisfactory after adjustment, the bearings should be replaced.

If the steering head bearings have been loose for any period of time, there is a chance that the bearings have pocketed the races. After adjusting the bearings, note any halting or unevenness in the fork move-

ment as it is turned from lock to lock which would indicate this condition. The bearings and races must then be replaced.

SWING ARM

The swing arm should be checked for bushing side-play periodically. There should be absolutely no play and the swing arm must not be bent or weakened by cracked welds, otherwise handling (especially at high speeds) will be erratic and dangerous.

Storage

If the bike is to be stored for a period of two months or more, follow this procedure to ensure minimum deterioration.

1. Wash the bike thoroughly, then ride it for at least fifteen minutes to evaporate any moisture that has been accumulated in or around the engine. Make sure that the bike is completely dry.

2. Drain and refill the transmission with new oil.

3. Run the engine for ten or fifteen minutes to circulate the new lubricant, then turn off the fuel petcock. Just before the engine dies, squirt some oil into the carburetor throat to help prevent the piston, cylinder and rings from rusting.

4. Make sure that the battery is fully charged before storing it and remember to lubricate the terminal connections with a heavy coat of grease or petroleum jelly. Recharge the battery every two months to keep it alive. If the storage location is rather wet or hot, remove the battery and store it in a cool, dry place.

5. Drain the carburetor, disconnect the fuel lines at the carburetor and seal the openings tightly.

6. Lubricate all points: grease fittings, cable ends, chain, etc.

7. Apply a heavy coat of wax on all painted, chromed, and polished surfaces. Grease offers more chrome protection, but makes the clean-up job much harder.

8. Set the machine up on its center stand (or block it up), then throw a porous (breathable) protective cover over it.

AFTER STORING

When taking the bike out of storage, go over it completely, checking all points of maintenance: spark plug, points, timing, battery charge, brakes, etc. Also inspect the carburetor and fuel petcock for any gum deposits. Disassemble and clean them if necessary. Always replace the fuel and check for any evidence of rusting. Don't forget to check the tire pressures.

Recommended Spark Plugs
BULTACO

Model	NGK	Model	NGK
100 cc Lobito	B7H or B7HC	100 cc Sherpa S	B8EN-B10EN
200 cc Metralla	B7EC	125 cc Sherpa S	B8EN-B10EN
125 cc Mercurio	B7HC	175 cc Sherpa S	B8EN-B10EN
175 cc Mercurio	B7EC	200 cc Sherpa S	B8EN-B10EN
175 cc Campera	B7EC or B77EC	250 cc Scrambler	B9EN or B10EN *
200 cc Matador	B7EC or B77EC	360 cc Motocross	
250 cc Matador	B77EC or B8EN	Scrambler	B9EN or B10EN *

(* Dual Plug B9EN and B10EN—The hotter plug on the carb. side; other on exhaust side).

Spark plug gap is 0.020 in. (0.5 mm) for all models.

MONTESA

Model	NGK	Bosch	Champion
Impala Sport	B7H	W 260 T1	L5
Impala	B6H	W 225 T1	L86
Commando 175	B6H	W 225 T1	L86
Kenya	B6H	W 225 T1	L86
Cota 25	B6H	W 225 T1	L86
250 Trial	B6H	W 225 T1	L86
Texas	B6H	W 225 T1	L86
Impala-Cross 175	NA	NA	NA
Impala-Cross 250	NA	NA	NA
Enduro 175	B7H	W 260 T1	L5
Sport 250	B7H	W 260 T1	L5
Cappra 250 MX	B8EN	W 310 T16	L57R
Cota 247	B4L	W 145 T1	L10
LaCross 250	B8EN	W 310 T16	L58R
Scorpion 250	B7H	W 260 T17	L5
Sport 250	B7H	W 260 T1	L5
Cota 123	B6H	W 225 T2	N4

Recommended Spark Plugs (cont.)

MONTESA

Model	NGK	Bosch	Champion
Cappra 250 MX	B8EN	W 310 T16	L57R
King Scorpion 250	B7H	W 260 T17	L5
Cappra 360 GP/DS	B8EN	W 310 T16	N58R
Cappra 250 Five	B8EN	W 310 T16	N58R
Cappra 250 GP	B8EN	W 310 T16	N58R

Spark plug gap for all models is 0.016–0.020 in. (0.4–0.5 mm).

OSSA

Model	NGK	Bosch	Champion
All	B7ES	W 240 T2	N4

Spark plug gap for all models is 0.016–0.020 in. (0.4–0.5 mm).

3 · Bultaco

Engine and Transmission

FOUR-SPEED MODELS

Engine Removal

1. Unscrew the plastic cap from the top of the carburetor and pull out the slide.

2. Unscrew the fuel line banjo cap-screw and remove the banjo, fuel filter and washer. Unscrew the retaining nuts and remove the carburetor.

3. Unscrew the gearbox and primary case filler plugs. Using a 19 mm wrench, remove the drainplug from the bottom of the primary chaincase, catching the oil in a suitable container.

4. Remove the kickstart lever and then

unscrew the four allen bolts securing the left side engine case.

5. Engage first gear in the transmission, and, while a helper holds the rear brake on, unscrew the nut securing the flywheel to the crankshaft. A magnet can be used to remove the two flat washers and one lock-washer from the end of the crankshaft.

6. Turn Bultaco Tool 132-015 (or Tool 11-32-015 for engines with the large taper shaft) completely into the flywheel center. (Use a small amount of grease on the end of the crankshaft and make sure that the center bolt is screwed all the way out so that the tool seats fully.) Tighten the center bolt until the flyweel pulls free

Draining the primary chain oil

Removing the flywheel nut. Arrow indicates clutch pushrod and felt washer

of the crankshaft. Remove the woodruff key from the crankshaft.

7. Mark the original position of the stator disc in relation to the engine case, as shown (for convenience when reassembling the engine). Pull the wires from the connector block, and unscrew the three screws and remove the stator disc assembly. Pull out all electrical wires leading to the frame through their rubber grommet.

8. Remove the six bolts holding the crankshaft oil seal housing and remove the cover and gasket.

9. Bend back the tabs of the lockwasher holding the countershaft nut and again,

Removing the magneto flywheel with the special tool (arrow)

Crankshaft oil seal housing bolts

Removing the countershaft sprocket nut

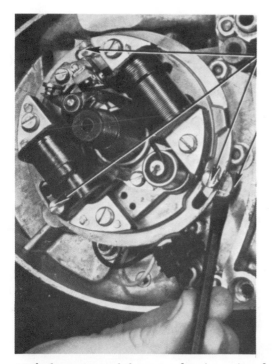

Mark the position of the stator disc (arrow) and remove the screws

holding the rear brake on, unscrew the nut.

10. On early models, unscrew the three countersunk screws retaining the countershaft seal holder and remove the holder, gasket, and spacer. On mid-1964 and later engines, the triangular plate has been relocated inside the transmission case. These later series engines use a larger countershaft ball-bearing assembly, which has the same part number as the main bearings. If

Removing the exhaust pipe flange nut

this bearing operates roughly or is worn, it should be replaced after the crankcases have been split.

11. Unbolt the rear exhaust pipe bracket.

While supporting the pipe, unscrew the flange nut at the cylinder head using a pin wrench, as shown.

12. Unscrew and completely remove the

Clutch safety wire (left); engine sprocket flywheel on models with duplex chain (right)

shift lever securing bolt, and slip the lever off the selector shaft. Unscrew the seven allen bolts and remove the right side engine cover.

13. Remove the safety wire on the clutch tension nuts. Gradually and evenly loosen the nuts, and then remove the springs, pressure plate, and clutch discs. Remove the clutch rod thrust pin.

14. Bend back the tabs of the clutch hub retaining nut (some models use a star washer) and, using the clutch tool to stop the clutch from turning, remove the nut. Use the same procedure to remove the inner hub nut. To remove the inner clutch hub and engine sprocket flywheel, screw two of the tension nuts to the studs on the opposite sides of the inner clutch hub and use two hooked pry bars against the outer clutch hub to remove it. Also, take care not to misplace the woodruff keys.

15. Remove the clutch sprocket and the engine sprocket together, using gear pullers if necessary. Use pry bars to pull the inner clutch hub spacer off the transmission shaft. Remove the O-ring after the spacer

and the woodruff key have been removed.

16. Unscrew the six bolts from the crankshaft seal cover. Before the cover can be removed from 250 cc scramblers and engines with duplex primary chains, it will be necessary to pry off the spacer in the same manner as described in the previous step. After removing the spacer and its O-ring, the seal cover can be pulled off.

NOTE: *On some models there is a notch in the seal holder. Upon reassembly, this notch must fit into the cylinder stud which extends down from the top of the case.*

17. Unscrew and remove the speedometer cable from the speedometer drive at the engine.

18. For assembly convenience, measure and record the end-play of the transmission mainshaft using a dial indicator or vernier caliper, as shown.

19. Pull off the cap and remove the sparkplug. Remove the drive chain master link and remove the chain. Unbolt and remove the chainguard.

20. Unscrew the three (four on recent

Removing the engine sprocket and clutch hub

Removing the crankshaft oil seal housing spacer

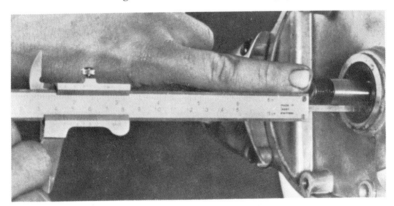

Measuring crankshaft end-play

models) engine mounting nuts and withdraw the bolts. Lift the front of the engine while lowering the rear until all of the frame flanges have been cleared, and remove the engine.

Engine Disassembly

1. Loosen the six cylinder head nuts, 3 ft. lbs. at a time, in reverse sequence of that shown in the illustration. Lift the head off the cylinder head studs.

2. Loosen and remove the seven nuts holding the cylinder to the crankcase. The two nuts below the intake flange can be removed after the cylinder has been lifted up slightly. Remove the cylinder, taking care not to let the piston and connecting rod fall against the case as they are withdrawn.

Cylinder head nut tightening sequence

Removing a piston wrist pin circlip

3. Pry out the wrist pin snap-rings, as shown, using a small screwdriver. A cloth placed around the crankcase opening will prevent them from falling inside. Wear safety glasses during this operation. Do not attempt to save the snap-rings; new ones should always be used.

4. Before attempting to remove the wrist pin, carefully remove any burrs that may be present around the snap ring grooves using a sharp scraper. Heat the piston gently, and push the wrist pin out of the piston with a drift, while supporting the connecting rod with your other hand.

CAUTION: *Do not, under any circumstances, hammer the drift or the connecting rod will be bent.*

5. Remove the three countersunk screws in the speedometer drive cover, and remove the small setscrew from the side of the speedometer drive housing. The drive cover can be removed by screwing a nut (or bolt on some models) onto the end and using this as a leverage point in order to pry the cover off.

NOTE: *The speedometer drive cover need not be removed at this point ex-cept on 125 and 155 cc Mercurios and 200 cc Matadors. In addition, it will be necessary to remove the speedometer drive bushing on these models. This can be accomplished by splitting the bushing and replacing it with a new one on assembly, or removing it with Bultaco Tool*

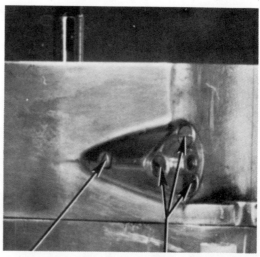

Speedometer drive bushing setscrew (left arrow) and cover screws

132-069 (*which can also be used to extract the speedometer drive cover*). *On all other models the cases can be split without removing the speedometer drive and bushing, but these parts must be removed before the cases can be reassembled.*

6. It is not necessary to remove the kickstarter spring or shaft in order to split the cases. However, if the spring or shaft are to be replaced, remove the spring at this time using a T-bar with a hook on one end or a screwdriver to force the spring end away from its retaining stud. Allow the spring to unwind around the shaft, then slip the kickstart lever onto its shaft and rotate it clockwise until the part of the spring that passes through the shaft is

Removing the kickstart return spring

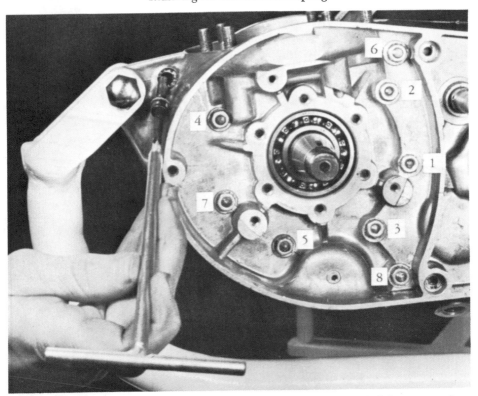

Removing the forward crankcase allen bolt, also showing the crankcase bolt loosening order

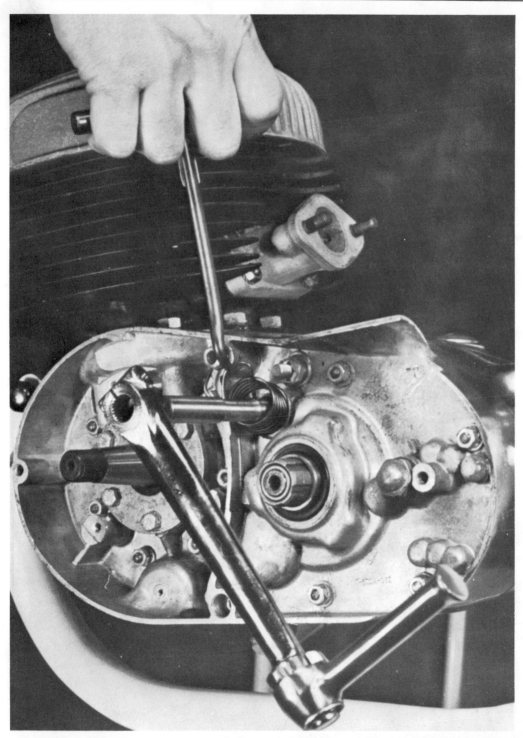

vertical. Then force the spring up until the end is clear of the hole in the shaft and pull it off the shaft.

7. Unscrew the 12 nuts that secure the crankcase studs in the order shown and remove the flatwashers and lockwashers. Remove the allen bolt and lockwasher located

behind the front engine mounting flange.

8. The crankcases are now ready to be separated. Before attempting this, heat the engine to approximately 300° F.

If the Bultaco crankcase puller (Tool 132-043) is not available, place the engine, magneto side down, on a bench.

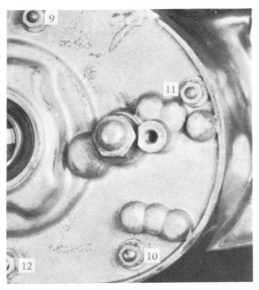

Crankcase bolt loosening order (rear bolts)

Grasping the cylinder studs of the crankcase half uppermost with the engine placed as above, lift the engine a few inches off the bench, and carefully tap, with a soft-faced mallet, around the circumference of the crankcase assembly on the joint until the cases begin to separate.

Transmission—Disassembly and Repair

NOTE: *The mainshaft gears are interchangeable among engines in all street machines and the Matador. The First,*

Separating the crankcases with the special tool

Second, and Third gears on the counter-shaft are interchangeable on all models except the 125 and 155 cc Mercurios and the Matador, which have a one-piece countershaft with non-removable gears. The First and Second gears in the Sherpa S have different ratios from those in other models (close ratio). Bandido gears are not interchangeable with any other model.

All of the transmission gears were re-designed early in 1965, the new gears differing both in size and shape. The new style gears can be used to replace the old ones, providing that they are replaced in mating pairs.

The following procedures apply to all models except the 250 Scrambler. If you are working on a 250 Scrambler transmission, note these constructional variations:

a) The internal shifting pattern is different. When shifting from 1st to 2nd gear, the 1st/3rd sliding dog moves out of engagement with the 1st gear idler and stops in a Neutral position between the 1st gear idler and 3rd gear idler. The 2nd/4th sliding dog moves over to engage the 2nd gear idler.

In all other transmissions, the 1st/2nd sliding dog is located between the 1st gear idler and 2nd gear idler on the mainshaft. When shifting from 1st to 2nd gear, the 1st/2nd sliding dog moves out of engagement with the 1st gear idler (mainshaft) and continues its travel until it has moved into engagement with the 2nd gear idler.

b) The dogs and their engaging slots are different. Care must be taken not to interchange one type of sliding and engaging dog with the other.

c) The pattern of the shifting cam plate in the 250 Scrambler is different, and cannot be interchanged with other models.

d) The 250 Scrambler uses a forged steel cam plate support bracket which can be used as an improved replacement part in other models if trouble is experienced with the forged aluminum bracket.

e) The 4th gear driving sprocket is wider than that used on other models. The wider sprocket necessitates the use of a different countershaft with a re-positioned snap ring groove.

Differences in the dogs and slots

Gearshift Selector Adjustment (Four-speed models)

On all models except the 250 Scrambler and Sherpa T, the selector mechanism can be adjusted with the engine in the frame.

1. Remove the shift lever from its shaft. Unscrew the three allen bolts and remove the triangular selector mechanism cover. (Hold down the cover until the bolts are removed or the selector fork spring will push it out with sufficient force to bend one of the screws.)

2. Check for a bent selector shaft by

checking it with a straightedge at several places around its diameter. A bent selector shaft can cause binding and erratic operation of the shift lever.

3. Note the machined aluminum surfaces in the engine case just above and below the selector shaft. These are the selector shaft stops, which limit the movement of the shift lever when shifting gears. The selector shaft is supposed to hit its stop at the same instant the spring-loaded cam plate plunger comes to rest in a notch in the cam plate. If the selector shaft hits its stop too soon or too late, the cam plate will not be rotated far enough (or will be rotated too far) for maximum engagement of the corresponding idler gear and sliding dog. The result will be either a false neutral or jumping out of gear. This can cause all sorts of wear or damage in the transmission if allowed to persist. To find out if the selector shaft is hitting the stop at the right time, proceed as follows:

4. Make sure the selector shaft thrust washer is in place. Install the selector cover while holding the selector shaft in position. (A small amount of grease will hold the gasket in place.) Make a special tool from a plunger sleeve nut, No. 111-020 (No. 11-11-020 for the 250 Scrambler). Drill a 6 mm hole in the outside end of the sleeve nut to enable the plunger spring to stick out. Install the sleeve nut, substituting it for the regular one, and push the protruding spring in with one hand. Shift gears in

Removing the gear shift selector shaft cover

Installing the selector shaft cover

both directions with your free hand; you will be able to feel the exact position of the plunger at the moment the selector shaft hits its stop. If the selector shaft hits its stop too soon, you will not feel the plunger slide into its notch in the cam plate. If it hits too late, you'll feel the plunger slide into its notch and then be forced back out again.

5. Remove the shift lever and the cover again. To remove the selector shaft, rock the splined end up and down while pushing forward and inward. This will free both ends of the selector hairpin spring from its anchor pin. (Do not remove the locknut from the spring anchor pin). Withdraw the selector assembly.

6. If the top or bottom of the selector shaft extension is not hitting its stop soon enough, the extension will have to be built up through brazing and filed smooth. Only trial and error can show how much added metal is necessary. If the shaft extensions hit too soon, grind a SMALL amount of metal off and retest it.

Top and bottom extensions

7. If the thrust surfaces of the selector fork fingers have become rounded (shown in illustration), replace the fork with a new one.

8. If the selector fork, shaft, or return spring have been replaced, several other checks will have to be made.

a) First, check to see if the shift lever sticks as you shift into or out of second gear (third gear on 250 Scramblers). If it does, remove the selector mechanism and grind the ends of the selector fork fingers. Remove no more than ½ mm of material and follow the original curves. Do not overheat the metal or it will lose its hardness. Reassemble and test the selector; continue this operation until the shift lever returns easily to the central position.

b) If the gearshift works stiffly or not at all, the selector fork is probably hanging up on its thrust peg. To remedy this, dress off any burrs or high spots that are interfering with the pivoting of the selector fork.

c) If you experience trouble shifting up into third or down into second gear, it is likely that the hairpin return spring is not adjusted correctly. If the problem is in shifting up from second to third, bend both legs of the spring up about 2 mm. If the gearbox will not shift from third to second, bend both legs down about 2 mm. Both legs must be bent the same distance in order to keep them parallel.

The Transmission Components

1. Lift out the countershaft cluster, taking care not to lose the thrust washer on each end.

2. Withdraw the shift fork shaft. Rotate the cam plate to the second gear position, then pivot the upper shift fork clockwise and remove it. Rotate the cam plate to the

Selector fork fingers

Removing the countershaft cluster

Temporary spacer (arrow)

third gear position and remove the remaining shift fork in the same manner.

3. Remove the spacer from the starter shaft. Using both hands, remove the mainshaft and the kickstart gear from the case together.

Removing the mainshaft and the kickstart gear

4. Clean all components thoroughly and check for wear and damage. Any part with a thrust surface that has turned blue should be replaced, as the blueing indicates that overheating has occurred.

5. Installation is in the reverse order of disassembly.

Component Checks

1. Using the amount of mainshaft end-play you recorded when disassembling, make a temporary spacer of the same thickness with a 14 mm hole in the center. Install the spacer onto the end of the mainshaft that slides into the sleeve gear. In-stall the mainshaft assembly with the spacer in place. Also, reinstall the selector forks and shaft in the left side engine case. With the cam plate in the first gear position, measure the gap between the first gear sliding dog and the first gear idler. (Take care not to deflect the selector fork shaft, which is normally supported by the right side engine case). Record the measurement and repeat the operation for second, third and fourth gears (with the cam plate in the appropriate positions). If any measurement amounts to more than 30% of the length of the engagement pegs, observe the following procedures.

Measuring sliding dog-idler gear clearance

a) Measure the width of the machined surface on the selector fork. It should not be less than 2.85 mm. The width of the groove in the sliding dog should not be greater than 3.2 mm. Replace any part that is worn beyond specification.

b) Measure the clearance between the shift fork cam plate follower and the slot in the cam plate. If greater than 0.65 mm, either or both parts should be replaced.

c) Check the end-play between each idler gear and its lock-ring. If necessary, place a shim between the ring and idler.

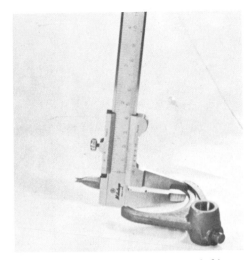

Measuring the width of the selector fork's machined surface

Checking transmission mainshaft straightness

Do not reduce clearance to less than 0.2 mm. If you are able to rotate a lock-ring with your fingers, it should be replaced with a new one. If the lock-ring grooves are not at least 0.3 mm deep, or if their edges have become rounded, the mainshaft should be replaced.

d) Check the straightness of the mainshaft by placing it in V-blocks, or between lathe centers, and rotating it while measuring with a dial indicator. If runout exceeds 0.04 mm, the mainshaft should be replaced.

2. Bend back the locktabs and unscrew the four bolts securing the cam plate bracket. Rock the cam plate back and forth until it is freed from its dowel pins. Check the straightness of the cam plate using an engineer's square, as shown. The bracket can sometimes be bent due to harsh shifting and it should be replaced if it is not in proper alignment.

3. If the countershaft or either of its two ball bearings are replaced, the end-play must be checked and adjusted. First, measure the distance between the two countershaft bearings in the crankcase halves. To accomplish this, measure the distance between the ball bearing inner face and the inner edge on each crankcase half and add the two figures. Add 0.4 mm to the result to compensate for gasket thickness. Next, install the two thrust washers on either end of the countershaft and measure the distance from the outside edge of one thrust washer to the outside edge of

Shift fork-to-cam plate follower clearance

Checking the cam plate for warpage

the other. Subtract this figure from the preceding one; the remainder is the countershaft end-play. If at least 0.2 mm end-play does not exist, file the thrust washers evenly until the desired amount is obtained.

4. Having already removed the kickstart return spring, you can now remove the kickstart shaft, the ratchet, the ratchet spring, and the washer. These components can be removed by rotating the kickstart shaft clockwise from the outside of the crankcase half, and lifting the assembly from the case.

5. If the crankstop in the left crankcase half is bent (a common occurrence in early 1964 models), it can be replaced with

Calculating countershaft end-play

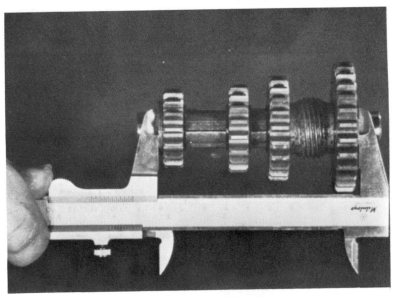

Measuring countershaft length

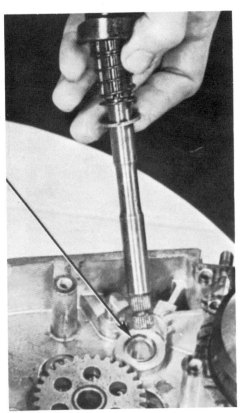

Crankstop (arrow)

Removing the sleeve gear

the later, improved one. The stop is secured by the chamfered nut, behind which the kickstart return spring is hooked.

6. Tap out the sleeve gear with a rubber hammer and inspect its support bearing for looseness or rough operation. Remove the O-ring, located between the support bearing and the spacer, and drive out the seal and sleeve from inside the case. Thoroughly clean the exposed countershaft bearing. If it is necessary to replace the countershaft bearing, remove the three screws from the retaining plate and lift off the plate. Heat the case to 300° F. and the countershaft bearing and crankshaft assembly will drop out of the case. A light tap with a soft-faced mallet may be necessary. To remove the bearing from the case, drop the case

from a height of exactly two feet, open side down onto a wooden bench. The bearing will then pop out. Install the new bearing while the case is still hot.

The Crankshaft Assembly

The transmission components need not be removed in order to work on the crankshaft. To remove the crank, heat the engine case to 300° F. While holding the gear clusters with one hand, tap the magneto end of the crankshaft with a rubber mallet until it is free.

1. Whenever connecting rod bearing failure has occurred, the first thing to suspect is crankcase pressure leakage. Check the crankshaft seals. If stiff, scratched or rough, they must be replaced. Leaky seals can cause main bearing failure and piston seizure due to insufficient lubrication.

2. Check connecting rod side play with a feeler gauge between the thrust washer and the cheek of the flywheel. This value should be about 0.016 in. for 100 and 125 cc engines; 0.018 in. for 175, 200, and 250 cc bikes, and 0.020 in. for the 326 and 360 cc machines. A value in excess of these will necessitate the replacement of the rod and bearing.

3. On engines with a solid crankpin assembly, the crankshaft can be pressed apart after a careful cleaning. On some 175 and 200 cc machines, the crankpin is hollow. Before pressing these assemblies apart, drill through the solid end of each expansion plug in the crankpin ends with a $\frac{5}{16}$ in. drill and knock out the plugs with a drift. (When reassembling a hollow crankpin assembly, do not press the expansion plugs into the crankpin until the crankshaft assembly has been perfectly aligned.)

4. To reassemble the crankshaft halves:

a) Press the crankpin into one of the crankshaft halves until the pin is flush with the outer surface of the flywheel. Install one of the thrust washers on the crankpin.

b) Pack the bearing cage with light grease and place a roller in each window of the cage.

c) Place the caged bearing on the crankpin and push each opposite pair of rollers inward until they touch the crankpin, then slip the connecting rod over the cage and put the other thrust washer on the crankpin.

d) Using a straightedge as a guide, press the other crankshaft half onto the crankpin until the outer surface of the flywheel is flush with the end of the crankpin. Insert the proper feeler gauge (0.016, 0.018, or 0.020 in.) between a thrust washer and flywheel, and press the crankshaft assembly together until the feeler gauge is a tight fit.

e) Place the crankshaft assembly in V-blocks or between lathe centers and check runout using two dial gauges against the bearing surfaces. Check whether the needles swing in unison or out of phase, and whether they move the same amount. If the needles neither swing the same distance nor start and end their swings at the same time, the crankshaft halves are both eccentric and non-parallel.

Checking crankshaft runout

To correct the eccentric condition, rotate the crankshaft until the drive side dial gauge reaches the point of maximum travel. Draw an imaginary line between the ends of the dial gauge shafts and make a chalk mark on the rim of the drive side flywheel at the place where the imaginary line would cross it. Remove the crankshaft assembly and, holding it on the magneto side, hit the chalk mark on the rim of the drive side flywheel with a bronze or lead hammer. This will (hopefully) rotate the flywheel slightly on the crankpin to bring it into alignment with the magneto side fly-

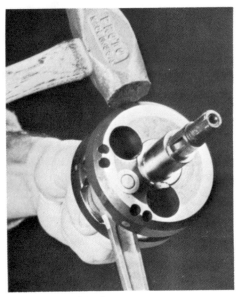

Aligning the crankshaft

wheel. Repeat this procedure until the gauge needles begin and end their swings at the same time.

To correct the non-parallel condition, rotate the crankshaft assembly until the dial gauge needles reach the high point of their travel. If the crankpin lies along an imaginary line drawn between the ends of the two dial gauge shafts, the flywheels are pinched together opposite

the crankpin. To correct this, rotate the crankshaft until the crankpin is at the bottom. Insert a wedge at the top of the flywheels and spread them slightly by tapping the wedge with a hammer. Check the alignment again; the assembly has been aligned properly if neither gauge needle travels more than 0.025 mm (0.001 in.). If necessary, continue this operation until this requirement is met.

If, in the above paragraph, the crankpin did not lie on or near the imaginary line between the dial gauge shafts but was opposite this line, the flywheels have been spread apart. To correct this, draw a chalk line on a flywheel (to match the imaginary line) from the driveshafts to the outer rim. Hold the assembly by the crankpin and lay the portions of the flywheels on the other side of the driveshafts flat on the bench with the chalk mark up. Hit the upper flywheel on the chalk mark with a mallet to bring the flywheels closer together. Retest, and continue this operation until neither dial gauge moves more than 0.025 mm (0.001 in.).

Aligning the flywheels

5. After completing crankshaft alignment, the expansion plugs can be inserted into the hollow crankpin (if applicable). Press the plugs in until they are flush with the ends of the crankpin. Take care to install the plugs straight; if they go in crooked, the end of the crankpin may split.

Aligning the flywheels

After installing the plugs recheck and correct, if necessary. flywheel parallelism.

6. Recheck connecting rod side-play as described earlier. If side-play is less than the prescribed amount, press the flywheels apart just enough to restore proper end-play.

Piston Size Information

1. Oversize pistons have the oversize number stamped on the crown. Four oversizes are available: 0.25 mm, 0.50 mm, 0.75 mm, and 1.0 mm.

2. Pistons are stamped with a "+" or "—" on the crown to indicate different machining tolerances.

The accompanying chart shows dimensions for "+" and "—" pistons up to 250 cc. In all cases, however, the cylinder must be bored to match the particular piston which will be fitted.

To properly fit a piston, the following dimensions must be obtained: cylinder barrel taper, concentricity, piston clearance, and piston ring end gap. These measurements are obtained as follows. Refer to the specifications chart for correct operating tolerances.

3. Wash the cylinder in hot, soapy water, and rinse thoroughly. Allow it to stand for two hours at room temperature. Measure the diameter of the cylinder bore, from front to back, at the lowest point of piston travel. Measure the diameter of the piston on an axis perpendicular to the wrist pin on the lower portion of the piston. Subtract the piston diameter from that of the bore to determine piston clearance. Check the value obtained with the correct value shown in the specifications chart.

4. To obtain the bore taper, take two measurements in the same plane across the bore. The first is taken ½ in. below the top of the bore, the other just below the intake port.

Piston-Cylinder Specifications

	100 cc	125 cc	175 cc	200 cc	250 cc	326 cc	360 cc
Maximum allowable bore taper (in.)	.0015	.0015	.0015	.002	.002	.0025	.0025
Maximum out-of-round before rebore (in.)	.0012	.0012	.0012	.0012	.0015	.0015	.0015
Maximum ring end gap (in.)	.020	.020	.030	.030	.035	.045	.045
Maximum piston clearance (in.)	.0055	.0057	.0065	.0065	.007	.0083	.0098
Piston clearance (New) (in.)	.001	.001	.0015	.0015	.002	.002	.0035
Trail—Enduro—Trials	.002	.002	.0025	.0025	.003	.0035	.0045
Competition	.0015 .0025	.0015 .0025	.0017 .003	.0017 .003	.0025 .0035	.0025 .0037	.0035 .0045

5. Check for bore concentricity, or out-of-round, with two measurements, at an angle of 90° apart, ½ in. below the top of the cylinder; two measurements at 90° in the area of the exhaust port, and two measurements at 90° below the intake port.

6. Piston ring end gap is obtained by inserting the ring into the top of the cylinder, and using the piston to push it down about 1 in. into the bore. Measure the end gap with a feeler gauge.

In all cases, values for the above dimensions should be within the specified tolerances shown in the chart.

7. After boring or honing a cylinder, it is necessary to bevel all of the port edges in the bore. A chamfer of 5° (0.5 mm radius) is correct.

8. If piston damage has occurred, it is important to check the cylinder liner for cracks, especially in the area of the lower transfer port cutouts in the portion of the liner below the cylinder barrel.

Installing A New Cylinder Liner

1. To remove the old liner, support the cylinder upside down in an oven so that the liner is free to drop out of the cylinder after reaching a temperature of 700° F. Do not exceed 800° F. or the aluminum alloy will be damaged.

2. The new liner can be inserted in the cylinder immediately after the old one has been withdrawn if the inside of the cylinder is very clean. If cleaning is necessary, reheat the cylinder before installing the new liner. Support the bottom fins of the hot cylinder so that the liner will not touch anything when it is in place. Insert the new liner and align the ports as closely as possible with the cylinder ports. Place a weight on the liner flange to keep it from

Bevel the port edges to a 0.5 mm radius

Cylinder Machining Tolerances

All figures are in mm

Engine Displacement	Model	Standard Piston		1st O.S. Piston		2nd O.S. Piston		3rd O.S. Piston		4th O.S. Piston	
		+	−	+	−	+	−	+	−	+	−
125 cc	TSS / Sherpa S	51.535 / 51.525	51.525 / 51.515	51.785 / 51.775	51.775 / 51.765	52.035 / 52.025	52.025 / 52.015	52.285 / 52.275	52.275 / 52.265	52.535 / 52.525	52.525 / 52.515
	Mercurio	51.525 / 51.515	51.515 / 51.505	51.775 / 51.765	51.765 / 51.755	52.025 / 52.015	52.015 / 52.005	52.275 / 52.265	52.265 / 52.255	52.525 / 52.515	52.515 / 52.505
155 cc	Mercurio	57.025 / 57.015	57.015 / 57.005	57.275 / 57.265	57.265 / 57.255	57.525 / 57.515	57.515 / 57.505	57.775 / 57.765	57.765 / 57.755	58.025 / 58.015	58.015 / 58.005
175 cc	Sherpa S / TSS	60.945 / 60.935	60.935 / 60.925	61.195 / 61.185	61.185 / 61.175	61.445 / 61.435	61.435 / 61.425	61.695 / 61.685	61.685 / 61.675	61.945 / 61.935	61.935 / 61.925
	Mercurio	60.935 / 60.925	60.925 / 60.915	61.185 / 61.175	61.175 / 61.165	61.435 / 61.425	61.425 / 61.415	61.685 / 61.675	61.675 / 61.665	61.935 / 61.925	61.925 / 61.915
200 cc	Metralla / Matador	64.525 / 64.515	64.515 / 64.505	64.775 / 64.765	64.765 / 64.755	65.525 / 65.515	65.515 / 65.505	65.275 / 65.265	65.265 / 65.255	65.525 / 65.515	65.515 / 65.505
	Sherpa S / TSS	64.545 / 64.535	64.535 / 64.525	64.795 / 64.785	64.785 / 64.775	65.045 / 65.035	65.035 / 65.025	65.295 / 65.285	65.285 / 65.275	65.545 / 65.535	65.535 / 65.525
250 cc	Metisse	72.060 / 72.050	72.050 / 72.040	72.310 / 72.300	72.300 / 72.290	72.560 / 72.550	72.550 / 72.540	72.810 / 72.800	72.800 / 72.790	73.060 / 73.050	73.050 / 73.040

shifting while cooling, or clamp it into position by fastening the cylinder head to its studs and torqueing the nuts to half the specified value.

3. Measure the outside diameter of the bottom of the new liner and the inside diameter of the crankcase opening to see if the new liner will fit in the crankcase. If not, the liner will have to be turned down. Before doing this, remove the connecting bridges at the bottom of the lower transfer ports in the liner with a hacksaw. Next, blend the edges that were sawed with a file. Then mount the cylinder in a lathe and remove only as much metal as necessary from the outside of the liner for it to fit into the case. The liner must be machined to the specifications shown in the accompanying illustration.

Cylinder Liner Specifications

Measurement	Model	Measurement mm	Inches
"A" bottom of transfer to top of sealing lip	350 cc & 360 cc eng.	64.0	2.520
	100 cc eng.	51.5	2.028
	125 cc to 327 cc eng.	60.0	2.362
"B" base of cylinder to top of sealing lip	350 cc & 360 cc eng.	96.7	3.807
	100 cc eng.	90.0	3.543
	125 cc to 327 cc eng.	95.8	3.772
Clearance between bottom of head and top of cylinder	All	minimum clearance 0.5 mm	.020

4. Follow the instructions in the preceding section to fit a new piston to the new liner. The liner must be bored to the proper specifications for piston clearance.

5. Match the ports in the liner with those in the cylinder by filing the port entrances in the liner until they form smooth exten-

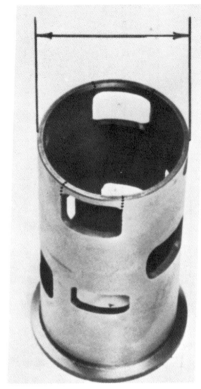

Outside diameter of a new liner (arrow) and the connecting bridges (dotted lines)

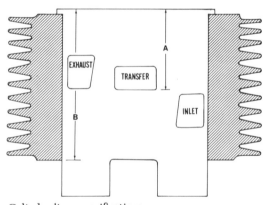

Cylinder liner specifications

sions to the ports in the aluminum cylinder. After matching the ports, carefully chamfer the edges of the ports with an 0.5 mm radius until they are smooth and round.

6. On 125 cc machines, there are two 10 mm rectangular reliefs in the bottom of the cylinder bore. Blend the holes in the new liner to match the tapered reliefs in the cylinder to provide clearance for the swing of the connecting rod. Remove metal from the bottoms of the holes in the liner until the taper of the cylinder reliefs is con-

Match the ports in the liner with those of the cylinder (arrows)

tinued in the liner holes; then file the edges until they are smooth and straight.

7. Finally, wash the cylinder in hot, soapy water, rinse, and dry with compressed air. Coat the cylinder bore with oil to protect it from rust.

ASSEMBLING THE ENGINE

NOTE: *Before reassembling the cases, replace any worn transmission bearings with new ones.*

1. Using an appropriately sized pipe or wrench socket, drive out the oil seal from the magneto side seal cover; then remove the seal cover gasket. Install the seal cover on the magneto side crankcase half with two of the seal cover mounting screws.

2. Heat the magneto side crankcase to 400° F. and slide the crankshaft into position, butting the main bearing against the seal cover. Hold the assembly in position until it has cooled enough to seize the main bearing, then allow it to cool for five minutes more and remove the seal cover. Turn the crankshaft to check that the bearing still rotates freely and smoothly. If it does

Removing the oil seal from the crankshaft seal housing

not, reheat the case, remove the crankshaft assembly, replace the bearing, and reassemble the crankshaft into the case.

3. While the case is still hot, fit the

sleeve gear into its bearing. If necessary, tap the gear lightly to seat it.

4. Reassemble the kickstart assembly by sliding the kickstart shaft, thrust washer, ratchet spring, and ratchet, as an assembly, into the kickstart shaft boss. Slide the ratchet onto the six large splines on the kickstart shaft so that when the ratchet is against its stop, the return spring hole in the shaft is as near horizontal as possible with the engine in its normal position. It may take several tries before you get the ratchet aligned properly.

Kickstart assembly in position

5. Install the cam plate bracket on its dowel pins and secure it with the four bolts and locktabs. The short tab plate should be under the two bolts that are at the top of the bracket when the engine is in its normal position. Torque the bolts to

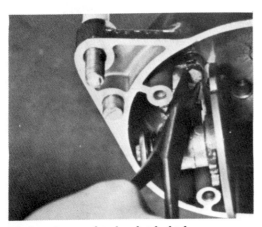

Bending the camplate bracket locktabs

5 ft. lbs. and lock them in place with the tabs.

6. Remove the homemade spacer from the transmission mainshaft and, while holding the kickstart gear in place, slip the mainshaft assembly into position. Install the kickstart shaft spacer.

7. Hold the 1st/2nd gear sliding dog up against the first gear idler on the mainshaft and, with your other hand, fit the countershaft assembly into its ball bearing in the crankcase. Make sure a thrust washer is fitted at each end of the layshaft (except engines with solid countershaft clusters).

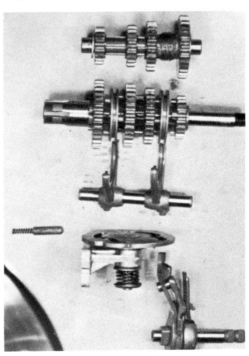

Transmission components

8. Rotate the cam plate to its third gear position (one position back from the clockwise limit of rotation as viewed from the crankshaft side). Install the shift fork with the longer cam plate follower into the 3rd/4th gear sliding dog, holding it so that the side toward which the follower is offset is facing the base of the cam plate bracket. Pivot the shift fork so that its follower fits into the cam plate, lifting the sliding dog as necessary to perform the operation.

9. Rotate the cam plate to the second gear position and install the other shift fork, holding it so that the side toward which the follower is offset is facing you.

The magneto side crankcase assembly ready for the drive side case to be installed

Pivot the fork so that the follower fits into the cam plate.

10. Push the shift fork shaft through the forks and into its support in the engine case. Install the cam plate plunger, plunger spring, and washer into the crankcase. Screw the plunger sleeve nut in. Liberally oil the transmission gears and bearings. Check that the two crankcase locating dowel pins are in place near the front and rear engine mount bosses.

11. Coat the magneto side crankcase mating surface with grease and fit a new gasket into position. If the drive side main bearing remained in the crankcase boss when the cases were separated, heat the crankcase to 400° F. and remove the bearing. Install the hot bearing on the drive side of the crankshaft and seat it against the flywheel. If a new bearing is to be installed on the crankshaft, heat it until the oil begins to smoke and slide it onto the shaft as above. In either case, allow the bearing to cool for ten minutes before proceeding further.

12. Prop the magneto side crankcase on the bench so that the crankshaft end is not touching the surface. Heat the drive side crankcase to 400° F. and mate it quickly to the drive side case, with the case studs started in their holes. While the case is still hot, tap it on each end with a rubber hammer to seat the ball bearing assemblies.

13. Install the twelve lockwashers and nuts on the crankcase studs and tighten them in the sequence shown, in 1 ft. lb. increments, to 5 ft. lbs. Use a thread locking compound on the nuts and studs to prevent the nuts from loosening due to vibration. Install the allen bolt and lockwasher just behind the front engine mount.

14. It is possible, when reassembling the crankcases, to disturb the crankshaft alignment. If the case was not hot enough and did not seat fully before cooling and contracting around the main bearing, the flywheels will have been forced together as the cases were drawn tight. For this reason it is necessary to check crankshaft runout at this point. Make up brackets to hold the dial gauges and install a gauge on both sides of the engine, so that the gauge shaft will contact a smooth, unbroken portion of the crankshaft. Rotate the crankshaft and watch the gauges. If the flywheels have been squeezed together, both needles will be at their highest point of travel when the connecting rod is at the bottom of its travel. If runout exceeds 0.025 mm (0.001 in.), rotate the crankshaft and stop

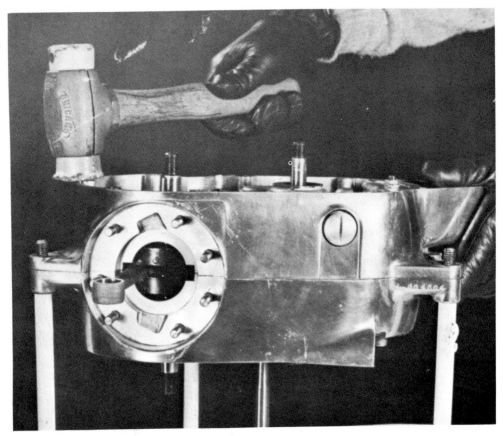

Seating the crankcase halves

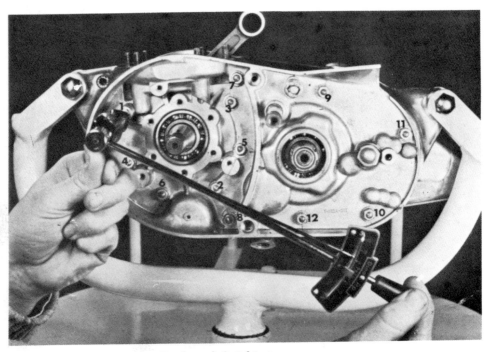

Crankcase bolt tightening sequence

at the point where the gauge needles are at their highest point of travel. Insert a wedge between the flywheels at top center and spread them until the needles move back to about half of their original travel. If you overdo it, the flywheels can close up by hitting both ends of the crankshaft. Recheck runout and repeat this procedure until alignment is within specification. It is important to align the crankshaft perfectly for accurate ignition timing and for long life of the main bearings and crankcase seals.

15. Remove the seal cover from the magneto side crankcase that you installed earlier to position the crankshaft assembly correctly. Remove the old seal from the other seal cover. To install a new seal in the cover, place the cover on the jaws of a vise. Position the jaws so that they are opened slightly wider than the diameter of the seal. Start a new seal into the cover with the open side up. Oil the seal lightly to ease installation. Use a piece of pipe or wrench socket that is slightly smaller than the outside diameter of the seal to drive

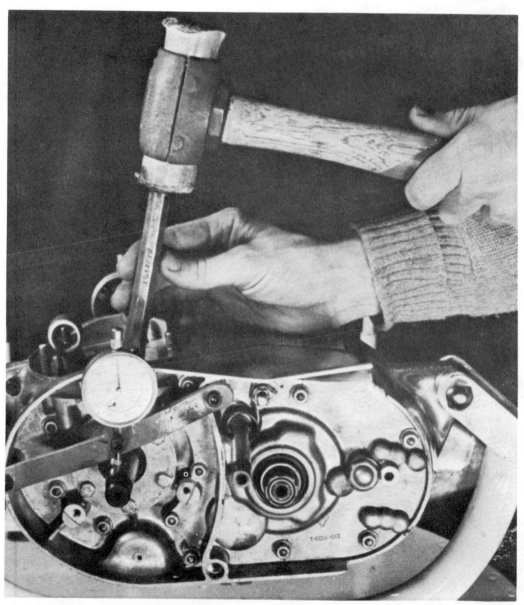

Correcting crankshaft runout after installation

it into the cover. Take care to start the seal squarely, and make sure it bottoms in the seal cover. Oil the seal lips and crankshaft ends with oil. Coat one side of each seal cover gasket lightly with grease, and place the gaskets on the seal covers. Slide the seal covers over the crankshaft ends with the open side of the seals facing in. (The larger crankshaft seal on the 250 cc Scrambler goes on the drive side.) Install and tighten the bolts until they just contact their star washers; then progressively tighten each opposite pair of bolts until you reach a torque of 5 ft. lbs.

16. Turn the kickstart shaft counterclockwise until it hits its stop in the crankcase. Install the kickstart return spring on the shaft, starting with the hook side first. Slide the kickstart lever on the shaft so that the lever is parallel with the spring mounting hole in the shaft; both should be horizontal at this time. Rotate the kickstart lever clockwise until it is pointing straight down, then install the straight end of the return spring in the hole drilled in the shaft. Grab the curved end of the spring with a hooked instrument and wind it around counter-

clockwise until it can be anchored behind its stop.

17. Install a new O-ring on the end of the countershaft on the magneto side of the engine. Install a new oil seal on the shouldered countershaft sprocket spacer and put the spacer, shouldered end first, on the countershaft. Using an appropriately sized pipe or socket, drive the seal in until it is flush with its housing.

18. Install the woodruff key in the slot in the drive side of the crankshaft. If the key is loose in the slot or is damaged, a new one should be used. Install new O-rings on the drive side crankshaft and transmission mainshaft and fit the shouldered spacers on the shafts. Install the woodruff key on the mainshaft.

19. Check the length of the clutch springs and replace any that measure less than 2 mm. Install the primary chain over the outer clutch housing and the engine sprocket. Slide this assembly onto the crankshaft and mainshaft as a unit, taking care not to knock the woodruff keys out of place.

20. Hold the outer clutch housing bush-

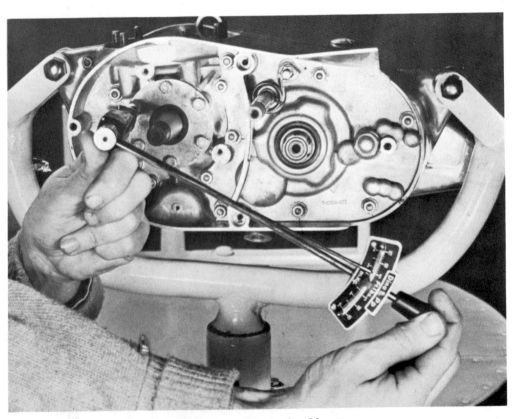

Installing the crankshaft oil seal housing

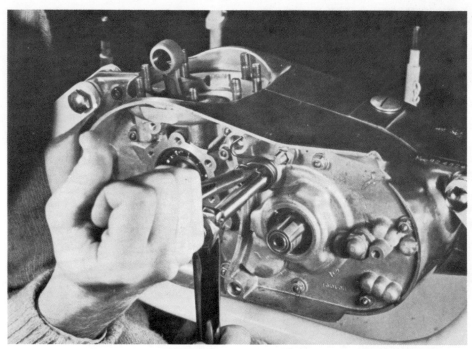

Installing the kickstart return spring

Installing the kickstart return spring

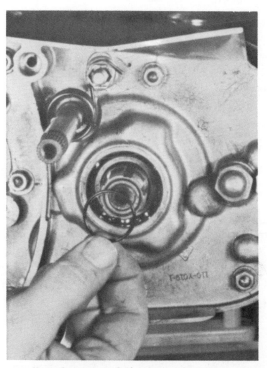

Installing the countershaft O-ring

ing tight against the woodruff key and, with your other hand, slide the inner clutch hub onto the mainshaft and start the inner hub on the woodruff key. Then, holding the outer clutch housing centered on the mainshaft, push the inner clutch hub through the bushing and up against the spacer. A slight tap may be necessary to seat the hub. Install the nuts and washers

Fitting the countershaft oil seal

on the mainshaft and crankshaft and run them up finger-tight. Torque the nuts after the engine has been reinstalled in the frame.

21. Install the magneto side crankshaft woodruff key into its slot. Lightly lubricate the felt lubricating pad attached to the stator disc with distributor cam grease. Install the stator disc (magneto backing plate), taking care to align the marks that you made when disassembling. If the stator is loose on its bosses, place strips of stiff paper cut 5 mm wide between the disc and bosses. The strips should be thick enough to take up the slack and you should barely be able to rotate the stator disc when the strips are in place and the mounting screws are loose. Finally, tighten the mounting screws.

22. Tie up the condenser-to-contact breaker points wire with a piece of strong string. If the wire drops too low it can rub against the points cam boss in the flywheel and be worn through. Carefully slide the magneto flywheel onto its shaft, taking care

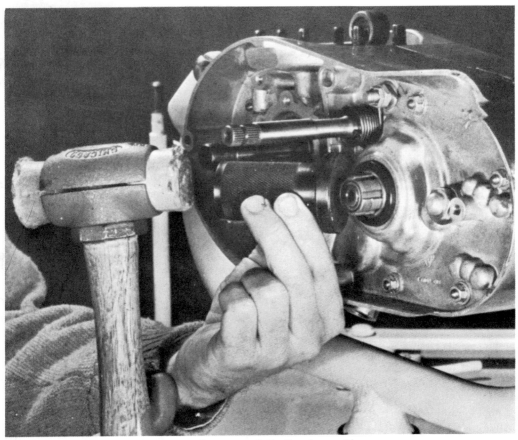

Seating the countershaft oil seal assembly

not to hit the contact breaker follower or the lubricating pad with the points boss on the flywheel. (Avoid this by eyeballing these components through one of the windows in the flywheel as you slide it on.) Install the one or two flat washers, the lockwasher, and the nut on the crankshaft. Tighten the nut to 75 ft. lbs.

23. Secure the electrical junction box to the crankcase, just below the flywheel. Securely tighten the mounting screw. Plug the black wire from the contact breaker points into the top left side of the junction box. Plug the yellow wire from the lighting coil into the bottom left socket in the box.

The Top End

1. Clean and inspect the piston and piston rings. Check for hairline cracks in the piston at the top edges of the transfer cutaways. Use a new piston if any are found.

2. Remove the carbon from the piston crown, taking care not to scratch the soft aluminum alloy. The thin hard bottom layer of carbon should be left alone.

3. Break an old piston ring in half and use it to clean the ring grooves. Insert the unbroken end into the ring groove and push the ring around the piston until the carbon deposits have been removed. Finally, use the end of a sharp knife to remove the thin band of carbon remaining between the top edge of the top groove and the top edge of the piston.

4. Take one of the piston rings and roll it around the top ring groove. If the ring sticks even slightly at one point, dress the top and bottom of the groove at that point with a 1 mm thick flat file until the ring no longer sticks. Repeat this for the bottom ring groove. Make absolutely certain that the rings don't stick, otherwise the engine will lose a lot of its power.

5. Check piston ring end-gap as directed in a preceding section.

6. Oil the wrist pin bearing assembly and place it in the connecting rod. If any of the needles are loose enough to fall out, the bearing should be replaced. It is always a good idea to stuff a rag into the crankcase opening to catch any parts that are dropped during assembly.

7. Heat the piston in a container of light oil to 100° F. or wrap it in rags soaked in hot water. Remove the piston from the oil and insert the wrist pin slightly beyond the first boss. Place one of the thrust washers inside the piston on the protruding wrist pin.

8. Holding the piston so that the shorter skirt faces the intake port, fit the piston to the connecting rod and push the wrist pin halfway through its bearing. Hold the other thrust washer in place between the connecting rod and the other piston boss and push the wrist pin through until it is centered. If the piston has cooled during this interval, wrap it with hot rags once more before inserting the wrist pin.

9. To install a snap-ring, hold it firmly

Installing the thrust washers and wrist pin

Installing a piston circlip

along its center section with a pair of broad-nosed pliers, as shown, and push it into its groove at the angle shown in the illustration. Take care to compress both sides of the ring evenly; do not attempt to hold it at one end and push the other end into the groove or you will bend it. When the ring has been pushed in far enough so that it

won't pop out, use the blunt end of the pliers to shove it in until it snaps into its groove. If, after installation, you are able to rotate the ring with only slight pressure, it should be replaced.

10. Install a new cylinder base gasket on the crankcase with the printed side down. If the gasket overhangs the transfer

Seating the circlip

Transfer port cutouts

that the dowel pin reliefs in the ends of the rings are deep enough so that the ring ends can touch when the ring is compressed. Deepen the reliefs, if necessary, using a small file.

12. Liberally oil the rings and the piston, and coat the cylinder with oil. Install a ring compressor around the piston and gently lower the cylinder over it until the rings are inside the cylinder. Remove the compressor and continue to lower the cylinder, keeping it aligned with its studs on the crankcase. Install a star washer and nut on each of the studs and progressively tighten each opposing pair of nuts.

13. Rotate the flywheel until the piston is at top dead center (TDC). The top edge of the top piston ring should be just below the top of the cylinder. If it protrudes even slightly, remove the cylinder, match a second cylinder base gasket to the first, and reinstall the cylinder with both gaskets in place. Install the cylinder head onto the cylinder and place a flat washer on each of the studs. Install and tighten the nuts lightly. Torque the nuts gradually and

port cutouts in the crankcase, tap the gasket lightly at the edges with a small ball-peen hammer. Remove the gasket and trim away the excess gasket with a razor.

11. Install the rings on the piston and position them so that their ends are butted against the small dowel pins. Check to see

Piston ring compressor in position

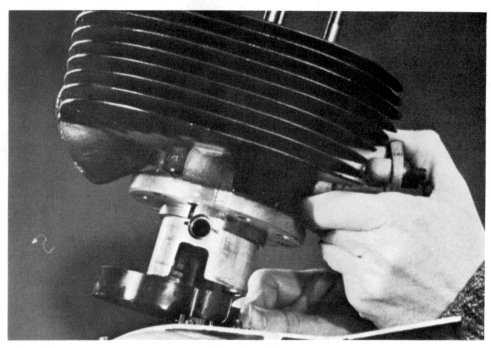

Installing the cylinder

evenly, 2 ft. lbs. at a time, to 12 ft. lbs. Tighten the nuts diagonally (opposing pairs), beginning with either of the two closest to the intake flange.

IGNITION TIMING

Breaker Point Ignition

1. Connect one lead of a continuity light with a built-in battery to the black wire going from the electrical junction box to the points, and ground the other lead on the crankcase.

2. Install a dial gauge, with a spark plug hole adapter, into the spark plug hole. (Dial gauges made specially for setting the ignition timing on motorcycles are available from almost any dealer that handles two-stroke motorcycles.)

3. Rotate the magneto flywheel until one of the windows is at 12 o'clock and the other at 10 o'clock. Turn the flywheel slightly in either direction until the gauge

Cylinder installed with piston at TDC

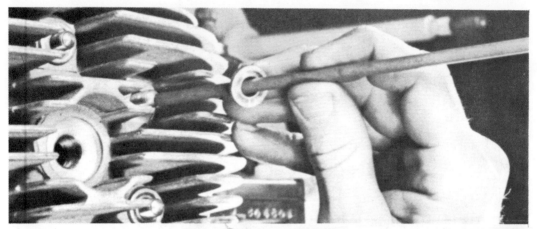

Replacing the cylinder head washers

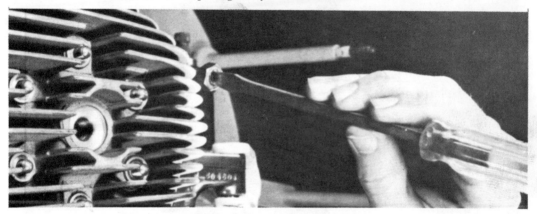

Starting the head nuts on the studs

needle reaches its point of maximum travel. This point of maximum travel is exact TDC. Zero the dial of the gauge on the needle, taking care not to disturb the piston or the gauge.

4. Refer to the following chart for the correct timing specifications for all models. Before checking the timing, make sure that the magneto flywheel is tightened fully to 75 ft. lbs., or the timing will be affected when it is tightened later. Your continuity light should be lit at this point (piston at TDC). If it is not, check the connections.

100 cc Lobito	3.00-3.25 mm
200 cc Metralla	3.00-3.25 mm
125 cc Mercurio	3.00 mm
175 cc Mercurio	3.00-3.25 mm
175 cc Campera	3.00-3.25 mm
200 cc Matador	3.00-3.25 mm
125 cc Sherpa S	3.25 mm
175 cc Sherpa S	3.25 mm
200 cc Sherpa S	3.25 mm
250 cc TT Scrambler	3.85-4.10 mm
250 cc Motocross Scrambler	3.85-4.10 mm
250 cc Matador	3.85-4.10 mm
250 cc Pursang MK IV	2.75-2.95 mm

(Note: Figures are all BTDC.)

5. Rotate the flywheel clockwise while observing both the dial gauge and light. Stop turning the flywheel as soon as the light goes out. If the light flickers during more than 0.02 mm of gauge travel, the points are dirty or pitted and should be cleaned or replaced.

6. Adjust the points gap until the points open (at which time the light will come on) within the figures given in the chart for your model. After adjustment, measure the points gap through the 10 o'clock window in the flywheel. The points gap should be 0.015 in. (0.35–0.45 mm). If it is not within tolerance you will have to remove the flywheel and reposition the stator disc. Rotate it clockwise if the points gap was too close or counterclockwise if the gap was too wide. After changing the stator disc position, replace the flywheel and repeat the

Test light properly connected, with the dial gauge in place in the plug hole

Checking point gap

operation in step 6 until the timing is spot-on and the points gap is within specification.

Femsatronic Ignition

1. Remove the spark plug.
2. Remove the left side engine case.
3. Fit a dial gauge into the spark plug hole and rotate the engine until the gauge shows a maximum reading. The piston is now at top dead center. Rock the piston back and forth several times to insure that it is correctly positioned. Zero the gauge at this point.
4. The rotor has a pin hole in it. A 2 mm pin should be inserted in this hole and the

rotor turned in a clockwise direction until the pin aligns with and will slip into the hole in the left hand corner of the upper coil. The pin will be approximately in the 9 o'clock position.

5. With the rotor aligned as described, the dial gauge should have indicated a total piston movement of 3.0–3.25 mm.

6. If adjustment is necessary, remove the rotor with the special tool and loosen the three screws which secure the stator plate.

7. Replace the rotor, but not the rotor nut. Leave the 2 mm pin in position.

8. Rotate the rotor and stator until they are in the correct timing position, as indicated by the dial gauge (3.0–3.25 mm BTDC).

9. Remove the rotor carefully, assuring that the stator does not move and tighten the stator screws securely.

10. Replace the rotor and rotor nut. Tighten the nut, and recheck the timing as described.

Installing the Speedometer Drive

1. If the speedometer drive bushing was removed during disassembly, insert it in its mounting boss. The end of the bushing farthest from the setscrew hole should be inserted first.

2. Carefully drive the bushing into its mounting boss until the setscrew holes in the bushing and mounting boss are aligned. Use the end of a file or a scribe to align them exactly. Install and tighten the setscrew with its fiber washer.

3. Install the speedometer drive seal to the cable driving end of the drive shaft, with the open end of the seal butted up against the shoulder of the shaft. Slide the drive assembly, splined end first, into the

bushing until you can feel the splines mesh with the drive spindle on the countershaft. Tap the oil seal into the boss until it is about 2 mm past the edge of the hole.

4. Lightly grease and install the thrust washers. Install the triangular cable mounting plate with its gasket. Tighten the screws and center-punch them at the edge of the slot to lock them in position.

INSTALLING THE ENGINE

1. Fit the engine into the frame and secure it with the three mounting bolts. Torque the bolts to 35 ft. lbs.

2. Grease the clutch pushrod and insert it in the mainshaft, flat end first.

3. Install the countershaft sprocket. Fit the drive chain over the rear wheel sprocket and the countershaft sprocket and join the ends with the master link. Make sure you install the master link clip with its closed end facing in the direction of normal chain rotation. Using a new locktab under the nut, tighten the countershaft securing nut to 75 ft. lbs. while holding the rear brake on. Secure the nut with the locktab.

4. Push the electrical wires through the grommet in the magneto side engine case. Plug the black or red ignition wire into the upper right socket in the junction box under the flywheel. Plug the yellow wire (if applicable) into the lower right socket.

5. Install the magneto side engine cover, fitting the two long screws to the top and bottom of the cover and the two short screws to the front and rear of the cover. Do not mix up the screws or the clutch will not function properly.

6. Slide the kickstart lever onto its shaft and secure it with the bolt. Locate the kickstart lever at about 10 o'clock. The lever should contact the peg before hitting

Aligning the holes in the bushing and mounting boss

the internal stop to avoid the chance of breaking the cases.

7. Apply the rear brake to keep the engine from turning over, and torque the clutch sprocket nut to 75 ft. lbs. and the engine sprocket nut to 90 ft. lbs.

8. If your model has steel clutch plates, insert alternately into the clutch assembly a driven plate (with rounded inner-drive tabs) and a drive plate (with holes in its thrust surface). The last plate installed will be a driven plate.

9. If the clutch plates have neoprene surfaces, first install only the driven plates with one bonded side and one plain side. The bonded side goes in first. Then alternately insert a bonded drive plate and a plain driven plate. The pressure plate is the last driven piece in this type of clutch.

10. Early engines have a short clutch rod and a clutch mushroom with loose ball bearings between the clutch rod and pressure plate. On this type, first install the mushroom. Then align the stud holes in the pressure plate with the studs on the inner clutch hub, and install the pressure plate.

11. Later model engines have a long clutch rod, and a pressure plate with a ball bearing thrust cover. Remove the thrust cover, pack the bearing with high temperature grease, and reinstall the cover. Fit the pressure plate on the clutch assembly, taking care not to let the thrust cover fall off and the bearings fall out before the thrust cover contacts the clutch rod.

12. The latest engines have the pressure plate thrust cover retained by a snap-ring. Squirt a few drops of 10 weight oil into the thrust cover cup. Align the tabs and slots and try fitting the pressure plate to the clutch assembly. It has been fitted properly if the inner clutch hub studs are centered in their holes in the pressure plate. If not, remove the pressure plate, rotate it clockwise until the next set of tabs and slots are aligned and install it again. If the studs are still not centered in the holes, repeat the process until you can push the pressure plate fully into position on the clutch assembly.

13. Install the spring cups on the inner clutch hub studs protruding through the pressure plate, then fit the clutch springs and nuts. Tighten each nut until the spring bottoms, then loosen each nut 4 full turns (3 turns on the 250 Scrambler).

14. Pull in the clutch lever on the handlebar and turn the engine over with the kickstarter while observing the rotation of the pressure plate. If the pressure plate is not parallel with the drive plate, it will wobble while rotating.

15. While the clutch is stationary, operate the clutch lever several times while watching the pressure plate. One side of the plate might be pushed out farther than the other side. If so, level the pressure plate by slightly tightening the clutch spring nuts nearest the high side of the plate. Repeat the testing and adjusting until the plate is

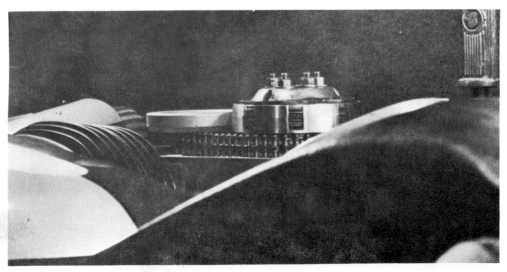

Checking clutch plate alignment

Safety wire in place on the clutch nuts

dead-level with the friction plates when the clutch lever is pulled to the handlebar grip.

16. After adjustment is complete, safety-wire the clutch spring nuts using 1 mm diameter stainless steel wire. Pull the wire through the hole in each nut, taking care not to tighten or loosen the nut in the process. When the wire is threaded through all the nuts, twist the ends together.

17. Coat the crankcase side of the primary case gasket lightly with grease and place it on the crankcase. Install the primary case and secure it with the 7 allen bolts.

18. Loosen the clutch lever adjuster knob at the handlebar. Remove the slotted clutch adjustment cover cap from the magneto side case and loosen the locknut. Screw in the slotted clutch rod adjustment screw until the clutch lever has about 4 mm free-play. Check to see if you can still pull the clutch lever all the way to the grip. If not, loosen the setscrew on the cable-clamping nipple. Move the nipple back toward the end of the cable and retighten the setscrew. Adjust the clutch rod screw inside the magneto cover again and check for full travel at the clutch lever. When you have obtained the correct adjustment, tighten the clutch rod adjusting screw locknut and replace the slotted cover cap in the magneto cover. Whenever you remove a clutch cable from its clamping nipple, this clutch rod adjustment procedure must be followed.

19. Install the carburetor on the cylinder and fit the slide in the carburetor. Replace the fuel line.

20. To install the exhaust system, align the rear mounting flange with its bracket on the frame and align the pipe with its mount in the cylinder. While holding the system in place, start the ring-nut into the cylinder, taking care not to cross-thread the cylinder threads. Use a pin-wrench to tighten the ring-nut securely. Install the bolts at the rear mounting flange. Do not force the rear mounting flange into place against the bracket, or you run the risk of distorting the cylinder. Instead, bend the flange or enlarge the holes so that the bolts can be tightened without putting a strain on the exhaust system.

21. On racing machines, safety-wire the exhaust ring-nut to the frame downtube.

22. Check the gearbox drainplug for tightness and pour 500 cc of SAE 90 gear lube into the gearbox filler hole. Reinstall the filler plug with its rubber gasket.

Clutch cable clamp nipple (arrow)

23. Check the drainplug for tightness and pour 250 cc of SAE 10W or 20W oil into the primary drive case through the filler hole.

CAUTION: *Never use ATF in any engine with neoprene clutch plates, as the fluid will deteriorate the neoprene.*

24. Install a spark plug of the correct heat range, tightening it sufficiently to compress the gasket. Do not overtighten. Fit the high tension lead onto the plug.

FIVE-SPEED MODELS

Disassembly and repair of five-speed Bultaco engines is similar to the basic four-speed engine. The major differences are:

1. The five-speed engine does not employ cylinder base nuts; instead, the cylinder is spigoted to the cases and held in place by the four head nuts on through-studs.

2. The drive side crankshaft half has two main bearings butted against each other. The engine sprocket flywheel is shaped differently, and the inner and outer clutch hubs are larger and stronger.

3. The shift forks are operated by a shift drum instead of a cam plate.

4. The gears and sliding dogs are arranged differently on the mainshaft and countershaft, but their operation is the same as in the four-speed engine.

Because of the many similarities between the four- and five-speed engines, this section will deal only with the variations in the five-speed engine. Use this section in conjunction with the preceding section on four-speed models.

ENGINE REMOVAL

Removing the Magneto Side Components

(Refer to the "Engine Removal" section on four-speed models.)

1. Remove the carburetor. Drain the primary case and the gearbox.

2. Remove the kickstart lever and unscrew the allen bolts from the magneto case.

3. Unscrew the magneto flywheel nut and remove the flywheel.

4. Mark the magneto backing plate and remove it. Pull back the wires and pull the wire connectors apart.

5. Remove the seal cover and its gasket.

6. Bend back the locktab and unscrew the countershaft nut.

7. Remove the exhaust system.

Removing the Primary Drive Components

1. Remove the outer gearshift linkage after taking off the right footpeg.

2. Unscrew the 10 mm nut from the fork that connects the shift lever with the selector shaft. Remove the fork from the shaft.

3. Unscrew the 8 allen bolts from the primary case and remove the case.

4. Remove the clutch plates.

5. Take off the engine sprocket nut.

6. To remove the inner clutch hub, first unscrew the inner clutch hub nut and remove the washer. Insert two prybars behind the outer hub ½ in. away from the engine case to avoid straining the primary chain. If the engine sprocket binds, use a gear puller on it and alternate between prying the outer clutch hub and engine sprocket until each one has moved ½ in. on its shaft.

7. Push the outer hub and the engine sprocket back against the engine case together.

8. Insert two prybars between the outer hub and inner hub and remove the inner hub from the mainshaft.

9. Remove the engine sprocket and outer hub.

10. Remove the spacer and O-ring from the crankshaft.

11. Remove the seal cover from the crankshaft.

Disassembling the Selector Mechanism

1. Lift out the selector shaft.

2. Bend back the locktabs behind the wide, slotted selector lever fixing cap bolt. Use a screwdriver with a wide bit to unscrew the bolt.

3. Lift off the selector lever with its welded pin.

4. Remove the three screws from the selector cover and remove the cover.

5. Remove the pawl carrier (trigger housing) with the two spring-loaded pawls from the shift drum.

Engine Removal

1. Remove the spark plug.

2. Uncouple the master link and remove the drive chain.

3. Unscrew the 4 engine mounting bolts. Lift up the rear of the engine until the crankcase boss clears the frame mounting flanges. Lift up the front of the engine and work the engine up higher until it can be lifted out from the left side.

REMOVING THE PISTON

1. Mount the engine on the bench in its normal position.

2. Consider the front of the engine as 12 o'clock on the face of the clock and loosen the four head studs in the following sequence: 2 o'clock, 8 o'clock, 10 o'clock and 4 o'clock. Loosen the nuts gradually and evenly, 3 ft. lbs. at a time.

3. Take off the nuts and remove the cylinder head.

4. Lift the cylinder off the crankcase, taking care not to let the piston and rod fall against the crankcase flange as they are freed.

5. Remove the two snap-rings from the piston. Before removing the wrist pin, check to see that the clips did not burr the piston. (Throw the old snap-rings away.) Push out the wrist pin and remove the piston from the rod. Remove the cylinder base gasket.

SPLITTING THE CRANKCASES

If you wish to remove the kickstart return spring, refer to the section on four-speed models. It is not necessary to do this in order to split the cases.

1. Unscrew the twelve 10 mm nuts on the magneto side of the engine.

2. Unscrew the allen bolt near the front of the cases.

3. Refer to the four-speed engine section for details on separating the cases. If you have the "standard Bultaco crankcase splitter", Tool No. 132-043, it will have to be modified to fit the five-speed engine. To accomplish this, fit the base of the tool to the right side engine case. Notice that on the right (more sharply angled) leg of the base, the lower mounting hole is not aligned with the primary case mounting hole. Elongate the hole in the tool base ⅛ in. Elongate the lower mounting hole in the left leg of the tool ⅛ in. also.

COMPONENT INSPECTION AND REPAIR

Transmission Components

1. To disassemble the transmission, remove the shift drum, shift fork assembly, countershaft assembly, and kickstarter gear assembly as a unit.

2. Remove the gears from the mainshaft. Two snap-rings must be removed to facilitate this; do not reuse the snap-rings.

3. Remove the gears from the countershaft, noting the warning in the previous step.

4. Clean and dry the components. Inspect them for wear, damage, and discoloration on their thrust surfaces. Replace any part showing a blue color at any thrust surface. This indicates that its temper has been lost due to heat.

5. If you have been experiencing shift indexing problems, examine the slot in the arm of the selector shaft and the pin on the selector lever.

6. Another factor that can cause the transmission to jump out of gear is excessive play between the sliding dogs and idler gears. Measure the thickness of the thrust surface (that bears against the sliding dog) on each shift fork. This measurement should be between 4.50–4.74 mm. Measure the width of the thrust groove in the sliding dog, at the widest part of the groove. Groove width should be between 4.80–5.20 mm.

7. Install the short shift drum follower of the largest shift fork into the bottom groove (nearest the detent cam) of the shift drum. Insert a wire feeler gauge between the follower of the fork and the side of the groove, and test the fit at several points along the groove. A 0.65 mm gauge is the largest that you should be able to fit between the follower and the groove.

8. Install the small, hooked shift fork in the top groove in the shift drum and repeat the measurement.

9. Install the third shift fork in the middle groove and test again. If any of the shift fork followers has excessive play, replace the shift drum and/or the shift fork. The follower pegs should be 5.50–5.80 mm in diameter. The slots in the shift drum should be 5.90–6.30 mm wide.

10. Check the snap-ring grooves on the mainshaft. Test the trueness of the mainshaft as described in the four-speed section.

11. To inspect the sleeve-gear (or countershaft) bearing, remove the kickstart return spring, the kickstart shaft, and the ratchet. Knock out the sleeve gear and remove the bearing. Test it for smooth operation. If it must be replaced, remove the bearing cover.

THE CRANKSHAFT ASSEMBLY

1. If it is necessary to service the crankshaft, remove it from the magneto side engine case.

2. Inspect the seals, seal cover gaskets, centercase gasket, and the connecting rod bearing as described in the four-speed section.

3. Before disassembling the crankshaft, remove the main bearings from the driveshafts. If the left side main bearing is still on the shaft, remove it with the main bearing extractor (Tool No. 132-067) or press it off.

4. To remove the outer main bearing from the right side shaft, fit the two halves of a knife-edge gear puller between the two bearings. Tighten the connecting bolts of the puller to force it into position between the bearings. The puller will force the outer bearing free of its interference fit. Be careful not to draw the edges of the puller toward each other enough to mar the shaft.

5. Remove the inner main bearing on the right side shaft with extractor No. 132-067 or with a press.

6. Drill out the expansion plugs in the crankpin as described in the four-speed section.

7. Press out the crankpin.

8. Reassemble and align the crankshaft assembly in the same manner as for the four-speed models.

PISTON SIZE INFORMATION

Refer back to this same section under the four-speed engine heading. The five-speed pistons are marked in the same manner.

CYLINDER MACHINING INFORMATION

Again, refer back to this same section under the four-speed engine heading. When determining the proper cylinder diameter for an overbore, use the data for the Metisse in the tolerances chart.

When installing a new cylinder liner, it is important to be aware that the fit of the liner in the five-speed crankcases is particularly important. There must not be more than 0.25 mm (0.001 in.) clearance between the outside diameter of the liner and the inside diameter of the crankcase mount.

ENGINE ASSEMBLY

Installing the Crankshaft

1. Before reassembling the cases, replace any badly worn transmission bearings.

2. Remove the crankshaft oil seal and the cover gasket from each seal cover. Install the smaller seal cover on the left side engine case.

3. Clean the main bearings with a solvent. If any dirt remains in the chamfers of the inner races, the seal surfaces of the shafts will be scored if the bearings are ever removed again, and the seals will leak.

4. To install the unsealed main bearing on the left side driveshaft, heat the bearing on a hotplate until the oil begins to smoke, then drop the bearing into position on the shaft.

5. Heat the left side engine case and install the crankshaft assembly in it.

6. Install the sleeve gear in the left side case.

7. If the kickstart assembly was removed, it should be installed at this point. In the five-speed engine, the kickstart assembly is fitted with a spacer between the thrust washer and the ratchet spring on the splines of the kickstart shaft.

Constructional Differences in the Five-Speed Transmission

In the five-speed gearbox, the simplified selector mechanism rotates a shift drum instead of a cam plate. The drum performs the same function as the cam plate, moving the shift forks back and forth along their shaft.

To save space, some of the driving sprockets are located on the mainshaft and others on the countershaft in the five-speed box. Each sprocket is splined to its shaft. Three of the sprockets have built-in sliding dogs and are positioned by the shift forks.

Two of these are located on the mainshaft, and the other is on the countershaft.

Starting from the clutch side, the gears on the mainshaft are laid out as follows:

1. 4th gear idler.
2. 1st gear drive sprocket (with 4th gear sliding dog attached).
3. 2nd gear idler.
4. 3rd gear drive sprocket (with 5th/2nd gear sliding dog).

The mainshaft fits inside the countershaft. The sleeve (countershaft) gear is mated with the transfer gear on the end of the countershaft, but the 5th/2nd gear sliding dog couples the sleeve gear directly to the mainshaft in 5th gear to provide direct drive.

Starting from the clutch side, the five gears on the countershaft are arranged as follows:

1. 4th gear drive sprocket.
2. 1st gear idler.
3. 2nd gear drive sprocket, with 1st/3rd gear sliding dog.
4. 3rd gear idler.
5. Countershaft transfer gear.

Transmission Assembly

1. Install the 25-tooth 2nd gear idler on the mainshaft by sliding the dished side of the gear on the unthreaded end of the mainshaft. Butt the gear against the raised splines of the mainshaft.

2. Install a snap-ring in its groove on the mainshaft next to the 2nd gear idler. Be sure that the pierced ends of the ring are beneath the sliding dog engaging holes in the 2nd gear idler. Grind down the ends of the snap-ring if necessary. The ring must be tight enough on the shaft so that you can't rotate it with your fingers.

3. Hold the mainshaft with the threaded end pointing up. Drop the 1st gear driving sprocket (19 teeth), with the 4th gear sliding dog attached, onto the mainshaft with the shift fork groove pointing down.

4. Install a second snap-ring on the mainshaft in the groove about 1 in. above the 1st gear drive sprocket. Check the fit and positioning of the ring as in Step 2.

5. Hold the mainshaft with the unthreaded end facing up. Install the 28-tooth 3rd gear drive sprocket, with the 5th/2nd gear sliding dog attached, on the unthreaded end of the mainshaft, with

3rd gear drive sprocket

the shift fork groove facing down. Hold the gear in position.

6. Turn the mainshaft over so that the threaded end is pointed up again, and install the 30-tooth 4th gear idler on the threaded end of the shaft with the dished side of the gear facing down.

4th gear idler

7. Install a snap-ring in the groove in the countershaft that is closest to the midpoint of the shaft.

8. Install the 28-tooth drive sprocket, with the 1st/3rd sliding dog attached, between the snap-ring grooves in the countershaft splines so that the shift fork groove faces the snap-ring that has been installed.

9. Install a snap-ring in the other groove in the countershaft.

10. Holding the countershaft so that the sliding dog groove in the sliding dog gear is facing up, put the 19-tooth 3rd gear idler on the shaft from the top with the dog-engaging slots of the gear facing down. Rotate the idler gear and make sure that the pierced ends of the snap-ring lie

beneath the engaging slots; if not, grind down the ends of the ring.

11. Install the thick spacer on the countershaft so that it butts against the 3rd gear idler.

12. Install the 16-tooth transfer gear on the countershaft so that it butts against the spacer.

13. Fit the thin spacer and butt it against the transfer gear. Coat the spacer with heavy grease to keep it from falling off. (Late Metrallas use a wider transfer gear that fits flush with the end of the splines. There is no thin washer.)

14. Turn the countershaft upside down, holding the gears and the spacer to keep them from falling off. Install the 28-tooth 1st gear idler with the dog-engaging slots facing down. Fit the 17-tooth 4th gear drive sprocket on the countershaft with the flat face of the gear facing down.

15. Hold the countershaft in a horizontal position. Pick up the mainshaft and mesh the gears on the two shafts, with the threaded end of the mainshaft at the same end as the 4th gear drive sprocket on the countershaft. All of the gears should mesh except for the transfer gear on the mainshaft which will mesh with the sleeve gear on the countershaft. The shafts will be parallel if the gears have been assembled correctly. Put the countershaft aside.

16. Mesh the 28-tooth kickstart with the 1st gear drive sprocket (4th gear sliding dog attached), with the ratchet teeth on the kickstart gear facing the unthreaded end of the mainshaft. Fit the unthreaded end of the mainshaft into the countershaft and fit the kickstart gear to the kickstart shaft simultaneously.

17. Hold the countershaft with the transfer gear facing the countershaft bearing. Rotate the countershaft gears so that they mesh with the mainshaft gears, and fit the countershaft into its bearing, taking care

not to dislodge the thin spacer from the splines of the transfer gear.

18. Unscrew the detent plunger capscrew from the other side of the engine case until the plunger is flush with its boss. Install the shift drum into its mounting boss. One of the notches on the detent cam at the rear of the drum is shallower than the others; rotate the drum so that the shallow notch is aligned with the detent plunger. Retighten the detent plunger capscrew. The shift drum is in Neutral at this point; assemble the transmission with the drum in this position.

19. Install the largest shift fork (the 2nd/5th gear fork) on the 2nd/5th gear sliding dog gear on the mainshaft next to the sleeve gear, with the follower peg on the fork pointing toward the shift drum. Pivot the fork until its follower peg engages with the rear cam groove (nearest the detent cam) on the shift drum.

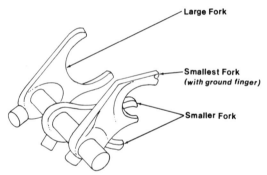

The order of shift fork assembly

20. Pick up the shift fork that has not had part of one of its fingers ground away and install it on the sliding dog gear on the countershaft, with the follower peg of the fork pointing toward the shift drum. Engage this 1st/3rd gear shift fork's follower peg in the middle cam groove of the shift drum.

21. Install the 4th gear shift fork on the 4th gear sliding dog, nearest the threaded end of the mainshaft, with the follower peg pointing toward the shift drum. Engage the peg in the front cam groove in the drum.

22. Insert the shift fork shaft through the holes in the forks and push it into the mounting boss in the engine case.

Assembling the Crankcases

1. Heat the two remaining main bearings until the oil begins to smoke. Drop the

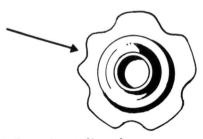

The shallower (Neutral) notch

unsealed bearing on the drive side crankshaft and allow it to cool for ten minutes.
Install the sealed bearing on the shaft so
that it butts up against the first bearing,
and allow it to cool for the same amount
of time. The cooling process can be speeded
up with compressed air. Make sure that you
install the center gasket before the cases
are mated.

2. Heat the right side case and install
it onto the left side case. Install and tighten
the case-stud nuts to 5 ft. lbs. Fit the allen
bolt just behind the front engine mount
boss.

3. After the cases have been mated,
check the flywheel alignment as described
in the four-speed section under "The Crankshaft Assembly".

4. Remove the magneto side seal cover
from the engine. Install new seals in the
magneto and drive side seal covers, fit new
gaskets to the covers, and install them on
the engine.

5. To install the kickstart spring, align
the spring mounting hole in the kickstart
shaft and fit the end of the spring into it.
Hook the other end of the spring over the
anchor nut.

6. Install a new O-ring on the countershaft and then mount the countershaft
spacer and oil seal.

7. Insert the two shift selector pawls,
round end first, into the slots of the pawl
carrier. If the square ends of the pawls
appear to have been hand filed, insert the
rounded ends of the pawls into the slots
of the carrier so that the filed edge of the
square corner of each pawl faces up.

8. Compress the pawls downward.
Holding the pawl carrier as before, with
the flats on the shaft in a vertical position,
fit the carrier into the shift drum. Neither
pawl will drop into a slot in the rim of
the drum.

9. Install the selector cover gasket on
the inner face of the cover. Fit the cover
to the shaft of the pawl carrier, with the
semi-circular notch in the cover facing
down. Install the three mounting screws.

10. Using pliers, rotate the pawl carrier
shaft clockwise until one of the pawls
drops into a slot.

11. Install the selector lever on the pawl
carrier shaft, with the arm of the lever
facing the rear of the engine and the pin
facing away from the engine. Bend down

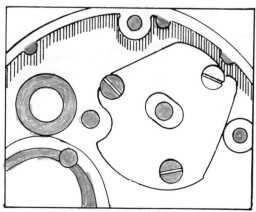

Selector cover installed

the tabs on the lever capscrew washer. Fit
the washer to the pawl carrier shaft, install
the capscrew, and tighten it. Bend up the
tabs of the washer to lock the capscrew in
place.

12. Install the selector shaft, with its arm
facing up, into its mount beneath the selector cover. Adjust the selector lever so
that its pin goes into the slot on the arm
of the shaft. Press the hairpin spring on the
rear of the selector shaft arm so that the
spring legs snap over the pin in the engine
case underneath the lever. Install the thrust
washer on the selector shaft with its chamfered side facing the engine.

13. Install the spacers, with new O-rings,
on the crankshaft and mainshaft.

14. Fit the woodruff keys on the primary side crankshaft and mainshaft. Check
the length of the clutch springs as described
in the four-speed section.

15. Fit the primary chain over the engine sprocket and outer clutch hub. Install
the assembly on the mainshaft and crankshaft. Install the inner clutch hub, and
then replace the mainshaft and crankshaft
nuts and washers. Torque the nuts after
the engine has been reinstalled in the
frame.

Assembling the Magneto Side Engine Components

Refer to the four-speed section. The procedures for five-speed models are the same.

Inspecting and Installing the Piston

Refer to the four-speed section.

Installing the Cylinder

1. Fit a ring compressor over the piston rings. Install the cylinder base gasket.

2. Install the cylinder over the four studs and gently lower it over the piston. When the cylinder has covered the rings, remove the compressor and bottom the cylinder against the crankcase.

3. Fit the cylinder head on the cylinder. Attach a head nut at the 2 o'clock and at the 8 o'clock positions. Torque the nuts to 3 ft. lbs., then unscrew the nuts again and remove the head.

4. Turn the flywheel until the piston is at top dead center and check the height of the piston relative to the top of the cylinder. (Refer to the four-speed section.)

5. Install the head again and fit a washer and nut on each of the studs. Tighten the nuts to 3 ft. lbs. in the following sequence: 2 o'clock, 8 o'clock, 10 o'clock, and 4 o'clock positions. Repeat the sequence in 3 ft. lb. increments until 12 ft. lbs. has been reached.

IGNITION TIMING

Refer to the four-speed section. Procedures are the same for five-speed models, with the following exception:

When grounding one of the test light leads on the engine case, attach the alligator clip so that it holds the exposed end of the green wire against the case.

ENGINE INSTALLATION

Refer to the four-speed section. The following notes apply to the five-speed models:

1. Insert the wires that are dangling from the frame up through the grommet in the bottom of the engine beneath the flywheel. Join the yellow wire to the yellow wire, the green to green, and the red wire to the black wire. Slide the insulators down over the exposed clips. Position the wires against the engine case beneath the flywheel and tighten the wire clamp screw to secure them.

2. Install the two long primary case allen bolts in the holes beneath the gearshift and "O" in "BULTACO" on the case.

3. Install the gear selector fork on the splined selector shaft so that it faces to the rear of the bike and lies parallel with an imaginary line drawn between the footpeg and the selector shaft.

4. After the shift lever and footpeg have been installed, engage the lever with the selector fork. Pull up on the lever to make sure that it can't slip out of engagement with the selector shaft fork. If it does, remove the fork from the shaft, rotate the fork one spline counterclockwise, and reinstall it. Check again by pulling up on the shift lever.

5. With the transmission in Neutral, rotate the rear wheel and press down on the shift lever to engage second gear. If the lever hits the exhaust pipe, loosen the 13 mm nut on the front side of the shift lever and rotate the eccentric pin to reposition it.

Engine Torque Specifications

(In ft. lbs.)

Flywheel retaining nut	75
Countershaft sprocket nut	75
Clutch hub nut	75
Engine sprocket	90
Head bolts	12
Case half nuts	5
Seal retainer screws	5
Primary & mag. cover screws	5
Engine mounting bolts	35

Fuel Systems

AMAL CARBURETORS

The Metering Systems

There are several metering systems in a carburetor. None of the metering systems start or stop abruptly, but blend gradually with each other to create a smooth throttle response.

THE PILOT SYSTEM

The pilot metering system consists of the low speed pilot (air) screw and the pilot jet, which regulates fuel flow. The pilot, or low-speed system, regulates fuel mixture at throttle openings ranging from 0–⅛ throttle. In this system, air enters the smaller of

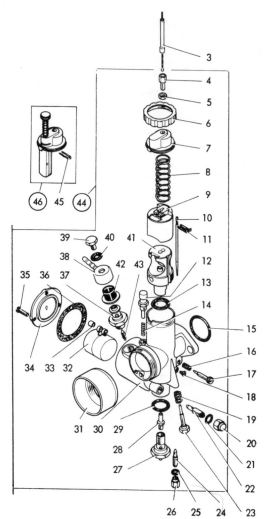

Exploded view of the Amal Monobloc carburetor

THE SLIDE CUTAWAY AND NEEDLE JET METERING SYSTEM

As the throttle is opened past ⅛ and up to about ¼ of maximum, the cutaway of the throttle slide (which regulates air flow direction) and the needle jet (which regulates fuel flow) come into operation. Because of the shape of the slide, air entering the mouth of the carburetor is forced downward in the bore and across the mouth of the spray nozzle, sucking fuel out into the airstream. The shape of the cutaway determines the richness of the mixture at this point, as at small throttle openings only the straight, untapered portion of the jet needle passes through the jet, which does not vary the fuel flow.

The size of the cutaway in the slide is measured from the bottom of the slide to the highest point in the cutaway, in sixteenths of an inch. The lower the cutaway, the richer the mixture.

Pilot mixture passages

Pilot fuel jet (arrow)

the two holes beneath the mouth of the carburetor. This hole leads to the low-speed air screw. Two small passages lead from a chamber on the other side of the air screw to the pilot jet.

When the engine is idling, a vacuum is created behind the throttle slide. Air enters the smaller hole beneath the mouth of the carburetor, passes the low-speed air screw, and enters the chamber just beyond. The second, larger, passage comes into operation as the throttle is opened and the slide uncovers it. It adds to the fuel fed to the engine by the first passage. As the throttle is opened beyond ⅛ of its travel, the vacuum in the venturi becomes great enough to pull fuel out of the needle jet and the low-speed system is overshadowed by the slide cutaway and needle jet metering system.

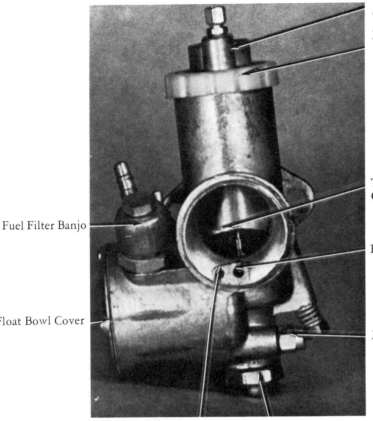

Carburetor Top
and
Top Nut

Throttle Slide
Cutaway

Fuel Filter Banjo

Booster System Inlet

Float Bowl Cover

Main Jet Nut

Pilot Air Metering Inlet   Needle Jet Holder

The Slide and Needle Metering System

From 1/4–3/4 throttle the slide is lifted far enough away from the bottom of the throttle bore and the needle is lifted out of the nozzle enough that the slide cutaway no longer has any effect on carburetion. A much larger volume of air is passing through the carburetor at this point. As the slide is raised and more air is admitted, the needle is lifted farther out of the nozzle.

Throttle Slide
Cutaway

Throttle Slide
Needle

The needle is tapered down toward the end that fits in the nozzle, and as it is raised more fuel is able to pass through the nozzle to match the increased air volume.

By varying the position of the needle in the slide (up or down), or by varying the taper of the needle, the fuel mixture at these mid-range throttle openings can be tuned to suit various requirements. Raising the needle richens the mixture, lowering the needle leans the mixture. In the same way, by fitting a needle with a greater taper the mixture can be richened, or, with a lesser taper, leaned.

The Main Jet Metering System

At openings between 3/4 to full throttle, the needle is completely withdrawn from the nozzle and the main jet takes over the fuel supply completely. As this point, there is virtually no restriction of fuel or air through the main jet and throttle bore, and only the size of the main jet determines

Main Jet Removed

Pilot Air Screw

Jet Block Locating Screw

Pilot Fuel Jet Nut

Throttle Slide-Stop Screw

mixture strength. This is why it is so important to fit the proper sized main jet.

THE FLOAT CHAMBER

In order to maintain the correct flow of fuel to the carburetor jets at all engine speeds and throttle openings, a sufficient amount of fuel under relatively constant delivery pressure must be available. The float chamber serves to accomplish this. Fuel entering the float chamber from the fuel tank must pass between the float

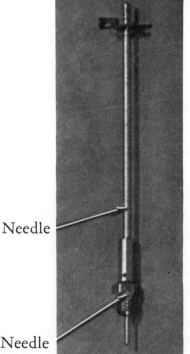

Needle

Needle
Jet

Float Metering Needle

Float Pivot Axle

Float

needle and seat. As fuel fills the chamber, the float rises with the fuel level and when a preset level is reached, the float shuts off flow by pressing the needle against the seat, closing the valve. As fuel is consumed and the level drops, the float follows the level and allows more fuel to enter so that a constant level is maintained.

Adjusting the Carburetor

The only external adjustment you can make on the carburetor is for idle speed and mixture.

1. Start the engine and warm it up.

2. Turn the low-speed air screw in until it bottoms GENTLY against its stop, and back it out ¾ turn.

3. Adjust the throttle stop screw so that the engine will idle smoothly with the throttle closed. Turn the air screw slowly, in very small amounts, in both directions until you find the point at which the engine runs the smoothest.

4. Back off the throttle stop screw until the engine turns over as slowly as possible and still runs smoothly. Open the throttle and let it snap back to idle. If the engine dies, adjust the throttle stop screw to lift the slide slightly more.

Tuning the Carburetor

The following changes can be made to tune the carburetor to meet various requirements:

1. Changing the size of the main jet.

2. Changing the position of the jet needle in the slide.

3. Changing the needle for one of a different taper.

4. Changing the throttle slide for one with a different cutaway.

5. Changing the size of the needle jet.

Before making any changes in the carburetor, make sure that there are no air leaks and that the ignition system is in perfect condition. To check the points gap and ignition timing, refer to the "Ignition Timing" section for your machine. To check for an air leak, bottom the low-speed air screw against its seat and back it out ¾ turn. If the engine then revs much faster than a normal idle speed, your problem is caused by an air leak, not by the carburetor.

The carburetor metering systems should be checked in the following sequence:

1. Warm up the engine. On level ground,

run the engine up to peak rpm in Second gear. Slowly back off the throttle until it is closed. While backing off, listen for a pinging sound, which indicates a lean mixture. Check also for *four-stroking* (engine firing every other stroke), which indicates a rich mixture. Try to determine the throttle openings at which the problem is noticeable.

2. If the engine was pinging between ¾–full throttle, install a larger main jet. If the engine was running too rich, fit a smaller main jet. Road test the machine again to make sure you have solved the problem.

3. If the engine was pinging between ½–¾ throttle, raise the jet needle one notch in the slide. If it was four-stroking, lower the needle one notch.

4. If the engine was pinging between ¼–½ throttle, install a slide with a smaller cutaway. If the engine was four-stroking, fit a slide with a higher cutaway.

5. Between ¼ and closed throttle, if the engine was pinging, fit a larger needle jet. If the engine was four-stroking, fit a smaller needle jet.

After changing any components, run through the following fine-tuning sequence.

1. Ride the motorcylce for at least ¼ mile with the throttle halfway between closed and ¼ open. Push the kill button and, at the same instant, pull in the clutch. Hold the clutch in, coast to a stop, and remove the spark plug. It should be dry and malt brown in color at the end of the porcelain insulator surrounding the center electrode. If it is white, the mixture is still too lean. If it is black and oily, the mixture is too rich. Change the needle jet to correct the condition.

2. Perform a plug check in the same manner as Step one, after having ridden the bike for at least ¼ mile at between ¼–½ throttle. If the mixture is not perfect, as indicated by the color of the plug, change the throttle slide as necessary.

3. Perform a plug check again, this time riding with the throttle open between ½–¾. If necessary, raise or lower the needle in the slide to get the correct spark plug reading.

4. Finally, ride the bike at least ¼ mile with the throttle wide open and check the plug again after pulling the clutch in and shutting the engine down cleanly. If neces-

sary, change the main jet. This completes carburetor tuning.

MONOBLOC CARBURETOR

Disassembly

1. Unscrew and remove the air cleaner.
2. Remove the fuel line from the fuel line banjo on the carburetor.
3. Unscrew the two carburetor mounting nuts and remove the carburetor from the engine.
4. Unscrew the plastic cover nut from the carburetor body, take off the carburetor top, and withdraw the slide from the carburetor body. Take off the needle retaining clip and remove the needle from the slide.
5. Hold the slide and carburetor top in one hand. Press them together to compress the slide return spring, and remove the throttle cable fitting from its slot in the top of the slide. Remove the cable from the slide and the carburetor top.
6. Take off the three mounting screws from the float bowl cover and remove the cover. Remove the float pivot spacer, the float, and the float needle from the carburetor.

7. Remove the tickler assembly from the top of the float bowl. Push the tickler assembly apart; it consists of the tickler button, the spring, and the crown-screw.
8. Remove the float needle jet holder (the float valve seat) from the top of the float bowl.
9. Unscrew the main jet cover nut and remove the main jet with a screwdriver.
10. Unscrew the pilot jet cover nut and then remove the pilot jet.
11. Remove the needle jet holder; catch the jet block as it falls out of the slide barrel.
12. Remove the needle jet from its holder. Remove the O-ring from the carburetor mounting flange.

Throttle slide barrel (top arrow), and jet block

INSPECTION AND REASSEMBLY

1. Separate the gaskets and plastic parts from the metal parts. Wash the metal parts

Tickler assembly (arrows)

in carburetor cleaner or other solvent, then blow dry with compressed air.

2. Fit a new jet block gasket (Part No. 815-132) to the bottom of the jet block and insert the block into the slide barrel of the carburetor. Make sure that the locating screw is in place.

3. If the bike is more than six months old or has covered more than 4,000 miles, replace the needle jet with a new one of the same size. Mount the needle jet in its holder and tighten it.

4. Install a new needle jet holder gasket (Part No. 815-130) to the needle jet holder.

5. Insert the needle jet holder into the bottom of the carburetor and screw it into the bottom of the jet block. The needle jet should be replaced if it is over a year old.

6. Fit a new gasket to the main jet (Part No. 715-089) and screw the jet firmly into its seat. Install and tighten the main jet cover nut.

7. Fit a new gasket to the pilot jet (Part No. 715-024) and screw the jet into its seat. Install and tighten the pilot jet cover nut.

8. Install and tighten the float needle jet holder into the top of the float bowl. Turn the carburetor upside down and, from the inside of the float bowl, drop the nylon float needle, pointed end first, down into the jet. Fit the float mounting bracket to the float pivot shaft with the narrow side of the bracket pressing against the float needle. Fit the pivot spacer to the float pivot shaft.

NOTE: *If carburetor flooding has been experienced, it is a good idea to replace the float needle and seat assembly. Also, check to see if the float is leaking by*

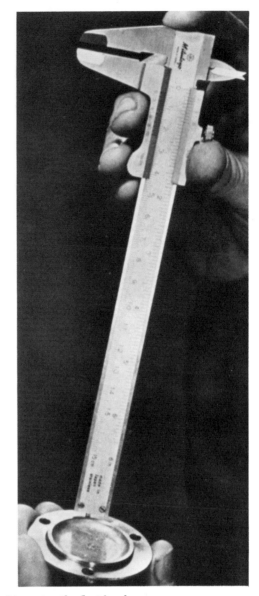

Measuring the float bowl cover

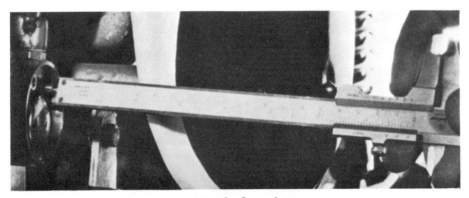

Measuring the float axle spacer

shaking it. If so, replace it. A few of the carburetors have float pivot spacers that are too thick, causing the lip of the float bowl cover to bind against the spacer and the float. To check for this, first measure the distance that the float bowl cover lip protrudes beyond its gasket. Then measure the distance from the edge of the float chamber to the top of the float pivot spacer, as shown. The first distance measured must be less than the second distance. If not, file the end of the float pivot spacer to provide the clearance.

9. Install a new gasket and fit the float bowl cover to the float bowl.

10. Put the open end of the tickler button into its mounting hole at the top of the float bowl. Fit the spring and crown screw to the button.

11. Smear a small amount of grease on a new O-ring and press it into its groove in the carburetor mounting flange.

12. Examine the nylon fuel filter. If there are any tears in the mesh, replace the filter element. Install the filter in its mounting spigot and place the banjo over the filter. Fit a new banjo screw gasket (Part No. 815-029) and tighten the screw.

13. Fit the throttle stop screw spring to the throttle stop screw. Turn the screw into its mounting boss.

14. Put the carburetor top plastic nut, the carburetor top, and the slide return spring, in that order, on the carburetor end of the throttle cable.

15. Measure the diameter of the slide at several points around its circumference with a vernier caliper. If the slide has worn oval more than ½ mm (0.020 in.), replace it.

16. Compress the slide return spring against the carburetor top so that a portion of the inner throttle cable protrudes past the end of the return spring.

17. Put the fitting on the end of the inner cable down into the hole in the top of the slide and work the cable back to the blind end of the slot. On the underside of the slide top is a round notch to accept the cable fitting. Allow the cable fitting to seat in this notch. Release the return spring.

18. Slide the notched end of the needle up into the rounded portion of the slot in the center of the top of the slide.

19. Fit a new needle clip to the center

Fit the cap tooth in the slot (arrow)

notch on the needle. Put the slide into the carburetor barrel, being careful to fit the needle into its hole in the center of the jet block. If the carburetor is equipped with a choke slide, make sure that the choke is positioned in its slot in the slide. Check to see that the slide cutaway is facing the mouth of the carburetor, and push the slide down into the barrel. It may be necessary to rotate the slide slightly so that the ridge inside the slide can find and enter the notch in the jet block. Push the slide all the way to the bottom of the barrel.

20. Hold the carburetor top pressed against the top of the barrel, and start the plastic top nut on its threads in the barrel. Make sure that the tooth on the bottom of the carburetor top is fitted into its slot in the top of the barrel. Tighten the plastic nut.

21. Look into the carburetor mouth and watch the action of the slide as you open and close the throttle twistgrip. Be sure that the slide is raised and lowered freely, with no binding, as you work the throttle.

22. Check to see that the O-ring is still in place on the mounting flange, and install the carburetor on the engine. Tighten the two nuts just enough to keep them from

loosening from engine vibration. If they are overtightened, the mounting flange may be warped. Locktite or safety wire the nuts to be safe.

23. Install the air cleaner.

24. Position the fuel filter banjo so that the fuel line can make an easy sweep from the tank to the fitting and connect the fuel line.

25. Again tighten the needle jet holder on the bottom of the carburetor. Start the engine and adjust the idle speed and mixture, as previously described.

CONCENTRIC CARBURETOR

Disassembly

1. Shut off the fuel tap, and disconnect the fuel line at the carburetor.

2. Lift up the rubber cover, and remove the carburetor cap, lifting out the throttle slide assembly.

3. If it is desired to dismantle the slide assembly, compress the return spring against the cap, take out the needle and clip. Remove the cable from the slide.

4. Disconnect the air cleaner hose, and unbolt and remove the carburetor from the engine.

5. Remove the float bowl banjo bolt.

6. Unscrew the float bowl screws, and remove the float bowl.

7. Lift out the float, complete with float needle and spindle.

8. Remove the throttle stop and pilot air screws from the carburetor body.

9. Remove the filter screen (if fitted) from the main jet. The main jet alone can be unscrewed from the jet holder, or the jet holder may be unscrewed which will effect the removal of both the main and needle jets. Both these jets may be cleaned while in place in the jet holder.

10. Unscrew the pilot fuel jet with a small screwdriver.

Inspection

1. All rubber O-rings must be in good condition. This is especially true of the carburetor flange O-ring. Replacement of the O-rings and float bowl and banjo gaskets is advised after disassembly.

2. The fuel passages in the float bowl must be clean. The needle seat in the float bowl must be clean, and free of deposits of any kind.

3. Check the float for leaks or punctures. The float needle must be in good condition.

4. Make sure that all jets are clear. Soak in solvent and blow them dry if necessary.

5. Soak the carburetor body in a solvent and blow it dry, paying close attention to all fuel and air passages.

6. Check the flange surface for warpage. Slight imperfections may be removed by grinding on a flat surface.

7. Clean the fuel filters.

8. Inspect the throttle slide. It should be free of wear or scratches.

9. The metering needle should be smooth and without signs of wear. The needle and the needle jet should both be replaced after many miles have been covered.

Assembly

Assembly is the reverse of the disassembly procedure. Note that the carburetor flange O-ring should be seated in its seat.

It is important that the flange bolts be tightened evenly and not overtightened.

If a plastic float banjo is used, care should be taken when tightening the banjo bolt. Leakage of gasoline at this point may be due to the bolt being too tight.

IRZ CARBURETORS

The constructional details and operation of IRZ carburetors is basically similar to the Amal concentric. The major variations are:

1. In the IRZ pilot metering system, air enters the carburetor through the larger of the two holes beneath the carburetor. Fuel for the pilot metering system enters the pilot jet directly; the jet protrudes down into the float bowl.

2. The slide in IRZ carburetors is grooved. The groove rides on the end of the slide stop to keep the slide positioned correctly.

3. In the IRZ, the spray nozzle is the upper part of the needle jet. The needle jet is stamped with two sets of numbers, indicating the size of the jet (three digits) and the size of the air holes in the jet (two digits).

4. The IRZ slide has its cutaway height marked in millimeters. A slide marked "75" has a cutaway height of 7.5 mm.

5. The air intake for the booster system in the IRZ carburetor is through the smaller hole beneath the mouth of the carburetor.

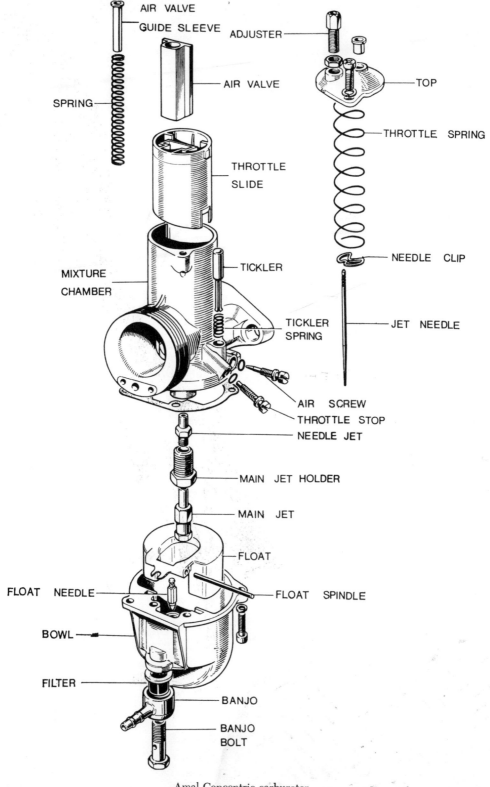

Amal Concentric carburetor

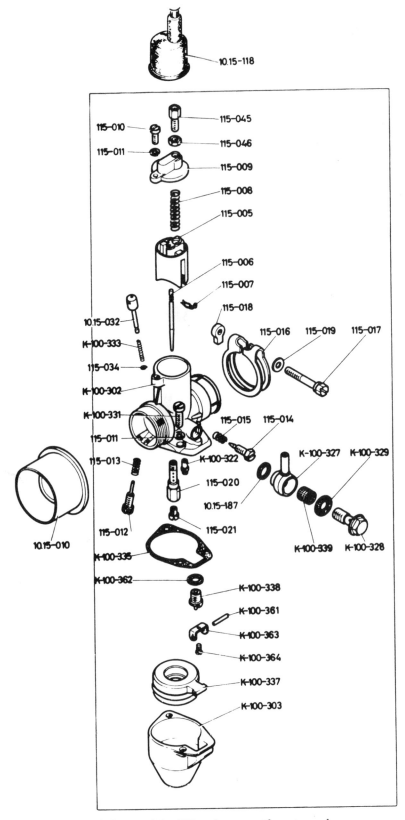

Exploded view of the IRZ carburetor with parts numbers

Tickler Button

Throttle Slide Stop

Pilot Air Inlet

Filter Banjo

Booster System
Air Inlet

Pilot Air Screw Mount

Air Screw Spring

Pilot Air Screw

Float Pivot Bracket

Tickler Retaining
Clip

Float   Pilot Fuel Jet

Pilot mixture inlet holes

The air is fed directly into six holes drilled into the needle jet body.

Disassembly

1. Loosen the air filter clamps and remove the hose from the mouth of the carburetor.

2. Remove the fuel line from the fuel filter banjo at the carburetor.

3. Loosen the mounting sleeve clamp and remove the carburetor from the intake manifold.

4. Take out the slotted screw from the carburetor top and remove the top. Withdraw the slide from the barrel.

5. Holding the slide and carburetor top as shown, push the slide and top toward each other to compress the slide return spring. Unhook the throttle cable fitting from the slot in the slide. Remove the slide, the spring, and the carburetor top from the cable.

6. Using your fingernail, remove the needle clip from the slide.

7. Unscrew the bolt from the fuel filter banjo and remove the banjo, the washer, and the filter element.

8. Unscrew and remove the low-speed air screw.

9. Take off the two screws and remove the float bowl.

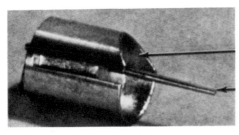

Throttle Slide Cutaway

Throttle Slide Needle

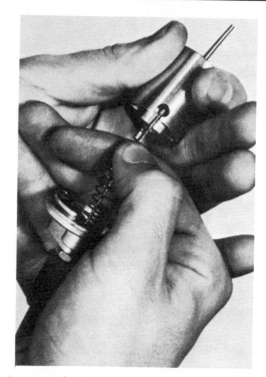

Removing the throttle cable

10. To remove the float, press against the end of the pivot shaft that protrudes from the slotted ear of the mounting bracket and remove the shaft.

11. Unscrew and remove the pilot jet from the bottom of the carburetor.

12. Unscrew the needle jet from the jet block in the bottom of the carburetor. Using a screwdriver, unscrew the main jet from the needle jet.

13. Using a pair of pliers with wide, smooth jaws, gently unscrew the float needle assembly by holding it on its center ridge.

14. Twist the mounting clip on the tickler button with a pair of pliers and remove the clip. Remove the tickler button and its spring from the other side of the carburetor body.

15. Unscrew and remove the slide stop screw.

Inspection and Reassembly

1. Separate the metal parts from the plastic parts and the gaskets.

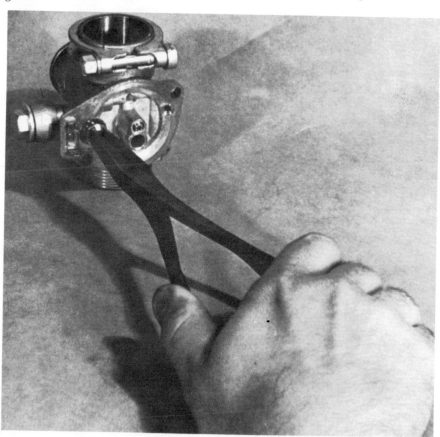

Removing the float needle assembly

2. Clean the metal parts in carburetor cleaner or other solvent. Blow dry with compressed air, taking care to clear all the fuel and air passages.

3. Install the needle jet in the jet block in the bottom of the carburetor. Install the main jet in the needle jet.

4. Install the pilot jet in the bottom of the carburetor.

5. Tighten the small screw that secures the float pivot mounting bracket. Check to see that the ears of the bracket are not bent toward or away from each other.

Straighten the float bracket ears if necessary

6. Hold the float needle and seat assembly in your fingers, with the protruding portion of the needle facing down. Press the needle up into its seat and release it quickly. If it binds, or is slow to drop down, replace the assembly. Using a new gasket, install the assembly into the bottom of the carburetor with the ridge facing away from the carburetor. Tighten it with pliers, taking care not to distort the ridge (which could cause the needle to bind).

7. Check to see if the float is leaking by shaking it. If you hear gasoline sloshing around, it should be replaced.

8. Position the pivot arm of the float between the ears of the float mounting bracket. The float should be positioned so that the flat side of the pivot arm presses against the bottom of the float needle. Insert the pivot shaft into the plain ear of the mounting bracket. Press against the shaft to force it into the slotted ear of the bracket. Press it far enough so that each end protrudes the same amount.

9. Fit the tickler button to its mount and work it up and down. If it has a tendency to bind, either the tickler button or its mount are bent. Sight down through the tickler mount to determine where the bend is, and straighten it or replace the bent part.

The tickler assembly (arrows)

10. Fit the spring to the tickler button and insert them into the mount from the top of the carburetor. Install the clip in the groove in the button.

11. Install the float bowl on the carburetor, using a new gasket. Put a lock washer on the two mounting screws and tighten them.

12. Fit the spring on the low-speed air screw and install it. Bottom the screw gently and then back it out one turn.

13. Fit a new washer (Part No. K-100-329) to the banjo mounting bolt. Install the screen on the bolt so that the screen covers the two fuel-feed holes. Fit the banjo to the bolt and install the small washer (Part No. 10.15-187) on the bolt. Install the bolt and run it down finger-tight.

14. Install the rubber cable adjuster cover on the outer throttle cable with the small end of the cover pointing away from the end of the cable.

15. Thread the inner throttle cable through the cable adjuster on the carbu-

retor top. Fit the slide return spring on the inner cable, and compress the spring against the top so that a short portion of the inner cable protrudes from the spring.

16. Fit the cable into the slot in the top of the slide and butt the cable against the blind end of the slot so that it is connected to the slide. Release the spring.

17. Insert the grooved end of the needle in the hole in the bottom of the slide. Align the center groove in the needle with the slot in the top of the slide, and insert the needle clip into the slot.

18. Install the slide in the carburetor barrel with the cutaway facing the mouth of the carb. Rotate the slide slightly in either direction until the groove mates with the

positioning end of the slide stop screw. Bottom the slide in the barrel.

19. Install the carburetor top on the barrel. Mount the screw with its lockwasher.

20. Fit the carburetor to the intake manifold. Rotate it until it is aligned (vertically) with the cylinder, then tighten the clamp screw.

21. Position the air cleaner hose on the mouth of the carburetor and tighten the clamp.

22. Position the banjo so that the fuel line can make a clean sweep from the tank to the connection, then tighten the banjo bolt and install the line.

23. Start the engine and adjust the idle speed and mixture.

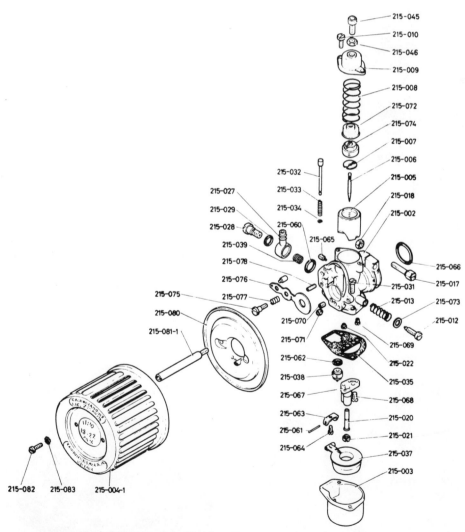

Exploded view of the Zenith carburetor, showing parts numbers

ZENITH CARBURETORS

The Zenith carburetor is quite like the Amal carburetor in design and operation. The major variations include:

1. In the pilot metering system of the Zenith carburetor, air enters the left hole of the three small holes beneath the mouth of the carburetor. The air travels through the pilot metering jet and along a passage to the pilot mixing chamber. Fuel is drawn from the float bowl through a hole drilled in the needle and main jet holder. The fuel travels through a passage to the pilot (fuel) metering jet and is then sucked into the mixing chamber. The mixture then travels to the pilot mixture metering jet, through which it enters the carburetor bore.

Pilot   Booster   Float   Throttle
Air   Air Inlet   Vent   Cutaway
Intake

2. The slide has an extra large cutaway. The cutaway directs incoming air toward the mouth of the pilot mixture passage and prevents the flow of fuel from the pilot jet

from increasing too rapidly. The Zenith carburetor provides outstanding low-speed throttle control because of the overlap between the first and second metering systems.

3. The size of the needle jet is given in letters because the flow capacity of the jet is determined by both its length and the number of holes drilled in it. The higher the letter, the more fuel the jet is capable of passing.

4. The number stamped into the bottom of the throttle slide represents the number of degrees from horizontal of the cutaway angle.

5. As the needle passes the halfway point, the movement of the slide is greatly increasing the volume of air taken into the engine. A booster system is used to speed up the flow of fuel out of the spray nozzle. Air enters the center hole of the three small holes beneath the carburetor mouth and is led to an air chamber surrounding the needle jet. The air is sucked into the needle jet through holes drilled in its shank. The mixing of fuel with air is begun in the needle jet and the rate of fuel flow increases.

6. The Zenith carburetor is equipped with a choke to aid cold starting.

Disassembly

1. Remove the bottom of the fuel line from the fuel filter banjo.

2. Loosen the carburetor mounting clamp and remove the carburetor from the intake manifold.

3. Take out the two screws from the top of the carburetor. Remove the carburetor top and pull the throttle slide out of the barrel.

4. Holding the slide upside down, pull the return spring down and away from the slide. This will allow the brass cable protector cup, which normally covers the top

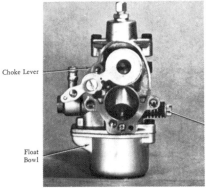

Choke Lever

Throttle
Slide
Adjustment
Screw

Float
Bowl

Pilot Mixture Jet   Needle Jet Mount

Float
Bowl

Pilot Fuel Jet

of the slide, to fall away. Move the throttle cable over to the enlarged end of the slot and remove the cable fitting from the slide.

5. Do not remove the nut from the top of the slide unless you wish to change the needle setting in the slide. If you wish to disassemble the slide, wrap a thick piece of leather around it and clamp it in a vise. Unscrew the top nut and lift out the needle.

6. Remove the brass cup, the slide return spring, and the carburetor top from the throttle cable.

7. Remove the retaining bolt from the fuel filter banjo. Remove the banjo, washer, and filter element.

8. Take out the throttle stop screw, its spring, and thrust washer from the carburetor.

9. Remove the two float bowl mounting screws and remove the bowl.

10. Press the end of the float pivot shaft that protrudes from the slotted ear of the mounting bracket and remove the shaft and float.

11. Remove the clip from the bottom of the tickler shaft. Remove the tickler shaft and its spring.

12. Remove the screw from the float pivot mounting bracket and take off the bracket.

13. Insert a 1/16 in. drill bit shank into each of the two holes in the brass float needle assembly. Insert a screwdriver blade between the two bits, perpendicular to them. Turn the drill bits counterclockwise

Removing the float needle assembly as described in Step 13

to unscrew the assembly from the carburetor body.

14. Unscrew the main jet from the bottom of the jet carrier.

15. Take out the screw from the base of the jet carrier and remove the jet carrier from the bottom of the carburetor.

16. Push the needle jet out through the bottom of the jet carrier.

17. Unscrew the two small jets remaining in the bottom of the carburetor. The mixture metering jet (with the larger number) is closest to the carburetor mounting flange, and the pilot fuel metering jet (stamped with the smaller number) is closest to the float needle assembly.

18. Take out the two screws from the front of the air cleaner.

19. Strike the air cleaner with the heel of your hand to separate it from the front of its carburetor mounting plate.

20. Unscrew the two slotted posts that secure the mounting plate to the carburetor and remove the plate.

21. Remove the choke lever mounting screw and its spring. Remove the choke lever. The choke lever spring is molded into the carburetor body; don't attempt to remove it.

22. Remove the unmarked jet from the center hole of the three small holes beneath the mouth of the carburetor.

Inspection and Reassembly

1. Separate the metal parts from the plastic ones and the gaskets.

2. Clean the metal parts in carburetor cleaner or other solvent and blow dry with compressed air. Take care to clear the passageways carefully.

3. Wash the air filter element in clean gasoline and dry it with compressed air. Spray the inside of the louvers on the outside of the element with an aerosol chain lubricant.

4. Install the pilot fuel metering jet (smaller number) in the threaded hole in the bottom of the carburetor nearest the float needle mount.

5. Install the pilot mixture metering jet (larger number) in the hole in the bottom of the carburetor nearest the mounting flange.

6. Test the movement of the float needle in its seat to make certain that it moves

freely without binding. If it binds even slightly, replace it.

7. Install the float needle and seat assembly, using a new gasket, in the same manner as it was removed.

8. Insert the needle jet into the unflanged end of the jet holder. Bottom the flange of the needle jet against the jet holder.

9. Screw the main jet into the bottom of the jet holder.

| Main
Jet | Needle
Jet | Jet
Holder |

10. Install a new float bowl gasket to the bottom of the carburetor. The gasket also serves as the jet holder gasket.

11. Fit the protruding end of the needle jet through the gasket and into the brass tube cast into the carburetor, and butt the jet holder against the bottom of the carburetor.

12. Align the mounting screw holes in the jet holder and carburetor. Install the screws.

13. Tighten the main jet.

14. Position the float pivot mounting bracket over its mount, so that the side of the base with the cut in it is next to the float needle and seat assembly. Secure the bracket with the self-tapping screw.

15. Fit the spring to the tickler shaft and insert the shaft into its mount from the top of the carburetor body. Depress the shaft and fit the clip to the groove. Crimp the clip with a pair of pliers. Release the tickler and allow it to spring back to make sure it is properly seated.

16. Position the float against the bottom of the carburetor body so that the ridge on the float pivot arm presses against the float needle. Insert the pivot shaft into the non-slotted ear of the mounting bracket and push it through the pivot arm of the float. Press the shaft into the slotted ear of the bracket; if it goes in too easily, crimp the slot in the ear. Align the float pivot shaft so that it protrudes an equal distance at each end.

17. Holding the carburetor so that the bottom faces down, push the float up against the bottom of the carburetor body and release it quickly. If it binds, spread the ears of the mounting bracket with needle-nose pliers.

18. Install the float bowl and tighten the two mounting screws.

19. Install a new gasket on the banjo mounting screw. Insert the screw into the

Float

Main
Jet

Mounting bracket cut (arrow)

side of the banjo with the smaller hole, and insert the filter screen between the screw and the banjo. Install the banjo, but don't tighten the screw fully at this point.

20. Fit the spring and washer to the throttle stop screw and install the screw.

21. Position the choke lever on the carburetor with the lever handle facing the rear of the carburetor. Install the choke screw spring on the screw, and insert the screw through the pivot hole in the choke lever. Install the assembly on the carburetor.

22. Install the unmarked jet in the center hole of the three holes beneath the mouth of the carburetor.

23. Fasten the air cleaner mounting plate to the carburetor with the two slotted posts.

24. Fit the air cleaner and its cover to

the mounting plate and install the two screws.

25. Pry the old rubber O-ring out of the manifold sleeve at the rear of the carburetor and install a new one.

26. Thread the inner throttle cable through the cable adjuster on the carburetor top. Fit the slide return spring to the inner cable and then install the brass cup so that its dome fits up into the return spring.

27. Force the cup and spring back against the carburetor top so that an inch of cable protrudes from the cup.

28. Insert the cable end into the slot in the top of the slide and move the cable over to the blind end of the slot. Release the spring.

29. Position the slide above the barrel of

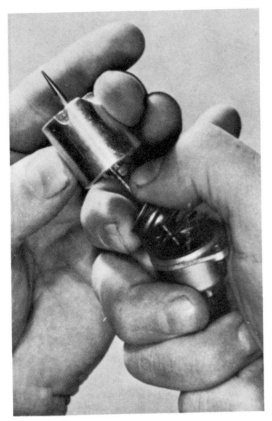

Installing the throttle cable

the carburetor so that the cutaway faces the mouth. Install the slide in the barrel, rotating it slightly to mate the groove in the slide with its location peg. Bottom the slide in the barrel, and install the carburetor top and its two mounting screws.

30. Install the carburetor on the intake manifold. Bottom the manifold against the rubber seal at the rear of the mounting sleeve.

31. Rotate the carburetor so that it is aligned vertically with the cylinder. Tighten the mounting clamp.

32. Position the banjo so that the fuel line makes a clean sweep from the tank to the connector and install the line.

33. Start the engine and allow it to warm up. Adjust the idle speed and mixture.

Electrical Systems

In almost all tests of the electrical system described in this chapter it will be neces-

sary to use a multimeter (volts/ohms/amps meter). You will be measuring ohms (resistance) and voltages. To measure resistance with the multimeter, plug the black test wire into the jack marked "common" or "—" on the meter. Plug the red test wire into the jack marked "+", and rotate the AC-DC switch to + DC.

For every resistance reading except from the secondary (high voltage) coil of the high tension coil, rotate the large center switch to the position marked "RX1". Read the resistance from the top scale on the dial.

For resistance readings from the secondary coil of the high tension coil, rotate the center switch to the position marked "RX100". Read the resistance from the top scale and multiply the number by 100.

Before taking a resistance reading, clip the test wires together and adjust the knob marked "zero ohms" until the meter needle is on the 0 mark on the top scale of the dial. The ohmmeter is meant to be used for taking resistance readings only when there is no current flowing in the system. *Never rotate the magneto flywheel when you have the meter attached to the electrical circuits to read resistance, or you will burn out the meter.*

To read voltage, leave the test wires plugged into the same jacks. Rotate the AC-DC switch to AC. You will be using the 2.5, 10 and 50 volt positions on the center switch. Read the voltage, when the center switch is positioned for 2.5 volts, on the lower red scale marked "2.5 V.A.C. ONLY". If you are using the 10 volt position of the center switch, read the figures just above the upper red scale. When using the 50 volt position, read the figures just above the upper red scale.

BUILDING A CREST VOLTAGE ATTACHMENT

A crest voltage (or peak-to-peak) attachment is necessary for testing the Femsatronic generator output. It is easy to build, and the materials cost only about five dollars. This attachment will absorb up to 700 volts; correct rated voltage will show on the scale of the meter.

1. You will need two capacitors of 350 volt, 2 microfarad capacity (Mallory Part No. TT350Z2). Two of these connected in

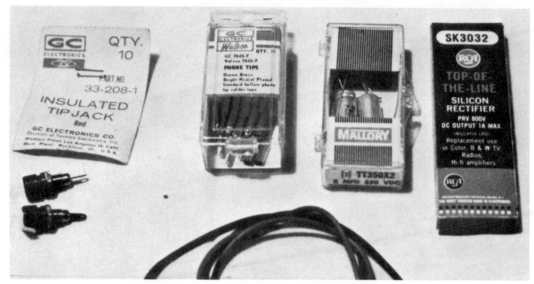

Materials needed to build the crest voltage attachment

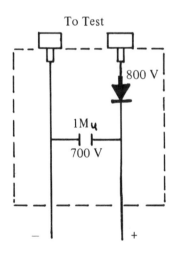

Capacitor wiring diagram

series result in 1 microfarad, with 700 volts capacity.

2. You will also need an 800 volt diode (Mallory Part No. SK3032). The arrow on the diode must point toward the meter side of the accessory.

3. Solder the components together as shown and use the plastic box the capacitors came in as a case. Use two tip jacks for receptacles for the test leads. Use two phone tips to allow the accessory to be plugged into the meter.

4. Using your crest voltage attachment, the Femsatronic generator should show at least 100 volts on crank speed and 400 to 420 volts at 7,000 rpm. Plug the attachment into the positive and negative sockets in the meter, then plug the probe wires into the accessory sockets. After it has been checked out, you can insulate the accessory by pouring the box full of fiberglass resin. Be sure to first coat the ends of the jacks with wax to prevent them from becoming plugged with resin.

The arrow on the diode must point toward the meter side of the attachment

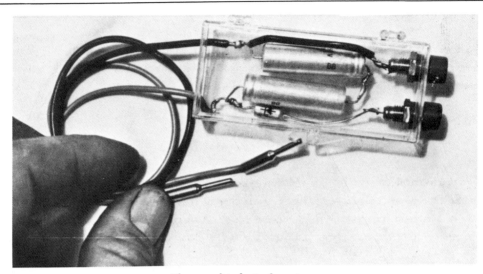

The completed attachment

RACING MODEL IGNITION SYSTEMS

Magneto Ignition System

DESCRIPTION

With a magneto ignition system, when the breaker points open, a surge of current from the magneto goes into the primary side of a step-up transformer (high tension coil). A surge of high voltage current goes out of the other side of the coil and arcs across the spark plug electrodes.

The Bultaco magneto is a simple alternator. It consists of a magneto flywheel, which contains two cast-in permanent magnets,

Bultaco Racing Models Ignition System Chart

| Model | Magneto | | Femsatronic | |
	Generator	Coil	Generator	Coil
Lobito AK-100	VAJ6-8	19.20-002		
Sherpa S Series MK-II	VAR-VAF 42-20-001	320-002 42-20-061		
Sherpa S Series MK III S100 MK III 125, 175 & 200			GEB1-3 GEA1-2	ELA1-1 ELA1-1
Pursang MK-I & MK-II MK-III MK-IV	VAR. 41-11 1101-001-1	320-002 42.20-001 OR	GEA1-2 GEA1-2	ELA1-1 ELA2-4
El Bandido MK-I & MK-II			GEA1-2	ELA2-4
TSS 125-250 cc	VAF-VAK	320-002		
TSS 125 MK-II TSS 250 MK-II TSS 350 MK-II			GEB1-1 GEB1-2 GEA1-2	ELA1-1 ELA1-1 ELA2-4

and a magneto backing plate, with two coils of wire. The ignition system makes use of only one magnet and coil. As a pole of the flywheel magnet begins to pass by the low tension ignition coil, the coil begins to gen-erate electrical current. The points are closed at this time, so the current flows out one end of the low tension ignition coil, through the points, and back to the other end of the low tension coil. As more area of

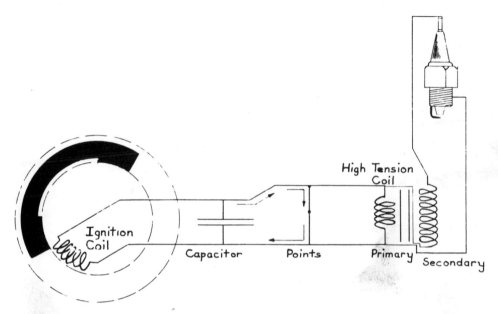

The points are closed and current is being built up and stored in the condenser

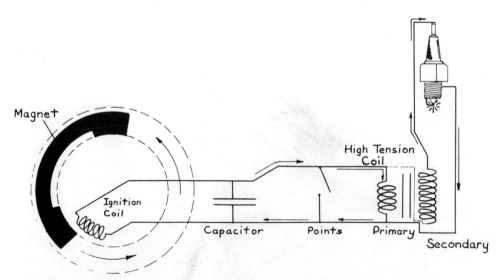

The points open and the current is discharged into the primary side of the high tension coil. A high voltage surge is induced in the secondary side and ignition occurs

the pole of the magnet passes over the coil, more current is generated. At the point when the maximum amount of current is being generated, the points open.

When the points open, the current is forced to flow into the primary coil of the high tension coil. The surge of current into the primary side of the high tension coil creates a magnetic field, which induces a high voltage surge in the secondary side of the high tension coil. This is the current that is sent to the spark plug and ignites the fuel mixture.

The condenser helps to regulate the flow of current and prevents the contact breaker points from becoming pitted too rapidly. Pitted points don't break evenly, and will prevent a strong surge of current from flowing into the high tension coil.

A kill button is wired into the circuit between the low tension coil and the breaker points. When the button is pressed the current is grounded through the frame, short-circuiting the ignition.

Testing the Magneto Ignition System

The following tests are to be performed to determine whether the individual components of the magneto system are functioning properly. Before these are undertaken, you should make general checks of all systems to isolate the *area* of the problem. If for instance, the engine won't start, maybe the fuel line is clogged. Refer to the "Troubleshooting" chapter before proceeding here, if you have not already done so.

High Tension Coil

1. Adjust the multimeter to read resistance (ohms). Zero the needle. Attach one of the test wires to the spark plug cable and ground the other on the cylinder head. The needle should read 30 on the top scale of the meter. If the needle reads infinity,

then a connection has come loose or a wire has broken somewhere between the coil and the spark plug. If the needle reads 30, continue the testing.

2. To test the secondary side of the high tension coil, remove the gas tank and scrape enough of the insulation from the end of the coil ground wire so that you can touch the test wire to it. Connect the other test wire to the spark plug cable. If you get a reading of 25–30, the coil is good, but the ground wire is not making good contact with the frame. If you get an open circuit reading the coil is defective and must be replaced.

3. To check the primary side of the coil disconnect the black wire from the small junction box taped to the frame near the coil. Connect the meter to the black wire and the spark plug cable. If you get an open circuit reading the coil is defective. If the meter reads 30, the coil is functioning. Check for full output by adjusting the meter to 2.5 volts AC. Disconnect the red wire from the junction box. Connect the test wires to the red wire and ground. If you get less than 2.0 volts, replace the coil.

NOTE: *If the coil is OK and you still have no spark, it would be a good idea at this point to make sure that the kill button on the handle bar is not short-circuiting. You can do this by simply bypassing the button using a jumper wire.*

Low Tension Coil

1. Rotate the AC-DC switch on the meter to the AC position. Turn the center switch to 2.5 volts.

2. Ground one of the test wires on the engine. Disconnect the black wire from the junction box under the gas tank and connect the other test wire to the black wire.

3. Turn the engine over with the kickstarter and watch the meter. If it reads 2.0–2.5 volts, the coil is good. If it does not

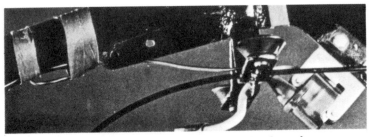

The coil is mounted on the frame, under the tank

Breaker Points

Capacitor

Low Tension Coil

read 2.0 volts, then either the coil or the magnet in the flywheel is bad.

POINTS AND CONDENSER

1. Remove the magneto flywheel. Take out the big screw that mounts the points to the magneto backing plate and remove the points. Disconnect the two black wires from the points.

2. Switch the meter to the + DC position and turn the center switch to the R x 10,000 notch. Zero the needle. Connect one of the test wires to the magneto backing plate. Watch the meter as you clip the other test wire to the end of the black wire from the condenser. The needle should immediately jump to 150 on the top scale and then go back to infinity. If it does not, the condenser is defective.

3. To doublecheck the condenser, run the same test again with the meter switched to 2.5 volts. You should get the same results.

4. To check the points, rotate the center switch on the meter to the R x 1 position and zero the needle. Connect the test wires to the points mounting bracket and the bracket where the electrical wires were mounted to the points assembly. The needle should read 0 (short circuit). Open the points. The needle should read infinity (open circuit). If both of these conditions are not met, replace the points.

NOTE: *If the low tension (ignition) coil, points, and condenser test out OK, check the wires on the magneto backing plate. It is possible that one of them has been rubbed by the flywheel or crimped when the backing plate was mounted.*

Femsatronic Ignition System

DESCRIPTION

Refer to the accompanying diagram while reading the following description of the Femsatronic system.

As the rotor on the end of the crankshaft spins, alternating current is generated in coil A. The current is rectified (changed from AC to DC) by the diode, D3, and then passes on to the condenser (C). The control diode (D) is connected in series with the primary winding of the high tension coil (B). Through the coil, the diode prevents discharge of current to the condenser.

At the instant of ignition, coil (P) generates an impulse of current which, in turn, makes diode (D) a conductor. The condenser then releases its spark, which travels through the primary winding of coil (B). This induces enough current into the secondary winding of the high tension coil to make the current jump across the spark plug gap.

PRELIMINARY CHECKS

1. Set the multimeter to read resistance and connect the test leads to the spark plug cable and ground. The needle should swing from infinity toward the other end of the scale if the unit is in working order, as this indicates a closed circuit. The meter should read 3.5K ohms when it is set on the 100K ohm scale. If you fail to get these readings, proceed with the next step. If it reads correctly, go on to step 3.

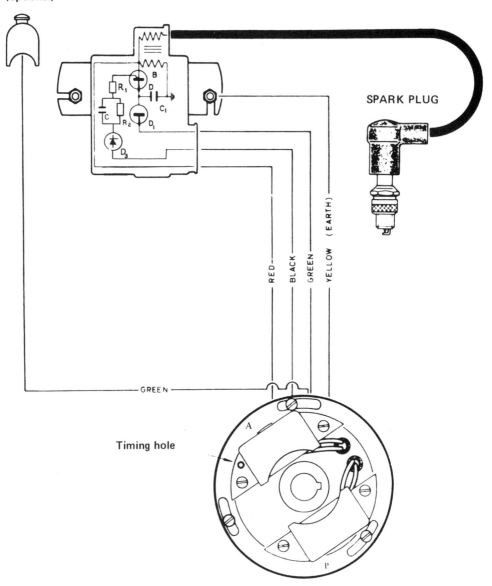

KILL BUTTON
(optional)

SPARK PLUG

RED

BLACK

GREEN

YELLOW (EARTH)

GREEN

Timing hole

FLYWHEEL MAGNETO

Femsatronic ignition

NOTE: *Make sure that the spark plug cap is securely connected to and is making good contact with the spark plug wire.*

2. Connect the test leads to the spark plug wire and the metal body of the coil. If you now get a closed circuit reading, the ground is bad between the coil and the frame at the mounting point. If the circuit is still open, the coil unit must be replaced.

3. Check to make sure that there is a good connection between the plug-in clip and the three-pronged plug that connects the coil to the Femsatronic generator in the flywheel. The connections should be clean and show no signs of discoloration from arcing. If necessary, clean the prongs with emery paper.

4. Pull the rubber cover back from the female portion of the plug and check for

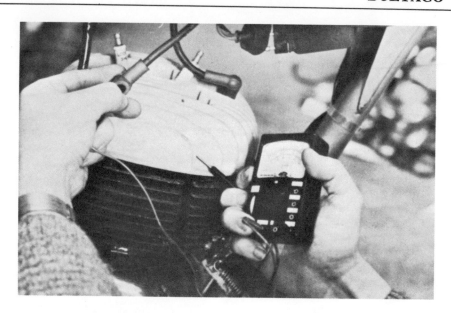

broken wires or for any water or other foreign material that could cause a short circuit.

5. Remove the left side engine cover and check to see if there is any play in it. Looseness can mean that it is coming loose from the hub or that the main bearings are worn. In either case, weak or erratic firing can be the result.

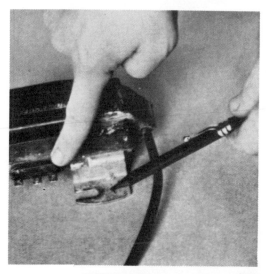

TESTING THE COMPONENTS

1. Check the condenser loading voltage by running the engine while a voltmeter with a peak-to-peak circuit (see the introduction to this chapter) is attached. Slide back the rubber covering from the female portion of the connector plug and check the

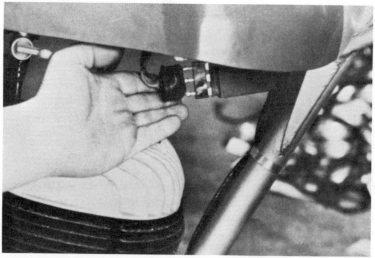

The flywheel has dragged on the coils and burnt them out as a result of looseness

voltage from the green wire to ground. (If there are two green wires, connect the test wire to both of them.) Start the engine and check the voltage. It must not be more than 400 volts or less than 300 at 5,000 or more rpm or it will burn out the coil. The generator should produce at last 250 volts below 5,000 rpm. A reading lower than 300 volts at high rpm means that either the flywheel is de-magnetized or there is an open circuit in the generator coils. In either case, replace the generator feeder and/or the flywheel. (The flywheel should lift one half of its weight if the magnets are in good shape.)

2. The generator should show at least 120 volts as the engine is kicked through. If it produces this voltage but will not spark,

The feeder on the right is typical of those used on light-equipped bikes; the feeder on the left is used on racing machines

the coil is faulty. If it shows no voltage, the generator should be replaced.

FEEDER CIRCUIT TESTS

If the engine will not run, the faulty component can be located without removing

Checking condenser loading voltage

anything from the bike. Check the circuits with the meter set to read resistance; all tests will be made at the point where the generator wiring harness plugs into the coil (generator feeder). In the accompanying illustration the feeder on the right is typical of the unit used on bikes equipped with lights, while the feeder on the left has ignition coils. Refer to the chart to determine the correct feeder model for circuit testing.

GAC Type Feeder

1. GAC6-1 feeder:

a) Check continuity between the green cable and the green cable. The ohmmeter should read about 870, plus or minus 60 ohms.

b) Check continuity between the red cable and ground. The reading should be about 1 ohm.

2. GAC-3, 5, 6, and 7 feeders:

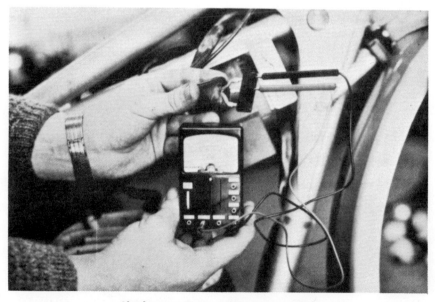

Checking continuity between two cables

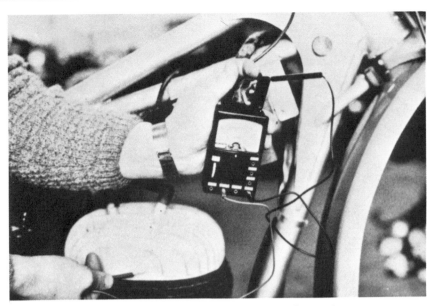

Checking continuity between a cable and ground

a) The continuity between the two green cables will be 1,900, plus or minus 200 ohms.

b) The continuity between the red cable and ground will be about 1.5 ohms.

GEA Type Feeders

1. Check the continuity between the green cable and ground. The meter should read 450, plus or minus 35 ohms.

2. Check continuity between the red and black cables. The reading should be about 0.35 ohms.

GEB Type Feeders

1. Check continuity between the green and yellow cables. The reading should be about 235, plus or minus 30 ohms.

2. Check the continuity between the red

and black cables. The reading should be about 0.25 ohms.

GED Type Feeders

1. Check the continuity between the green cable and ground. The reading should be about 1,800, plus or minus 200 ohms.

2. Check continuity between the red cable and ground. The reading should be about 3 ohms.

TESTING THE FEMSATRONIC COIL WITH THE ENGINE OFF

To check the coil units the wiring harness must be unplugged from the coil. Be sure that the positive and negative probes are attached in the manner described be-

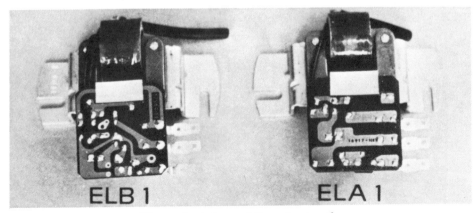

The two basic types of Femsatronic coils

low, as the diodes in the circuit are designed to pass electricity in one direction only.

The terminals are identified as follows: No. 1—the terminal farthest from the central one, No. 2—the central terminal,

No. 3—the terminal closest to the central one.

If either coil or the generator fails the above tests, they must be replaced with a new unit. Since the coil and feeder units are sealed, do not attempt to repair them.

Checking ohm value between terminals 2 and 3

Checking ohm value between terminal 1 and ground

Femsatronic Coil Test Data

Positive Test Point On	Negative Test Point On	See Ohmmeter On Scale Below (ohms)	Correct Reading	Incorrect Reading
a. *The ELA Type Coil*				
1	Ground	100K	∞	< ∞
Ground	1	100K	∞	< ∞
2	3	100K	∞	< ∞
3 *	2	100K	40K Ohms	< ∞ or < 40K Ohms
High Tension Lead	Ground	10K	3.5K Ohms	∞ or < 3.5K Ohms
b. *The ELB Type Coil*				
2 or 3	3 or 2	100K	∞	< ∞
2	Ground	100K	∞	< ∞
3	Ground	100K	∞	< ∞
Ground **	2	100	≅ 80	0 or ∞
Ground **	3	100	≅ 80	0 or ∞
1	Ground	100K	≅ 40K	∞ or 40K
Ground	1	100K	∞	∞ or 40K
High Tension	Ground	10K	3.5K	∞ or < 3.5K

∞ means infinity   < means less than   ≅ means approx.   K = 1000
* Values may vary from 40K ohms due to other components included in the circuit.
** Check for continuity is satisfactory regardless of meter reading.

Femsatronic Type Identification Chart

Models	Generator	Coil Unit
El Bandito MK-I and MK-II	GEA1-2	ELA2-4
Campera MK-II	GAC6-5	ELB1-2
Lobito MK-III 125 cc	GAC6-5	ELB1-2
Matador MK-III	GAC6-7	ELB1-2
El Montadero MK-II	GAC6-6	ELB2-7

Models	Generator	Coil Unit
Pursang MK-III and MK-IV	GEA1-2	ELA2-4
Sherpa S 100	GEB1-3	ELA1-1
Sherpa S 125, 175 and 200 MK-II	GEA1-2	ELA1-1
TSS 125	GEB1-1	ELA1-1
TSS 250	GEB1-2	ELA1-1
TSS 350	GEA1-2	ELA2-4

Ignition-Lighting Chart for Bultaco Machines Equipped with Lights

Model	Magneto Generator	Coil	Femsatronic Generator	Coil	Accessories
All Models up to 1965	VAF	320-002			Abril
Mercurio 175 cc	VAR 41-11	320-002			Abril-Femsa
Mercurio 200 cc	VAR 41-11	320-002			Lucas-Femsa
El Tigre 200 cc	VAR 41-11	320-002			Lucas-Femsa
Campera MK-I	VAR 41-11	320-002			Abril-Femsa
Campera MK-II			GAC 6-5	ELB 1-2	Lucas
Matador MK-I 200	VAR 41-11	320-002			Abril-Femsa
Matador MK-II-III	4920-001	320-002			Femsa-Lucas
Matador MK-III			CAC 6-7	ELB 1-2	Lucas
Metralla MK-I 200	VAR 41-21	320-002			Abril-Femsa
Metralla MK-II 200	2620-001	220-002			Femsa-Lucas
Metralla MK-III			GAC 6-5	ELB2-7	Lucas
Lobito MK-I	VAJ 6-8	19.20-002			Femsa-Lucas
100 cc 125 cc MK-II	VAJ 6-8	19.20-002			Lucas
MK-III			GAC 6-5	ELB 1-2	Lucas
El Montadero MK-I & MK-II			GAC 6-6	ELB 2-7	Lucas
Sherpa T MK-I	VAR 125-4	320-002			Femsa
MK-II	VAR 41-9	320-002			Femsa
49 Series MK-III	49.20-001	320-061			Femsa

Wiring diagram for magnetic ignition bikes
equipped with lights

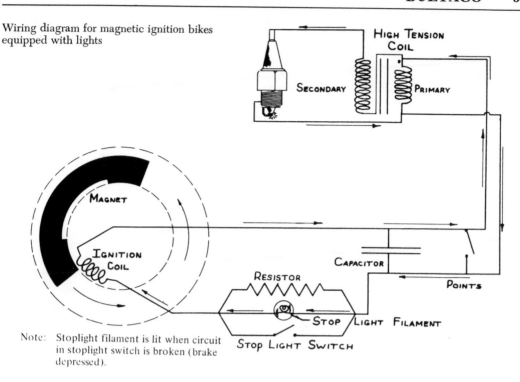

Note: Stoplight filament is lit when circuit
in stoplight switch is broken (brake
depressed).

STREET MODEL IGNITION SYSTEMS

Magneto Ignition System

The Bultaco magneto systems are the
same for racing and light-equipped models
except that the stoplight has been included
in the ignition system and a kill switch is
also part of the system.

Femsatronic Ignition System

All Femsatronic-equipped machines with
lighting systems have the same ignition and
circuitry as the Femsatronic type racing
bikes. Refer to the racing model section for
test procedures for both types of ignition
systems.

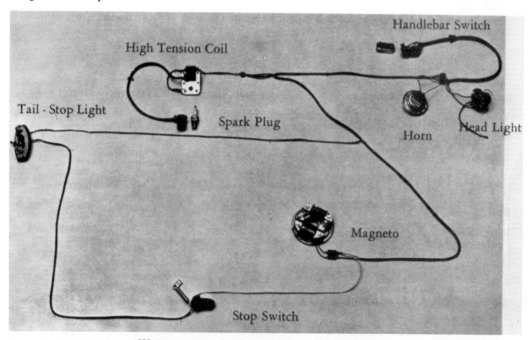

Wiring circuitry for Femsatronic ignition with lights

LIGHTING SYSTEM

Magneto Models

The Bultaco lighting system is fed by a lighting coil in the magneto, which operates in the same way that the ignition coil works.

If you are experiencing problems with bulbs burning out rapidly, it is recommended that you install a zener diode in the system. Zener diode kits are available at Bultaco dealerships. The diode will absorb the excessive voltage produced by the lighting coil and high rpm, and help to stabilize the lighting system. In addition, Bultaco dealers carry a sealed beam headlight kit and an improved type of taillight assembly that uses a heavy duty bulb.

Femsatronic Models

The power supply for battery equipped models comes from the Femsatronic generator. This type of generator is easily identified from the earlier magneto type because it is totally encased in resin.

Zener diode assembly (left) and high tension coil (right)

Testing the rectifier

CHECKING GENERATOR OUTPUT

Remove the four allen bolts from the timing side of the engine so that the wiring harness is accessible. Use a sharp probe to pierce the insulation on the blue wire, and connect a voltmeter to the blue wire and ground. Start the engine; the meter should read 18 or more volts AC. Perform the same test using the black wire. If improper voltage is obtained, the generator must be replaced.

CHECKING THE RECTIFIER

The rectifier is the unit located on the frame, under the fuel tank. It functions to convert the AC produced by the generator to DC.

The rectifier has four plugs; refer to the accompanying illustration when making the following tests.

1. Set the multimeter on R x 1 ohms. Place the negative probe on terminal 1 and the positive probe on terminal 4. You should get a continuity reading. Reverse the probes and test from number 4 to number 1. You should read continuity again. If the meter reads infinity in either case, the diode has failed and the rectifier unit must be replaced.

2. Place the negative probe on terminal 2 and the positive probe on terminal 3. You should get a continuity reading. Reverse the probes as above. The meter needle should not move. If it shows continuity, the second diode is faulty and the rectifier must be replaced.

Wiring Diagrams

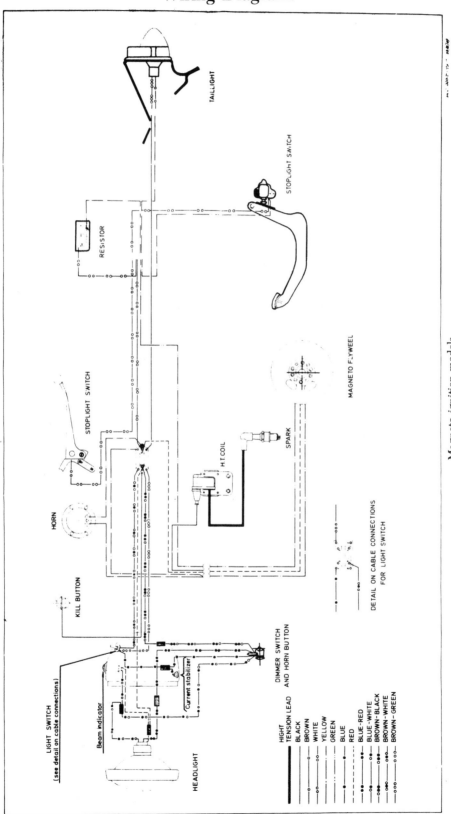

Magneto ignition models

TAILLIGHT

STOPLIGHT SWITCH

RESISTOR

STOPLIGHT SWITCH

MAGNETO FLYWEEL

HORN

H.T. COIL

SPARK

KILL BUTTON

DETAIL ON CABLE CONNECTIONS
FOR LIGHT SWITCH

LIGHT SWITCH
(see detail on cable connections)

Beam indicator

Current stabilizer

DIMMER SWITCH
AND HORN BUTTON

HEADLIGHT

HIGHT
TENSION LEAD
BLACK
BROWN
WHITE
YELLOW
GREEN
BLUE
RED
BLUE-RED
BLUE-WHITE
BROWN-BLACK
BROWN-WHITE
BROWN-GREEN

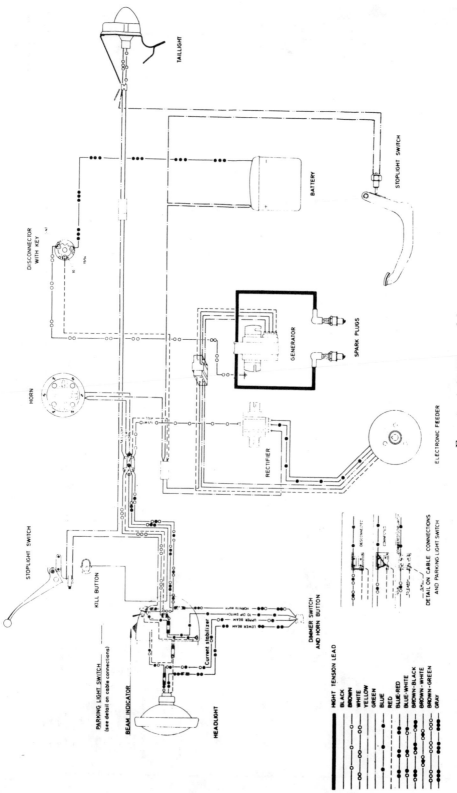

Femsatronic ignition models

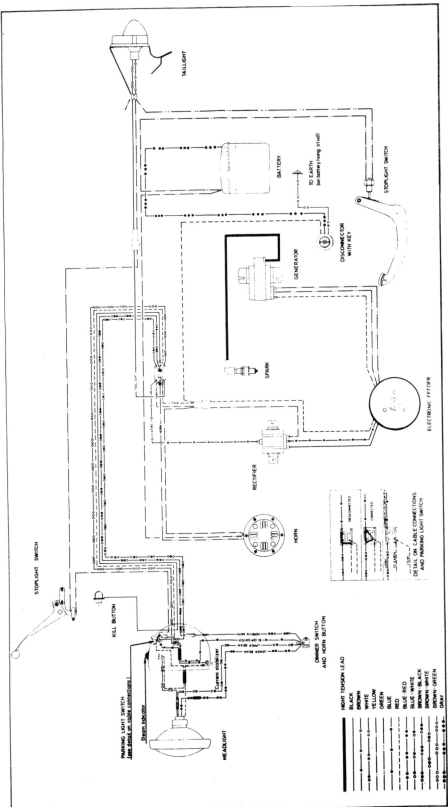

Femsatronic ignition models

Chassis

FRONT FORKS AND STEERING

1965–66 250 cc Scrambler

Oil Changes

Take note of the following:

1. Oil capacity of each leg is 160 cc. 20 or 30 weight oil is recommended.

2. After refilling the legs with oil, torque the stanchion plugs to 100 ft. lbs., and then work the forks up and down. If any oil escapes from the valve holes in the stanchion plugs or if you can hear air re-entering the valves when the forks are rebounding, the ball bearings in the stanchion plugs will have to be reseated.

3. To reseat the bearings, remove the screw from the top of the plug and insert a magnet to lift out the spring. Insert a $\frac{3}{16}$ in. drift into the valve hole so that the drift bears against the ball. Tap the drift lightly to reset the ball. Reinstall the spring and screw, and retest the forks again to make sure the ball is seated.

Disassembly

1. Loosen the clamp bolt on the front brake cable nipple and remove the nipple from the cable. Remove the brake cable and the spring from the brake arm on the front wheel. Remove the cable from the forks. Unscrew the drain plug from each of the fork legs and pump the oil out.

2. Prop up the bike so that the front wheel is off the ground and remove the two bolts that mount the brake anchor strap to the right fork leg.

3. Unscrew the front axle nut and then loosen the two axle clamp nuts. Withdraw the axle and remove the wheel.

4. Take off the two fender mounting clamps from the slider legs. Slide the front fender down the forks to remove it.

5. Using a 28 mm socket, rotate each stanchion plug five turns to loosen it.

6. On early models with steel top and bottom brackets, loosen the two clamp bolts on each bracket.

7. On late models with a forged alloy top bracket, loosen the four clamp bolts on each bracket.

8. Loosen the stanchion tubes in the top bracket by hitting each plug with a rubber mallet until the plug bottoms against the top bracket. Remove the plugs from the stanchion tubes.

9. Remove the top bracket mounting nut on top of the bracket. Loosen the steering shaft clamp bolt on the top bracket. Remove the top bracket by tapping it upward with a rubber mallet.

10. Loosen the handlebar mounting bolts and pull each stanchion tube downward

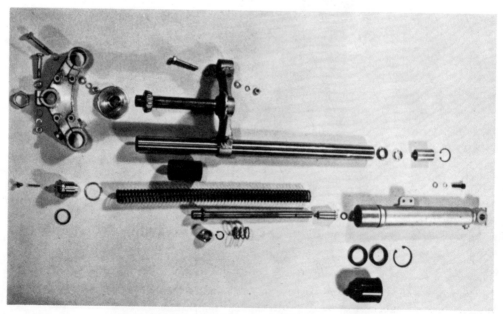

The front forks and steering head—disassembled

Removing the top bracket

out of the top bracket far enough so that the handlebar can be removed.

11. Tap each stanchion tube downward through the steering damper stop. When the tube is free of the stop it can be removed.

12. Unscrew the steering head bearing locking collar.

13. Hit the top of the steering shaft with a hammer, using a piece of wood to protect the shaft. This will free the upper steering

bearing from the shaft and the bottom bracket will fall off. (Catch it.)

14. Lift the inner race of the upper steering head bearing out of the top of the steering head.

15. If it is necessary to remove the bottom steering bearing, clamp the bottom bracket upside down in a vise and hammer alternately on the two protruding portions of the dust shield with a hammer and drift.

16. If you wish to remove the outer

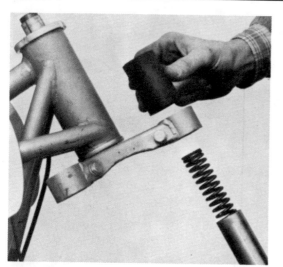

Removing a stanchion tube

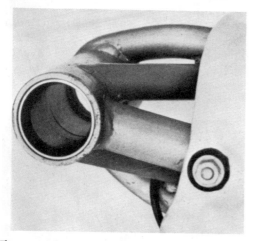

The outer bearing races remain in the steering head

races of the steering bearings, insert a drift from the opposite end of the steering head and drive them out squarely. Take care in this; if they come out at an angle you can distort the steering head.

17. To remove the stanchion tube from its slider leg, unscrew the allen bolt from the bottom of the slider leg. The slider and stanchion can then be pulled apart.

NOTE: *Sometimes the components inside the leg will rotate with the allen bolt, and you can't loosen it. If this happens, use the following procedure:*

a) Drill a ⅛ in. hole into the damper cylinder support inside the slider leg through the oil drain hole, taking care not to chew up the hole threads.

b) Pack some grease on the end of a thin drift and insert the drift into the

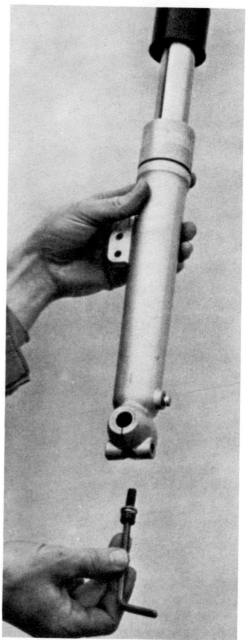

Removing the fork slider allen bolt

drain plug hole to remove the metal chips. Repeat this as many times as is necessary to remove all the chips.

c) Insert the drift again and use it to hold the damper components in place while you unscrew the allen bolt.

18. Remove the fork spring through the top of the stanchion tube.

19. Turn the stanchion tube upside down and the valve tube assembly will fall out.

If the damper cylinder support sticks in the bottom of the tube, screw the allen bolt back into the bottom of the tube a few turns and tap it with a hammer to free the support.

20. Remove the snap-ring from the bottom of the stanchion tube.

Removing the snap-ring from the bottom of a stanchion tube

21. Insert a squared-off broomstick into the top of the stanchion tube and push out the remaining damper components.

22. Remove the rubber dust guard and the snap-ring from the top of the slider leg. Pry out the oil seals with a blunt screwdriver, taking care not to gouge the soft walls of the slider leg.

INSPECTION

1. Measure the length of the fork springs. If they are less than $17^{11}\!/_{16}$ in. long, or are unequal in length, they should be replaced.

2. If you have found that the springs were bottoming regularly, make up two 1 in. spacers and fit them between the top of each spring and the bottom of the stanchion plug.

3. If the distributor ring spring washer on the valve tube has broken or lost its tension, replace it.

4. Examine the threads of the allen bolt and the threads in the bottom of the fork leg where the allen bolt screws in. If worn, replace the bolt and the valve tube.

5. Each time the forks are disassembled, the following components should be replaced:

a) Oil seals (4);
b) O-ring (2);
c) Dust guard (2);
d) Oil drain plug washer (2);
e) Stanchion plug O-ring (2);
f) 30 mm internal snap-ring (2);
g) 16 mm external snap-ring (2);
h) Rubber damper cylinder support washer (2).

6. To compensate for normal wear, the following components should be replaced once a year:

a) Distributor ring assembly (2);
b) Damper piston (2);
c) Valve washer (2);
d) Valve support cylinder (2).

REASSEMBLY

1. Thoroughly clean all steering head and damper components before reassembly.

2. Install the upper and lower outer steering bearing races in the steering head. Drive them in squarely, using a piece of pipe with an outside diameter slightly smaller than the inside diameter of the steering head. Check often to make sure that the races are going in straight.

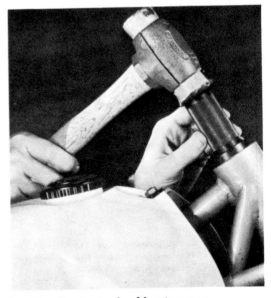

Installing the steering head bearing races

3. Install the inner race of the lower steering bearing on the steering shaft, with the smaller end up, using a suitably sized pipe. Before driving the race into position, fit the bottom dust cover to the shaft with the dished edge facing up and the three drain holes facing the rear of the bottom bracket.

4. Grease the inner races of both bearings with wheel bearing grease.

5. Insert the steering shaft in the steering head from the bottom.

6. Screw the locking collar onto the steering shaft and tighten it until the inner race of the upper bearing is forced into its outer race. When the collar has been tightened enough, you will need to give the bottom bracket a gentle push to rotate it from lock to lock. If you feel any roughness or binding while moving the bracket, there is probably dirt in the bearings, and they will have to be removed and cleaned.

Inserting a stanchion tube

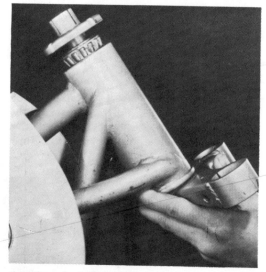

Installing the locking collar

7. After adjusting the locking collar, rap the top of the steering shaft with a hammer (protecting it with a piece of wood). If the effort required to move the bottom bracket from side to side remains the same as it was before, the bearings are fully seated and properly adjusted. If the bottom bracket has loosened, readjust the locking collar again.

8. Install the top bracket on the steering shaft.

9. Screw the top nut on the steering shaft down finger-tight.

10. Coat the inner surfaces of the steering damper stops with light oil or liquid detergent so they will slide down the stanchion tubes easily. Lay the stops and the handlebars near the front end of the bike.

11. Insert a stanchion tube from the bottom of the bottom bracket. Fit a rubber

stop to the top of the tube and work it down in the tube.

12. Fit a handlebar to the stanchion tube. Seat the tube in the top bracket by bumping the bottom of the tube lightly with a rubber mallet. Install the other tube in the same manner.

13. Tighten the stanchion tube clamp bolts on the top bracket enough to hold the tube in place while the damper components are installed.

Installing the damping components

14. Fit the damping piston on the end of the valve tube away from the flange. The recessed end of the piston should face away from the flange. Butt the piston against the flange on the valve tube.

15. Spread the 16 mm snap-ring just enough so that it can be slid along the

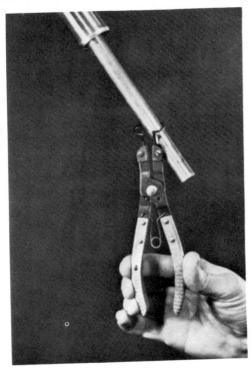

Refitting the snap-ring

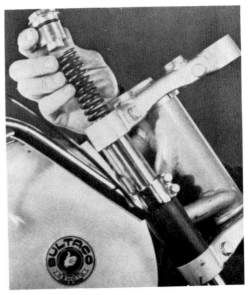

Installing the spring and stanchion plug

valve tube into its groove next to the piston.

16. Put the valve tube retaining spring on the valve tube and butt the spring against the piston.

17. Put the distributor ring assembly on the valve tube with the spring washer facing away from the valve tube retaining spring. Butt the distributor ring assembly against the spring.

18. Put the valve spacer on the valve tube. Butt the spacer against the spring washer.

19. Put the valve support cylinder on the valve tube so that the washer fits into the counterbored end of the cylinder. Assemble the other valve tube assembly in the same manner.

20. Insert the flanged end of the valve tube into the bottom end of a stanchion tube, while holding the damper components in place.

21. Push the valve tube up into the stanchion tube. The distributor ring will seat against a machined lip near the bottom of the stanchion tube, and the valve support cylinder will come to rest against the distributor ring. Install the 30 mm snap-ring in its groove in the bottom of the tube.

The ring should be installed with the sharp edge facing the bottom of the stanchion tube; make sure that the ring is seated perfectly in its groove. Fit the damping components to the other stanchion tube in the same manner.

22. Install the spring into the top of each stanchion tube. Fit the washer to each stanchion plug and install the plugs finger-tight in the top of the tubes.

23. Smear the oil seal with grease and install it, open end down, into the slider leg. Install the seal squarely. Fit the other seal in the same manner, until it butts up against the first seal. Install the snap-ring in the mouth of the leg.

24. Install the two seals in the other slider leg in the same manner.

25. Fit the dust guards to the slider legs.

26. Pry out the old O-ring and install a new one in the damper cylinder support.

27. Fit the damper cylinder support to the bottom end of the valve tube, which is sticking out of the bottom end of the stanchion tube. If the support won't stay in position, smear grease on it and reinstall it.

28. Thoroughly coat the dust guard and seals with light oil. Fit the slider leg to the stanchion tube and move it up until the damper cylinder support reaches the bottom of the inside of the leg.

29. To bottom the support in the leg, you may need to guide the nipple of the support into the anchor screw hole of the

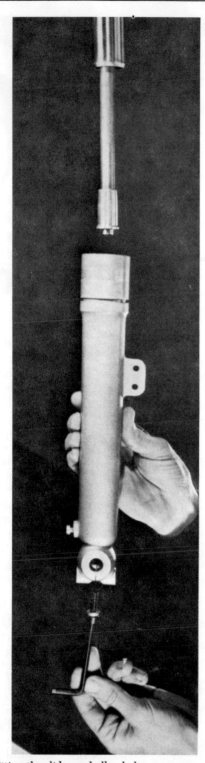

Refitting the slider and allen bolt

leg by fitting a thin drift into the hole and centering the nipple.

30. Hold the slider leg in position and install the flat washer, lockwasher, and allen bolt in the anchor hole. Tighten the bolt securely.

31. Install the other slider leg on its stanchion tube in the same manner.

32. Install the fork oil drain plugs, using new washers.

33. Fit the rubber fender tab guards to the slider legs and slide the fender up the legs into position. Tighten the fender clamps finger-tight.

34. Position the handlebars and tighten the clamps securely. The clamp bolts must be tightened alternately, a little at a time, in order to secure each handlebar effectively.

35. Check to see that the flanged spacers are still pressed into the wheel bearing oil seals in the front wheel. Position the wheel between the forks and insert the axle from the left side. Fit the flat washer and lockwasher, and run the nut up finger-tight.

36. Align the two mounting holes in the brake anchor strap with the holes in the lug on the right slider leg. Install and tighten the brake anchor nuts and bolts.

37. Straddle the front wheel, holding it between your knees, and work the handlebars to align the wheel with the forks.

38. Thread the inner brake cable through the outer cable stop on the right slider leg. Retract the cable adjuster on the front brake handlebar lever into its mount.

39. Install the coil spring on the inner brake cable. Fit the cable through the slot in the brake arm and install the cable nipple on the inner cable.

40. Using pliers, force the nipple up the cable to lift the brake arm until the brake doesn't quite drag when you spin the front wheel, then tighten the nipple clamp bolt.

41. Remove the stanchion plugs and pour 160 cc of SAE 20 or 30W oil into each stanchion tube. Install the washers on the plugs and tighten them to 100 ft. lbs.

42. On early models with steel top brackets, tighten the top and bottom clamp bolts to 15 ft. lbs.

43. On late models with alloy top brackets, tighten the top and bottom clamp bolts to 6 ft. lbs.

44. Torque the steering shaft top nut to 35 ft. lbs.

45. Torque the steering shaft clamp bolt on the top bracket to 15 ft. lbs.

46. Snug down, but do not fully tighten, the two front axle clamp nuts. Tighten the

front axle nut until it is compressing its lock-washer, then torque the two clamp nuts to 60 ft. lbs.

47. Finally, tighten the front fender mounting clamps.

NOTE: *It is very important to follow the sequence of tightening and observe the torque specifications given above. Proper fork operation depends upon this.*

1966–67 Matador and 1966–67 Sherpa S

Oil Changes

Refer to the previous section on the 250 cc Scrambler. Procedures are the same, except that the stanchion plugs should be torqued to 50 ft. lbs.

Disassembly, Inspection, and Reassembly

Refer to the previous section on the 250 cc Scrambler. Procedures are the same, except that:

1. When reassembling the stanchion tube and slider leg assemblies, insert a stanchion tube from the bottom of the bottom bracket. Slide the tube up through the bracket and fit a handlebar to the top of the tube. Seat the tube in the top bracket by tapping it with a rubber mallet.

2. Be sure to observe this final tightening sequence:

　　a) Stanchion plugs—50 ft. lbs.;
　　b) Top bracket fixing nut—tight;
　　c) Steering shaft clamp bolt on top bracket—15 ft. lbs.;
　　d) Front axle nuts—30 ft. lbs.;
　　e) Front axle clamp bolts—6 ft. lbs.;
　　f) Stanchion tube clamp bolts on bottom bracket—15 ft. lbs.

1964–67 Mercurio, 1964–67 Metralla, 1965 Sherpa S, and 1964–65 Matador

Oil Changes

To change the oil in the forks on any of these models, it is necessary to remove the slider legs, pour out the old oil, add 85 cc of oil into each leg, and reassemble the forks. The necessary steps are described in the following sections.

Loosening the locknut at the bottom of the plug

Unscrewing a stanchion plug

DISASSEMBLY

1. With the bike off its stand, sit on the tank to compress the forks. Unscrew the two stanchion plugs from the stanchion tubes.

2. Loosen the locknut at the bottom of the stanchion plug.

3. Prop the bike so that the front wheel is off the ground.

4. Loosen the front brake cable nipple and remove it. Disconnect the brake cable and its spring from the brake arm, and remove the cable from the front forks.

5. On the Metralla and Matador, unscrew the two bolts securing the brake anchor strap to the front forks.

6. Remove the front axle nut.

7. On the Metralla and Matador, loosen the four axle clamp bolts.

8. Withdraw the front axle and remove the front wheel.

9. Take off the bolts and nuts and remove the front fender. Loosen the clamps and work the dust guards off the slider legs (Matador).

10. Press upward on a slider leg and remove the stanchion plug and washer. Pull the leg down off its stanchion tube and re-

The front wheel assembly of the Metralla

Removing the stanchion plug and washer

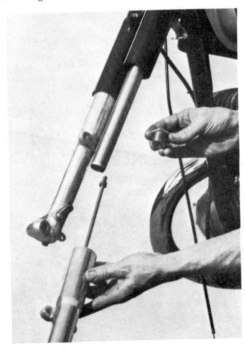

Removing a slider leg

move it. The fork spring will fall off the tube. This completes the partial disassembly necessary for changing the fork oil.

11. Remove the allen bolt from the bottom of the slider leg. If the damper rod

assembly rotates with the bolt, preventing the bolt from loosening, slide a deep 16 mm socket down the damper rod and fit it to the nut down inside the leg. Hold the socket and unscrew the allen bolt.

12. To disassemble the damper rod assembly remove the nut from the top of the cylinder, and remove the rod from the cylinder.

13. Wash the piston at the bottom of the damper rod in solvent and examine it for wear. If it is worn badly, replace the entire damper rod assembly.

14. It is very important that the piston is tightly attached to the damper rod. If it is loose, back off the locknut and tighten the piston until the ball bearing, visible through the bottom of the piston, is seated tightly against the rod. Then, loosen the piston 1/8 in. and tighten the locknut.

15. To remove the oil seal, it is necessary to make a special tool. Procure a length of 1 in. I.D. water pipe, with a tapered thread on one end. Squeeze the threaded end in a vise until it is oval, 36 mm across the widest part. Thread the pipe into the oil seal in the slider leg, and clamp the other end in a vise. Insert a bar in the axle hole in the slider leg and yank the bar firmly to pull the leg free of the oil seal.

16. Loosen the two stanchion tube clamp bolts in the bottom bracket. On the Matador, it is also necessary to loosen the two mounting bolts on each handlebar, and to unscrew the two allen bolts from the headlight brackets and remove the headlight.

Tapping a stanchion tube out

17. Turn each stanchion plug ¾ of the way down its tube. Hit the plug with a hammer (protecting the plug with a piece of wood) until it bottoms on the top bracket. Catch the stanchion tube as it falls away. (It may be necessary to pry open the clamps on the bottom bracket to free the tubes.)

18. Take out the three screws and remove the dust guard. If necessary, pry out the rubber suspension stop from the top of the guard.

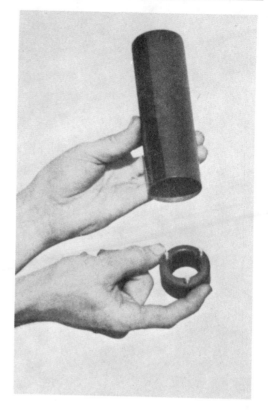

Take out the three screws to remove the dust guard

20. Unscrew and remove the top bracket securing nut.

21. Loosen the steering shaft clamp bolt on the top bracket. Tap the bracket up and off the steering head.

22. Loosen the steering bearing locking collar and unscrew it from the shaft.

23. Remove the headlight assembly from the Metralla and Mercurio at this point.

19. Unscrew the steering damper knob and lift it out. Remove the spacer from the top bracket. Remove the two washers and the steering damper anchor from beneath the bottom bracket. On the Metralla and Mercurio, remove the handlebar and let it hang by the cables.

Removing the top bracket

Unscrewing the top nut

24. Spread a cloth beneath the steering head to catch the bearings, and rap the top of the steering shaft with a rubber mallet to drive the bottom bracket out. Catch it as it falls.

Tapping the steering shaft out

Check the bearing races for pitting and roughness

25. Lift off the inner race of the upper bearing. Remove the ball bearings from the outer race of the upper bearing, and the inner race of the lower bearing. Wash the bearing components in solvent and dry them. There should be 22 balls per bearing. If any of the races or balls show pitting or wear, the entire bearing assembly must be replaced.

26. If it is necessary to remove the inner race of the lower steering bearing, in-

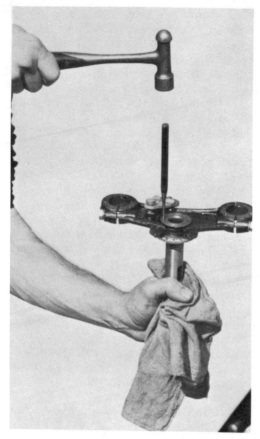

Drifting out the inner race of the lower bearing

The disassembled fork and steering head components

    a) Dust guard clamps (Matador);
    b) Front suspension stops;
    c) Damper rod assemblies;
    d) Fork springs;
    e) Suspension stop springs and washers;
    f) The 6 mm nuts;
    g) Steering head bearing assemblies;
    h) Fiber washers in the steering head;
    i) Handlebar bolts.

sert a drift in one of the holes in the steering shaft, as shown, and tap the race out squarely, moving the drift back and forth between the two holes. If you need to remove one of the outer races, drift it evenly out of the steering head.

INSPECTION

1. Measure the fork springs. If one is shorter than the other, or they are less than $7\%_{16}$ in. long, replace them.

2. Replace any damper components that are damaged or worn.

3. Each time the forks are disassembled, the following components should be replaced:
    a) Rubber dust guards (Matador only);
    b) Oil seals;
    c) O-rings;
    d) 8 mm lockwashers;
    e) Brake cable rubber grommet;
    f) 6 mm lockwashers.

4. Replace the following parts at yearly intervals:

REASSEMBLY

1. Install the outer steering head bearing races in the steering head using an appropriately sized pipe to drive them in. Take care to install them squarely.

2. Install the inner race of the lower bearing in the bottom bracket. Place the bracket on a bench so that the shaft is pointing up, and fit the race with its dished face up and the three drain holes facing the rear of the bracket (the clamp bolts for the stanchion tubes are at the rear of the bracket).

3. Place the inner race of the lower steering bearing on the steering shaft with the small end of the race facing up. Drive the inner race and the dust cover down the shaft until they butt against the bracket.

4. Cover the outer race of the upper

bearing in the steering head with a layer of wheel bearing grease. Put 22 balls in race and cover them with another layer of grease. Place the inner race on the balls.

5. Coat the inner race of the lower bearing on the bottom bracket with a layer of grease and place 22 balls on the race. Cover the balls with another layer of grease.

6. Work the steering shaft up into the steering head as far as it will go, holding down the inner race of the upper bearing to prevent the balls from coming loose.

7. Start the locking collar on the steering shaft and tighten it until the balls on the lower inner race are tight against the outer race. As the collar is tightened, guide the bottom bracket so that none of the balls in the lower bearing are shaken out.

8. Continue tightening the locking collar until the bottom bracket, when centered, will just swing away to either side under its own weight.

9. On the Mercurio, position the headlight assembly on the bottom bracket and place a rubber gasket on top of each headlight bracket. On the Metralla, fit a headlight bracket gasket to the counterbored bottom of each of the two bracket spacers, and position the two spacers on the bottom bracket. Install the headlight on top of the spacers, and place a gasket on top of each bracket.

10. Place the top bracket on the steering shaft.

11. Mount the dust guards (or supports) on the bottom of the bottom bracket. Insert a rubber suspension stop into a dust guard, with the flat end of the stop going in first. Align the mounting holes in the stop with those in the guard and position the three screws. (Use a thread locking compound on the screws to keep them from loosening.)

12. Position the guard beneath the bottom bracket and mount the three screws to the bottom bracket. Do not overtighten the screws.

13. Fit one end of a rubber boot to the short metal dust guard (Matador). Tighten the clamp, and mount the other boot in the same manner. Position the handlebars on the bracket so that they can be mounted on the stanchion tubes before the tubes are inserted in the top bracket.

14. Check the cables and electrical wires to make sure that they will be routed correctly after the tubes are installed.

15. Start the top bracket securing nut on the steering shaft; run it down finger-tight.

16. Insert a stanchion tube from the bottom of the bottom bracket.

17. On the Metralla and Mercurio, slide the stanchion tube up through the headlight bracket and into the top bracket. On the Matador, fit the handlebar to the stanchion tube and slide the tube up into the top bracket.

18. Tap the bottom of the tube to start it into its taper in the top bracket.

19. Tighten the tube clamp bolts on the bottom bracket only enough to hold them in place while the damper components are installed.

20. Install the damper oil seals in the slider legs with the open end of the seal facing in. Coat the seal with oil before inserting it; drive it down so that it seats against its flange.

21. Insert the damper rod, piston end first, into the damper cylinder. Tighten the damper cylinder nut into the top of the damper cylinder.

22. Install a new O-ring on the bottom of the damper rod.

NOTE: *If the damper rod assembly is not machined at the bottom to accept an O-ring, it is recommended that this early type (6 mm diameter) assembly be replaced with the later type (8 mm) assembly. The later type is much stronger.*

23. Install the allen screw in the bottom of the slider leg and tighten it firmly.

24. Pour 85 cc of oil into each slider leg. Use SAE 20 or 30W oil.

25. Work the damper rod up and down until the oil has been sucked down into the damper cylinder.

26. Fit the slider leg to the stanchion tube; the fork spring goes outside and the damper rod goes inside the tube.

27. Pull up the damper rod and run the stanchion plug locknut down to the bottom of the threads on the damper rod. Pull the rod over to the side of the tube and hook the stanchion plug locknut on the top edge of the top bracket.

28. Screw the stanchion plug to the damper rod and run it down until it bottoms. Lift the stanchion plug so that its locknut no longer bears against the top

bracket, and tighten the nut against the bottom of the plug.

29. Screw the plug into the stanchion tube until the plug bottoms against the top bracket.

30. Assemble the other slider leg in the same manner after adding the required amount of oil.

31. Work the bottom of the rubber fork boots down over the slider legs on the Matador and tighten the clamps.

32. Tighten the top bracket securing nut securely (75 ft. lbs.).

33. Mount and secure the handlebars in the position you like them.

34. Install the front fender.

35. Check to see that the flanged spacers are still pressed into the oil seals, and position the front wheel between the forks.

36. Insert the front axle from the left side and start the axle nut on it.

37. Install and tighten the two front brake anchor straps on the Metralla and Matador.

38. Install the front brake cable, connecting it to the brake lever and the brake arm. Retract the handlebar lever cable adjuster into its mount. Fit the cable nipple to the bottom end of the inner cable. Using pliers, pull the nipple up the cable so that it moves the brake arm up; when you reach the point where the front brake does not quite drag when you spin the wheel, tighten the cable nipple clamp bolt.

39. Tighten the front axle nut finger-tight. Straddle the front wheel with your knees pressed against it and work the handlebars to align the wheel with the forks.

40. Tighten the stanchion nuts securely (50 ft. lbs.).

41. Torque the steering shaft clamp bolt at the rear of the top bracket to 6 ft. lbs.

42. Tap the top and bottom of the bottom bracket on both sides of the stanchion tube clamp bolts using a hammer and piece of wood. It is important that this is done at this point to avoid placing strain on the top bracket.

43. Torque the two stanchion tube clamp bolts on the bottom bracket to 15 ft. lbs.

44. Tighten the front axle nut until it has just compressed its lockwasher, then torque the four axle clamp nuts to 6 ft. lbs. (Metralla and Matador).

45. Torque the front axle nut to 30 ft. lbs.

46. Reassemble the steering damper components in the following sequence:

a) Place the plastic spacer on the top bracket.

b) Swing the damper adjuster away from the bottom of the steering shaft.

c) Fit the damper anchor (bent prongs down) to the gusset on the frame downtube. Press the circular portion of the anchor up against the fiber washer on the bottom bracket. Position the other fiber washer against the bottom of the anchor.

d) Swing the adjuster into alignment beneath the fiber washer, and insert the damper into its spacer and down through the steering head. Screw the damper into the adjuster.

1966–67 Campera and 1963–64 Sherpa S

OIL CHANGES

To change the oil in these forks it will be necessary to remove the slider legs, pour out the old oil, add fresh oil, and re-install the legs. This procedure can be gleaned out of the disassembly and assembly methods below. Each fork leg should contain 85 cc of 20 or 30 weight oil.

DISASSEMBLY

1. Unscrew the stanchion plugs from the tubes (Campera).

2. Remove the allen bolt from the top of each stanchion plug (Sherpa S), and unscrew the plugs from the tubes.

3. Sit on the gas tank to compress the forks (Campera) and loosen the locknut on the bottom of the stanchion plugs.

4. Remove the front fender and take off the front brake anchor strap nut.

5. Remove the nipple from the brake end of the front brake cable. Remove the cable from the front forks.

6. Remove the lower clamp from the rubber boots (Sherpa S) and push the boots up off the slider legs.

7. Prop the bike so that the front wheel is free and remove the front axle nut.

8. Withdraw the axle and remove the wheel.

9. On the Campera, press up on the slider leg and unscrew the stanchion plug from the damper rod.

10. Pull the slider legs off the stanchion tubes.

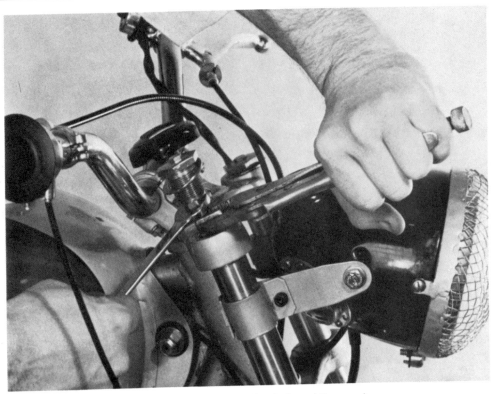

Loosening the stanchion plug locknut (Campera)

11. Hold the fork spring in a vise (Sherpa S). Unscrew the spring carrier using pliers, and push the spring down and away from the carrier locknut. Put a wrench on the locknut and remove the carrier with pliers.

12. Remove the fork springs and carriers from the slider legs (Campera).

13. Turn the slider leg upside down and pump the damper rod to expel the oil. Disassembly for changing the damper oil is now complete.

14. Unscrew the allen bolt at the bottom of the slider leg. If the damper rod assembly rotates with the bolt, preventing it from loosening, slide a 16 mm deep socket down the damper rod and fit it to the nut. Hold the socket and unscrew the bolt.

15. Remove the damper rod assembly from the leg. Remove and discard the O-ring in the groove in the cylinder.

16. Remove and discard the fiber washer from the damper cylinder (Sherpa S).

17. Find the two O-rings that are supposed to be on the outside of the damper cylinder but are now probably inside the slider leg.

18. Unscrew the damper cylinder nut

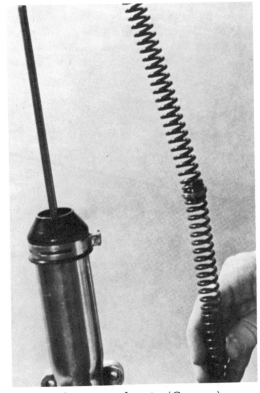

The two fork springs and carrier (Campera)

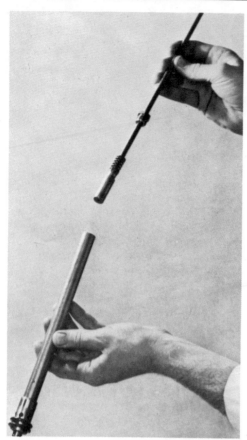

Removing the damper cylinder from the damper rod (Campera)

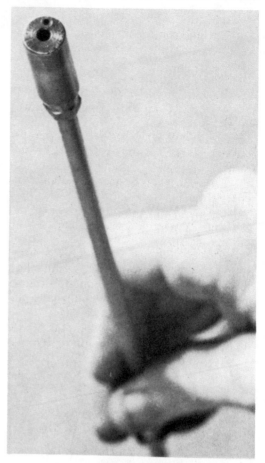

Piston and damper rod (Campera)

and remove the cylinder from the rod (Campera).

19. Clamp the round damper cylinder nut in a vise, grab the bottom of the cylinder with vise-grips, and unscrew it from the nut (Sherpa S).

20. Wash the piston at the bottom of the damper rod with solvent and dry it. Check it for wear. If it is worn badly, the damper rod assembly should be replaced.

NOTE: *(Sherpa S)—It is very important that the piston be tightly attached to the damper rod. If it is loose, back off the damper piston locknut and tighten the piston on the rod until the ball, visible through the bottom of the piston, is seated tightly against the end of the rod. Back the piston off ⅛ in. down the threads of the rod and tighten the locknut against it. (Don't clamp the piston in a vise or mar its friction surface.)*

NOTE: *(Campera)—It is very important that the piston be tightly attached*

to the damper rod. If it is loose, back off the damper locknut and tighten the piston on the damper rod until the ball, visible through the bottom of the piston, is seated tightly by the end of the rod. Leave it that way; the ball is not supposed to operate as a check valve in the Campera. Tighten the locknut against the piston.

21. To remove the oil seal from a slider leg on the Campera, first loosen and remove the dust guard from the mouth of the slider leg.

22. To remove an oil seal from the slider leg of either model, it is necessary to make up a special tool. Refer to the "Disassembly" section for the Mercurio and Metralla, Step 15. The procedure is the same for the Campera and Sherpa S.

23. If you wish to disassemble the steering head, refer to the previous section on the Mercurio and Metralla. The Campera and Sherpa S use the same assembly.

INSPECTION

1. The following components should be replaced each time the forks are disassembled:

Campera—damper cylinder O-rings, dust guards, stanchion plug O-rings, suspension stop O-rings, clamp bolt star washers, and slider leg oil seals.

Sherpa S—slider leg oil seals, damper cylinder O-rings, and clamp bolt star washers.

2. The following components should be replaced once a year:

Campera—top fork springs, damper rod assemblies, dust guard clamps, and bottom fork springs.

Sherpa S—damper cylinder assemblies, rubber suspension stops, fork springs, fork boots, fork clamps, suspension stop screws and washers, and the axle clamp nuts and bolts.

3. The Campera stanchion tubes are fitted with adjustable fork spring tensioners. These tensioners allow you to compensate for weakened springs or varying riding conditions. Normally, the tensioners

Stanchion plug ball and spring

should be positioned 35 mm below the top edge of the stanchion tubes.

4. If you have found, when the forks are rebounding (Campera), that oil escapes from the small hole in the stanchion plug cap screw (or you can hear air escaping), reseat the ball in the plug as follows:

a) Remove the cap screw.

b) Remove the spring and ball, and clean the ball with solvent. Replace the ball in the stanchion plug.

c) Insert a thin drift so that it rests against the ball, and tap it lightly several times to reseat the ball on its valve seat.

d) Reinstall the spring and cap screw.

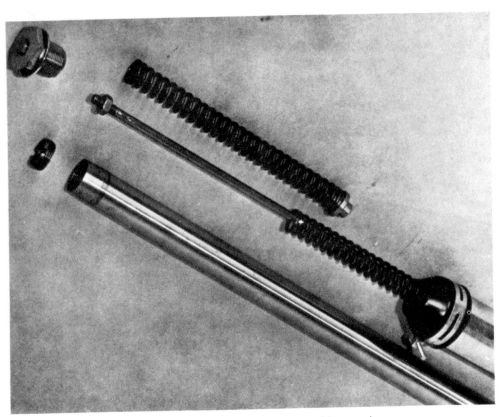

Fork springs and adjustable tensioners (Campera)

REASSEMBLY

1. If you took apart the steering head, reassemble it as described in the Metralla/Mercurio section.

2. Install new oil seals in the slider legs, with the open side facing in, after the seals have been coated with oil. Drive each seal onto its flange in the leg.

3. Fit the rubber dust guard to the mouth of each slider leg and tighten the clamp.

4. Campera—Insert the damper rod, piston end first, into the damper cylinder. Be sure that the piston spring is located between the damper cylinder nut and the piston on the damper rod. Screw the cylinder nut tightly into the damper cylinder; if necessary, hold the bottom of the cylinder with vise-grips.

5. Sherpa S—Insert the damper rod into the damper cylinder, piston end first. Tighten the damper cylinder nut as described above for the Campera.

6. Install a new O-ring in the groove at the bottom of the damper cylinder.

7. Install the two O-rings on the lower part of the damper cylinder, beneath the holes drilled in the face of the boss (Campera).

8. Install a new fiber washer on the bottom of the damper cylinder (Sherpa S).

9. Insert the damper rod assembly into the slider leg and install the allen bolt in the bottom of the leg.

10. Pour 85 cc of SAE 20 or 30W oil into each slider leg. Work the damper rod up and down until the oil has been sucked down into the cylinder and the unit is working satisfactorily.

11. Put the fork spring on the damper rod and screw the spring on the top of the damper cylinder (Sherpa S).

12. Connect the two fork springs to their carrier and fit them to the damper rod (Campera).

13. Fit the slider leg to the bottom of the stanchion tube and work the slider leg up.

14. Campera—Pull the damper rod up and hold it with a pair of pliers. Fit the locknut to the damper rod and screw it down to the bottom of the threads. Put the stanchion plug washer on the rod and then install the plug, turning it down until it bottoms. Hold the stanchion plug and tighten the locknut up against it. Gently release the pliers and screw the plug into the tube until it bottoms.

15. Sherpa S—Pull up the damper rod and hold it with pliers. Screw the spring carrier to the damper rod and run the plug down until it bottoms. Tighten the locknut against the bottom of the spring carrier. Release the pliers and hold the spring so that the slider leg won't fall. Hold the leg down slightly and insert the stanchion plug into the tube. Tighten the plug and push the slider leg back up so that the spring carrier is held against the plug. Insert the allen bolt and lockwasher into the plug and tighten the bolt securely.

16. Pull the bottom of the boot down over the slider leg and tighten the clamp (Sherpa S).

17. If you disassembled the steering head, turn back to the Metralla/Mercurio section and complete the assembly of the front end under the "Reassembly" heading, Steps 32–45. If the steering head was not disassembled, continue with this section.

18. Install the front fender (the shorter length faces the rear).

19. Check to see that the flanged spacers are still in place in the front wheel oil seals. Align the wheel with the forks and insert the axle from the left side. Install and

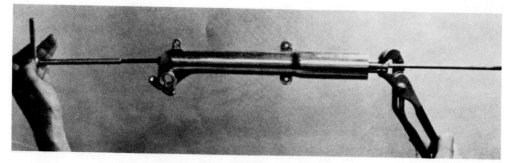

Installing the allen bolt in the slider leg

Installing the locknut on the damper rod (Campera)

tighten the axle nut until it just begins to compress its lockwasher.

20. Position the brake anchor plate and the right fender brace against the lug on the right slider leg. Install and tighten the two fender bolts and nuts, and tighten the anchor plate nut on the brake plate.

21. Connect the brake cable to the brake arm and handlebar lever. Fit the nipple to the inner brake cable and pull the nipple up the cable so that it lifts the brake arm until the brake does not quite drag when you spin the front wheel. Tighten the nipple clamp bolt.

22. Align the front wheel so that it is parallel with the forks.

23. Tighten the four axle clamp nuts to 6 ft lbs (Campera).

24. Torque the axle nut to 30 ft lbs.

25. Tighten the stanchion plugs securely (50 ft lbs).

26. Rap the top and bottom of the bottom steering bracket on the side of each stanchion tube clamp bolt, using a hammer and piece of wood. Torque the two stanchion clamp bolts to 15 ft lbs.

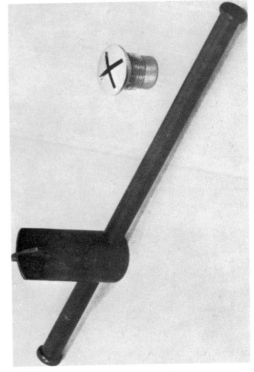

Stanchion plug wrench (Sherpa S)

1966–67 Lobito

OIL CHANGES

1. Remove the slotted drain plug near the bottom of each slider leg.

2. Work the front forks up and down to expel the oil from the legs.

3. Reinstall the drain plugs, using new fiber washers.

4. Remove the handlebars and unscrew the two stanchion plugs. Pour 70 cc of SAE 20 or 30W oil into each slider leg.

5. Loosen the stanchion tube clamp bolts on the bottom bracket. Screw the stanchion plugs into the tubes and torque them to 50 ft lbs. Tap the top and bottom of each side of the bottom bracket with a mallet to relieve any strain. Torque the clamp bolts on the bottom bracket to 15 ft lbs.

NOTE: *Whenever you loosen the stanchion plugs on the Lobito, it is very important to loosen the stanchion tube clamp bolts on the bottom bracket, torque the plugs, and then torque the clamp bolts. This must be done to avoid straining the top bracket.*

DISASSEMBLY, INSPECTION, AND REASSEMBLY

The Lobito forks are similar in design to the forks on the 1965–66 250 Scrambler. Refer to that section for fork repair procedures. If it is necessary to strip the steering head, refer to the Mercurio/Metralla section, as these models use the same type of steering head bearings as the Lobito. Perform the following checks on the fork components after disassembly:

1. Check the top bracket for cracks. If you find any, the bracket must be replaced. The bracket will not crack if the correct assembly procedure is followed.

2. Measure the fork springs. Minimum spring length is 5 in. for the bottom spring, 7¾ in. for the top spring.

3. Each time the forks are disassembled, these components should be replaced: oil seals, damper cylinder O-rings, rubber boots, oil drain plug washers, stanchion plug O-rings, and all snap-rings.

4. Replace these components at yearly intervals: distributor ring assemblies, damper pistons, valve washers, and valve support cylinders.

5. Front fork seal leaks on Lobito models Mk I through Mk III may be rectified in the following manner:

a. Replace the old seals with stock items in which the seal springs have been removed and replaced with a rubber O-ring about 1⅛ in. inside diameter and ³⁄₃₂ in. thick.

b. Grease the seals well before installation.

c. Check and clean the ball check valves in the stanchion plugs (if fitted).

Topping out of the forks on 1972 models (indicated by a clanking noise when the front wheel leaves the ground) may be remedied by increasing the amount of oil in the fork legs. The amount may be increased to about 195 cc of oil in each leg.

Fork Leg Capacities

Model	Quantity each leg	Weight (SAE #)
100 cc Lobito "K"	70 cc	20 (30 or 40 optional)
100 cc Lobito Trail	70 cc	20
175 cc Mercurio	85 cc	20
175 cc Campera	85 cc	20 (30 or 50 optional)
200 cc Matador	85 cc	30–50
125 cc Sherpa S 4 speed	85 cc	20–50
175 cc Sherpa S 4 speed	85 cc	20–50
200 cc Sherpa S 4 speed	85 cc	20–50
250 cc TT Pursang	160 cc	10–30
250 cc Motocross Pursang	160 cc	10–30
250 cc Matador Mk II, Mk III	160 cc	10–30

Fork Leg Capacities (cont.)

Model	Quantity each leg	Weight (SAE #)
100 cc Lobito 5 speed	80 cc	30
125 cc Lobito 5 speed	80 cc	30
175 cc Campera 5 speed	80 cc	30
250 cc El Tigre	85 cc	30
200 cc El Tigre	55 cc	30
100 cc Sherpa S 5 speed	80 cc	20
125 cc Sherpa S 5 speed	150 cc	20
175 cc Sherpa S 5 speed	150 cc	20
200 cc Sherpa S 5 speed	150 cc	20
360 cc Bandido Scrambler	160 cc	20
360 cc El Montadero	160 cc	20
250 cc Metralla	85 cc	20

BRAKE SERVICE

Front Brake Inspection

Remove the front wheel and pull the brake panel off the drum. Examine the drum for scoring and excessive wear. Normally, the drum will not become scored unless the brake lining has been worn completely away. If necessary, replace the drum.

Measure the thinnest part of both brake linings. When any part of the lining has worn to less than 0.080 in. (2 mm), both shoe assemblies should be replaced. If any of the brake shoe return springs are stretched, replace them also. Lightly grease the shoe cam and pivots upon reassembly.

Rear Brake Inspection

The rear brake shoes should be replaced when the brake operating lever moves over-center as the brake is applied. The brake shoes can be replaced after the rear wheel has been removed. Refer to the preceding section for additional information.

Adjustment

Front and rear brake adjustment is covered in Chapter 2.

REAR SUSPENSION

Shock Absorber and Spring Replacement

The spring/shock absorber unit can be removed after the upper and lower mounting bolts have been taken out. To remove the spring, compress it slightly by hand and remove the retainers. To check the effectiveness of the shock, compress and extend the unit by hand. More resistance should be encountered on the extension stroke if the shock is operating correctly. Replace it if it is leaking or if damping is unsatisfactory.

SWING ARM SERVICE

Dissassembly

1. Remove the muffler (if applicable).
2. Remove the rear wheel.
3. Take off the shock absorber units.
4. Remove the swing arm pivot nut and withdraw the pivot shaft. The swing arm can now be removed from the frame.

Inspection

Check the swing arm carefully for cracks and distortion. It is very important that the swing arm is aligned properly and in perfect condition. It is also very important that the pivot shaft and bushings are not worn or damaged. Replace the bushings as necessary; replace the shaft if it is bent or damaged in any other way.

Assembly

Installation is in reverse order of removal. Observe the following points:

1. Liberally grease the pivot shaft before installing.
2. Lubricate the swing arm pivot at the grease fittings after it is assembled, and make sure that no more than 0.02 in. (0.5 mm) of free-play exists at the pivot.

The swing arm pivot bolts should be torqued to 75 ft. lbs.

Chassis Torque Specifications
(In ft. lbs.)

Front Forks

Stanchion Plugs	100
Axle Clamp Bolts	6
Axle Nut	30
Top Bracket Fixing Nut	30
Top Bracket—steering shaft clamp	15
Bottom Bracket—stanchion tube clamp	15

Rear Suspension

Swing Arm Pivot Bolts	75
Rear Axle Nut	30
Sprocket Bolts	20

4 · Montesa

Engine and Transmission

REMOVAL AND INSTALLATION

1. Remove the drain plugs and allow the oil to drain from the gearbox and the primary case.

2. Turn the fuel valve off and disconnect the fuel line from the carburetor.

3. Disconnect the exhaust pipe from the cylinder flange.

4. Remove the air filter (or disconnect the rubber tube) from the carburetor.

5. Disconnect the clutch and throttle cables from the engine.

6. Disconnect the high tension cable and remove the spark plug.

7. Remove the kickstart and shift levers.

8. Take out the screws and remove the

Removing the crankcase drain plug

120

right side crankcase cover (left side on the Cota 123).

9. Remove the master link and take off the drive chain.

10. Disconnect the wires from the magneto.

11. Unscrew the engine mounting bolts and lift the engine out of the frame.

12. To install the engine, reverse the preceding operations. The master link clip should always be installed so that its closed end faces in the direction of forward chain rotation.

TOP END SERVICE

Cylinder Head

REMOVAL AND INSTALLATION

1. Unscrew the head nuts gradually and evenly, in a criss-cross pattern, and remove the bolts (if applicable). Tap the head with a rubber mallet to break the seal and lift it off the cylinder.

2. Installation is in the reverse order of removal. Torque the head nuts to the following specification:

250 Trial, Cota 247, King Scorpion, Cappra 250 (all), and Cota 123—25 ft lbs.

All other models—15 ft lbs.

No torque specification is given for head bolts.

Cylinder Service

REMOVAL AND INSPECTION

1. Unscrew and remove the cylinder securing bolts (if applicable). Otherwise, simply lift the cylinder off the crankcase. Take care not to let the piston or connecting rod fall against the case flange.

2. Measure the diameter of the cylinder bore in the following manner to check for excessive wear and concentricity:

Measure the bore at three points, the first being about 1 in. below the top of the cylinder, the second in the middle and the last about 1 in. from the bottom. The maximum reading should not exceed the standard bore value by more than 0.006 in. (0.15 mm).

Take three more readings in a plane 90° from the first series. This is a check for cylinder concentricity (out-of-round) and the readings obtained must not exceed the first series by more than 0.002 in. (0.05 mm).

3. The cylinder can be bored, if necessary, allowing the proper clearances for piston and cylinder. Refer to the accompanying chart.

4. If a new liner is to be fitted, it should be bored AFTER installation.

5. After boring a cylinder, the ports must be chamfered slightly to reduce the possibility of their catching a piston ring. The chamfer should be about 0.5 mm.

Standard Cylinder Diameter

| Model | Diameter | |
	Inches	Millimeters
Impala Sport	2.3988	(60.93)
Impala	2.3988	(60.93)
Comando 175	2.3988	(60.93)
Kenya	2.3988	(60.93)
250 Trial	2.8563	(72.55)
Impala Cross 175	2.3988	(60.93)
Texas	2.3988	(60.93)
Impala Cross 250	2.8541	(72.49)
Enduro	2.3988	(60.93)
Sport 250	2.8563	(72.55)
Cota 247	2.8563	(72.55)
La Cross	2.8568	(72.56)
Scorpion 250	2.8563	(72.55)
Cappra 250	2.8568	(72.56)
King Scorpion	2.8563	(72.55)
Cappra 360 GP/DS	3.0724	(78.04)
Cappra 125 MX	2.0276	(51.50)
Cota 123	2.1263	(54.01)

Piston-to-Cylinder Clearance

Model	Inches	Millimeters
Impala Sport	0.0012	0.030
Impala	0.0012	0.030
Comando 175	0.0012	0.030
Kenya	0.0012	0.030
250 Trial	0.0033	0.085
Impala Cross 175	0.0012	0.030
Impala Cross 250	0.0010	0.025
Enduro	0.0012	0.030
Sport 250	0.0033	0.085
Cota 247	0.0033	0.085
La Cross	0.0039	0.099
Scorpion 250	0.0033	0.085
Cappra 250	0.0039	0.099
King Scorpion	0.0014	0.035
Cappra 360	0.0033	0.085
Cappra 125 MX	0.0019	0.048
Cota 123	0.0017	0.045
Texas	0.0012	0.030

CYLINDER LINER REPLACEMENT

Heat the cylinder to 1100° F. to remove the liner and then hold the new liner in position using a press (75 psi) while the cylinder cools. The liner must be bored to the proper specifications after installation. Send the cylinder liner and cylinder to a competent machine shop for these operations.

CYLINDER INSTALLATION

1. Check to see that the small pin in each ring groove is between the ends of the rings.

2. Install a new cylinder base gasket.

3. Oil the piston and cylinder bore and slide the cylinder down over the piston. Carefully compress each ring so that it slips easily into the bore (or use a ring compresser).

4. Seat the cylinder on the crankcase and install and torque the securing bolts to 15 ft lbs (18 ft lbs on the King Scorpion).

Piston Service

REMOVAL

1. Stuff a towel into the crankcase flange to prevent any foreign material from entering.

2. Remove the wrist pin snap-rings with needle nose pliers.

3. Heat the crown of the piston with an electric iron or with rags soaked in hot water, then push the wrist pin out using a drift that is slightly smaller in diameter than the pin. On bikes with uncaged needle bearings, take care not to loose the needles. Inspect the wrist pin and bearing needles for wear and excessive clearance; replace if necessary.

Piston Rings

REMOVAL AND INSPECTION

1. Carefully remove the rings using a ring spreader or by spreading the ends gently with your thumbs.

2. Clean the ring grooves with a scraper or with a broken piece of a ring.

3. Place each ring, in turn, into the cylinder and push it to the middle with the piston. Measure the end-gap. End-gap tolerance for all except 360 cc models is 0.0078–0.0137 in. (0.20–0.35 mm). On 360

Top end assembly

cc models, the specification is 0.0118–0.0177 in. (0.30–0.45 mm).

4. "Roll" the rings completely around their grooves to check for any binding. Measure the clearance between the top of the ring and the groove at several places; this measurement should not exceed 0.0067 in. (0.07 mm).

5. When installing the rings, take care to align the notch in the ring ends with the small pin in the ring groove. If one of the rings is chrome plated, it is installed in the top groove. Do not spread the rings any more than necessary when installing them.

INSTALLATION

1. Installation is basically a reversal of the removal procedure. The piston crown is usually marked "ESCAPE" with an arrow pointing toward one side. This arrow must be made to point toward the exhaust port. If the piston is not marked, the longer skirt should be positioned toward the front of the engine.

2. On models with uncaged needle bearings at the connecting rod small end, a special tool is used, as shown, to arrange

Fitting the small end needle bearings into the special tool

Fitting the needle bearings into the connecting rod

the needles for reassembly. Some stiff grease is used to hold them in place.

3. Use new wrist pin circlips upon reassembly.

LOWER END AND TRANSMISSION SERVICE

Engine Sprocket

REMOVAL

1. Remove the right side engine cover.
2. Bend the locktab away from the sprocket nut.
3. Use the special tool, or wrap a length of chain around the sprocket, and clamp the ends in a vise. Unscrew the nut. It has a LEFT-HAND thread.

4. Pull the sprocket off its shaft with a gear puller. Remove the woodruff key from the shaft.

Magneto

REMOVAL AND INSTALLATION

1. Remove the right side engine cover.
2. Hold the flywheel in position and unscrew the securing nut (LEFT-HAND thread). Note that the lock washer also has a special left-hand bias.
3. Install a flywheel puller and pull the flywheel off the shaft. Mark the position of the magneto plate with one or more scribed lines to facilitate reassembly. Remove the three screws and take off the **magneto plate**.

Magneto flywheel with removal tool in position

4. Installation is the reverse of the removal procedures. Torque the flywheel nut to 72 ft lbs. Check and, if necessary, adjust the ignition timing.

Removing the magneto flywheel

Auxiliary Flywheel

REMOVAL AND INSTALLATION

On models equipped with an auxiliary flywheel on the left side of the engine:
1. Remove the left side engine case.
2. Remove the lockwire from the flywheel securing nut.

Left side crankcase components

Right side crankcase disassembled

3. Unscrew and remove the flywheel nut.
4. Pull the flywheel off the crankshaft with a flywheel puller. Remove the woodruff key from the shaft.
5. Install the flywheel in the reverse order of removal. When installing new lockwire, position it so that it will tend to tighten the nut, rather than loosen it.

Clutch Service

REMOVAL

1. Remove the left side engine cover.
2. Pull the pronged release mechanism plate out of the clutch hub.
3. Bend back the locktab and unscrew the clutch hub nut. (Note that the shoulder of the nut faces inward.)
4. Withdraw the clutch plates from the hub.
5. Pull off the bushing and remove the clutch hub from the shaft.
6. Remove the spacer(s) from the shaft.

The thicker of the two spacers (if applicable) should be closer to the engine.

CLUTCH HUB INSPECTION

Check the hub teeth for wear and damage. Minor damage can be repaired with an oilstone. If the teeth are in bad shape, replace the hub.

Check the operation of the center bearing. If it does not operate smoothly and noiselessly, it should be replaced. If necessary, remove the snap-ring and press out the bearing.

If the small brass piece in the release mechanism shows signs of wear, replace it. When reassembling, install it so that the chamfer faces the release lever.

CLUTCH DISC REPLACEMENT

1. Mount the clutch disc assembly on a press, so that the disc tabs are securely located.
2. Apply pressure to the spring plate until it is compressed enough so that the pins can be removed. Release the press slowly.
3. Remove the spring plate, discs, and springs.
4. Install the new discs in the same

Clutch hub

Clutch plate assembly and hub

manner and tighten the retaining nut to
15 ft lbs.

NOTE: *Do not change the order of the
clutch plates. They are prearranged at
the factory.*

Clutch Adjustment

Rotate the clutch adjustment nut to provide about half an inch of free-play at the
end of the clutch lever. Retighten the locknut after adjustment.

Primary Drive Gear

Removal

1. Unscrew and remove the gear securing nut.

2. Pull the gear off the shaft using a
suitable gear puller. *Do not attempt to pry
or heat the gear in order to remove it.*

3. If, on your machine, the gear is in-
tegral with the auxiliary flywheel, use the
tapped holes in the flywheel to mount a
puller.

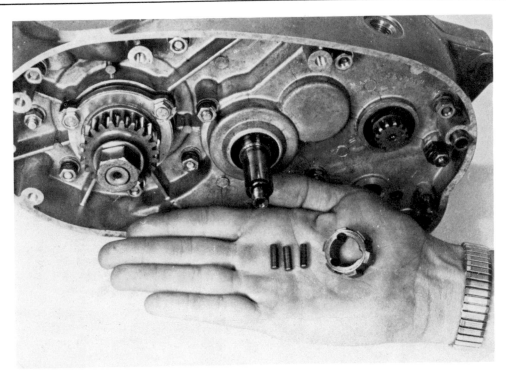

Clutch hub bearing components

Fitting the crankshaft (primary) gear

INSPECTION

If the gear is badly damaged or worn, replace it. Minor defects can be repaired with an oilstone.

INSTALLATION

When installing the gear, take particular care to clean the crankshaft and gear tapers. Wipe them with a non-oily solvent before assembly. Tighten the securing nut to 72 ft lbs.

Shifter Mechanism

MODELS WITH THE MECHANISM LOCATED UNDER THE LEFT CRANKCASE COVER

NOTE: *If inspection or repair of the shifter mechanism is not required, the mechanism may be removed, complete with its shaft, after the crankcases have been separated.*

Disassembly

1. Unscrew and remove the shifter detent plunger.
2. Bend back the locking tabs and remove the two bolts on the shifter mechanism.
3. Remove the shifter return spring and plates.
4. Remove the two shifter pawls. Take care when removing the pawls; they are positioned with springs.
5. Take off the sector gear. Remove the securing nut, then the adjusting cam.
6. Remove the stop plate after marking it so that it can be reinstalled in the same position.

Removing the detent plunger

Inspection

Replace any parts which show excessive wear. Examine the gear teeth and the detents on the stop plate; these items are more subject to damage.

Assembly

Assembly is the reverse of the disassembly procedure. Note the following points:

1. The transmission should be in Neutral during reassembly.

2. The diagonal slot in the end of the selector shaft (into which the pawls are installed) is closer to the TOP bolt hole.

3. Align the slash mark located on the third tooth from the right of the sector gear with the punch mark on the shift drum gear.

4. Screw in one of the two shifter assembly bolts, then move the shift lever to align the other bolt with its hole.

Gear selector mechanism

Adjustment

1. Loosen the locknut and set the adjustment cam on its center position. Retighten the nut.

2. Select each gear with the shift lever. If any gear won't engage properly, select First gear and then rotate the transmission input shaft a small amount. Continue to turn the shaft and check gear operation until all gears engage properly.

3. Loosen the locknut again and turn the adjusting cam so that when the plunger bottoms in each detent, the pawl engages its stop. Tighten the locknut.

MODELS WITH THE SHIFTER MECHANISM LOCATED UNDER THE RIGHT CRANKCASE COVER

Disassembly

1. Unscrew the shifter detent screw at the left, top of the crankcases and remove the detent ball with a magnetic screwdriver or suitable substitute.

2. Remove the retainer and take off the small shift cam gear.

3. Remove the snap-ring and washer from the end of the selector shaft and remove the shaft.

4. Take off the shift pawl cover (three screws), taking care not to lose the pawls.

Inspection

Check the tips of the pawls, the gears, and the rack guide bushing for wear. Replace parts as necessary.

Assembly

Assemble the shifter mechanism in reverse order of disassembly, noting the following points:

1. The transmission must be in Neutral during assembly.

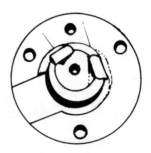

Gear selector pawls positioned for installation

Gear shift mechanism correctly positioned

2. Position the square shaft midway between its stops.

3. Install the small gear on its shaft so that its mark aligns with the mark on the rack.

Kickstart Mechanism

On some models, the kickstart mechanism is housed in the crankcase. This type of kickstarter is covered in the "Transmission Section." The other type of kickstart mechanism is accessible upon removal of the right side crankcase cover. Service procedures for this type are as follows.

DISASSEMBLY

1. Unhook the return spring from its anchor and pull out the kick gear assembly.

2. Remove the clutch gear from its shaft.

3. Remove the spacer, keeping it separate from the other one.

4. Remove the snap-ring and washer, then pull the idler gear from its shaft.

5. The kick gear assembly can be disassembled by removing the thrust washer, spring guide, and snap-ring.

INSPECTION

Check the splines in the kick gear and its shaft. The gear must be able to slide smoothly. Examine the gears for worn or broken teeth. Make sure that the return spring is healthy and in one piece.

ASSEMBLY

Assemble the kickstart mechanism in the reverse order of disassembly.

SPLITTING THE CRANKCASES

1. Perform the following operations, as previously described:
    a. Remove the crankcase covers.
    b. Disassemble the clutch.
    c. Remove the magneto flywheel.
    d. Remove the engine sprockets.

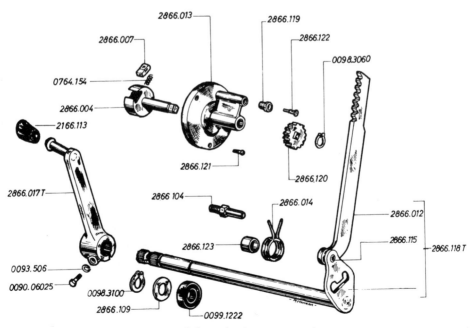

Gear shift mechanism components

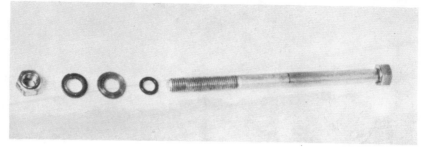

Crankcase bolt and components

Removing the crankshaft oil seal housing

e. Remove the cylinder head and cylinder.

f. Remove the piston, if desired.

2. Remove the crankshaft oil seal housings on either side of the crankshaft. Watch for any shims behind the seals and note their location.

3. Unscrew and remove the crankcase securing bolts and nuts. Note that one of the bolts has a flat washer under the bolt and nut heads. This bolt and washer must be replaced in their original positions. Do not take out the nut above and to the left of the kickstarter shaft. On models with the shifter mechanism located under the right crankcase cover, the kickstarter spring anchor serves as a crankcase bolt.

4. If there are any scratches or nicks on the gear shift selector shaft, smooth them

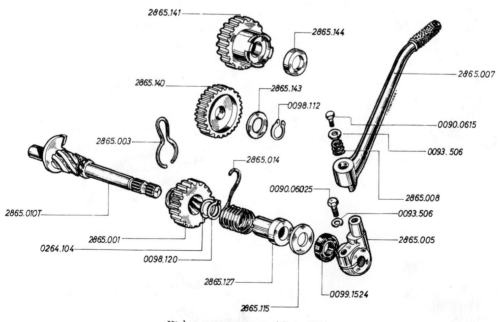

Kickstart components (Cota 123)

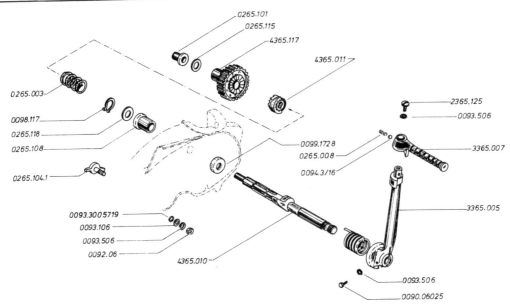

0265.101
0265.115
4365.117
4365.011
0265.003
0098.117
0265.118
0265.108
0265.104.1
2365.125
0093.506
0099.1728
0265.008
0094.3/16
3365.007
0093.3005719
0093.106
0093.506
0092.06
4365.010
3365.005
0093.506
0090.06025

Kickstart components (Cappra 250-VR)

with emery cloth before separating the cases.

5. Place the engine on the bench and carefully heat the area around the left side bearing.

6. Lift the engine, holding the left side of the engine up, and tap on the crankcase halves' mating surface with a soft-faced mallet until the cases separate.

Gear cluster shims

Kickstart ratchet

Gear cluster positioned as installed

Transmission Removal

SLIDING GEARS ON MAINSHAFT

After the cases have been separated, proceed as follows:

1. Remove the kickstart gear, ratchet and spring.

2. Unscrew the detent plunger from the case.

3. Lift out the mainshaft while tapping lightly on the countershaft with a soft-faced mallet. Take out the countershaft, along with the shift drum and forks.

4. Remove and tag the shims on the shafts and disassemble the gears on the countershaft.

5. If it is necessary to remove the bearings or bushings from the crankcase, heat it to about 325° F. and then drive them out.

6. To remove the gears from the mainshaft, it may be necessary to use a press.

7. Cut the safety wire, unscrew the guide pegs and remove the shift forks.

8. To remove the selector shaft, take out the snap-ring and its washer.

MODELS THAT HAVE SLIDING GEARS ON THE MAINSHAFT

Refer to the preceding section. The only difference is that the mainshaft, countershaft, and shifter mechanism must be lifted out of the case together.

Crankshaft Removal

After the transmission has been removed, the crankshaft may be removed from the crankcase half by heating the case to about 325° F. and driving out the crankshaft and bearing. Note the location of any shim washers on the crankshaft.

The crankshaft is pressed together and must be disassembled and reassembled in

Crankshaft assembly with shims

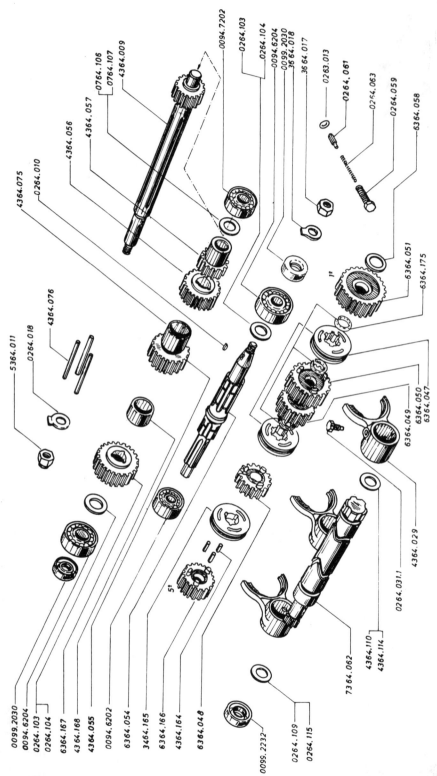

0094.7202
0264.103
0264.104
0094.6204
0099.2030
3664.018
3664.017
0263.013
0264.061
0264.063
0264.059
6364.058

0764.106
0764.107
4364.009
4364.057
4364.056
0264.010
4364.075

6364.051
6364.175

4364.076
5364.011
0264.018

1ª

5ª

Transmission components (Cappra 250-VR)

6364.049
6364.050
6364.047
4364.029
0264.031.1
4364.110
4364.114
7364.062

0099.2030
0094.6204
0264.103
0264.104
6364.167
4364.168
4364.055
0094.6202
6364.054
3464.165
6364.166
4364.164
6364.048

0099.2232
0264.109
0264.115

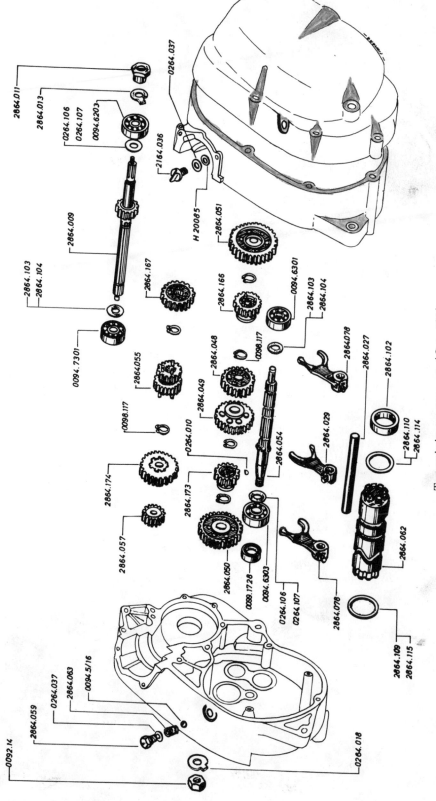

Transmission components (Cota 123)

Left and right crankcases stripped except for transmission bearings

the same way. Any play in the connecting rod big end bearing will require this operation.

Assembly and Alignment

Refer to Chapter Three, Bultaco four-speed models under "Crankshaft Assembly," Steps 4 and 6. Note that some Montesa models use caged connecting rod bearings.

Crankshaft Main Bearings

These bearings should be removed from the crank with the special tool, aided by heating.

Installation

As on removal, heat the case and drive the crankshaft bearing home. Note that the side of the crankshaft which is slotted for a woodruff key must be inserted into the drive side crankcase.

Transmission Inspection and Installation

1. Examine all gears for wear or damage. If the gear teeth are pitted or broken, replace the gear in question and its mating gear as a set.

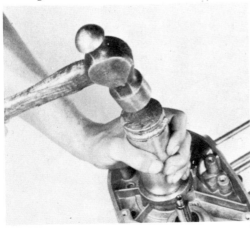

Installing a crankshaft bearing

Right side crankshaft bearing

2. Carefully check the dogs on the gears. If they are badly worn or broken, replace the gear. Light wear or chipping can usually be repaired with an oilstone. If the dogs are in poor condition, chances are that the slots in the engaging gears are also damaged.

3. Make sure that the shift forks do not bind. There should not be excessive wear on the shift fork sides. Clearance between each shift fork and the groove in its gears should not be greater than about 0.20 in.

4. To install new bearings or bushings in the crankcases, heat the cases to 325° F. Drive the bearings in quickly.

5. It is necessary to check and adjust the end-play if any of the transmission shaft components or bearings have been replaced. The procedure is as follows.

a. Refer to the accompanying illustration. Measure the dimensions of H, Hs, and Hp on the right side crankcase.

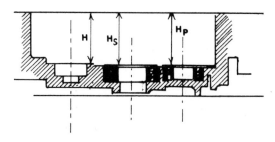

H = height from the crankcase surface to the bottom of the shift drum.

Hs = height from the crankcase surface to the top of the inner race of the countershaft bearing.

Hp = height from the crankcase surface to the top of the inner race of the mainshaft bearing.

b. Refer to the next illustration; measure the dimensions of h, hs, and hp on the left side crankcase.

h = height from the crankcase surface to the surface of the shift drum.

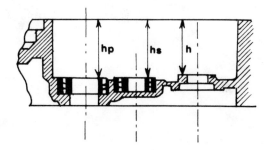

hs = height from the crankcase surface to the top of the inner race of the countershaft bearing.

hp = height from the crankcase surface to the top of the inner race of the mainshaft bearing.

c. Add the measurements obtained as shown below, also adding the thickness of the center crankcase gasket (S).

1) h + H + S = A
2) hs + Hs + S = B
3) hp + Hp + S = C

d. Measure the length of the shift drum (the result to be referred to as dimension (a). Assemble the gears onto the countershaft and measure the distance between the outer sides of the two end gears (to be referred to as dimension (b). Finally, assemble the gears onto the mainshaft and, as for the countershaft, measure the distance between the outer sides of the two end gears dimension (c).

e. To determine the end-play of the shafts, perform the following computations:

a) A—a = shift drum end-play (Xa)
b) B—b = countershaft end-play (Xb)
c) C—c = mainshaft end-play (Xc)

f. Since you now know the end-play of each shaft without any shims in place, it will be easy to determine the correct number of shims to use. The correct end-play for all of the shafts is 0.1–0.2 mm. Proper shim thickness (Z) can be determined in this manner:

Xa, Xb, or Xc − 0.15 mm = Z.

The mainshaft shims should be installed on the left side of the shaft.

The countershaft shims should be installed on the right side of the shaft.

6. Install the mainshaft, countershaft, and shift drum (with forks in place) in the right side crankcase, and operate the drum. Distribute the shims on each side of the shift drum so that there is equal distance between each sliding gear and its engaging gears.

CRANKCASE ASSEMBLY

1. With the transmission gear clusters and the crankshaft in place in the right side crankcase, install a new crankcase gasket, held in place by a small amount of gasket compound if necessary.

Installing the crankshaft

2. Gently heat the left side crankshaft bearing and fit the crankcase halves together.

3. Check immediately for free rotation of the crankshaft in the assembled cases, as it is quite possible for the flywheel to hit the cases if bearing alignment is not correct. The connecting rod small end should be exactly centered on the crankcase mating surface.

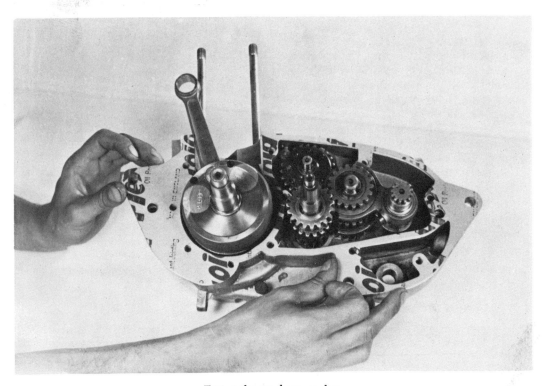

Fitting the crankcase gasket

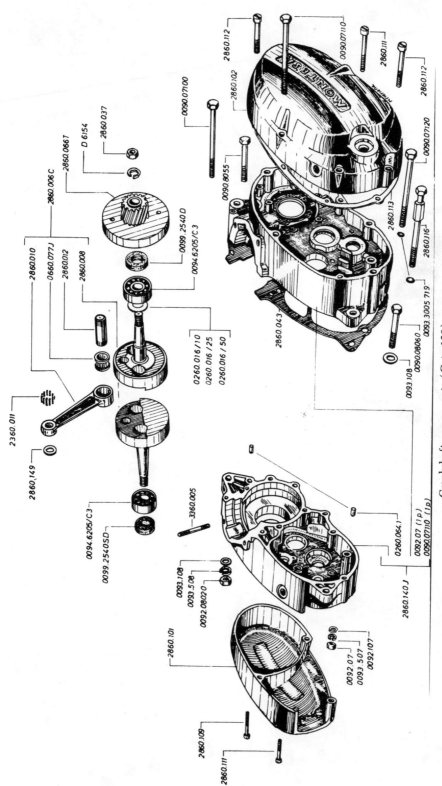

Crankshaft components (Cota 123)

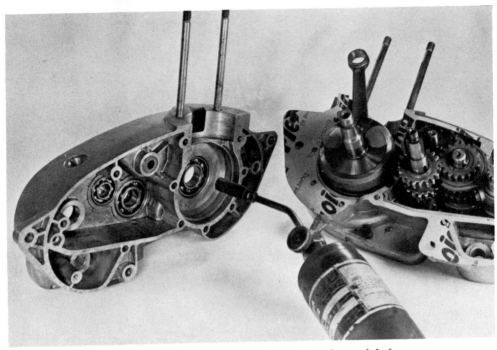

Heating the crankshaft bearing prior to fitting the crankshaft

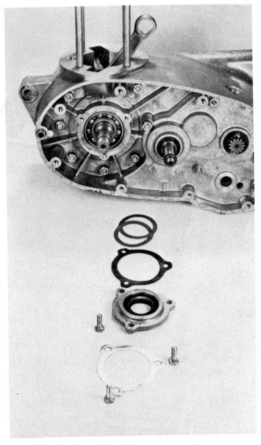

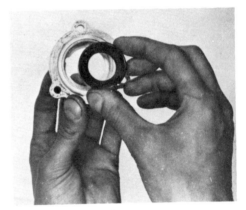

Crankshaft oil seal and housing

Crankshaft oil seal housing components

Fitting the oil seal to the housing

4. Refit the crankcase bolts, washers, and nuts in the correct order. Fit the crankcase oil seal assemblies. New seals should be used. These are pressed into the seal housings as shown.

IGNITION TIMING

Breaker Point Ignition

1. Disconnect the wire from the No. 1 terminal at the ignition coil and connect one lead of a continuity light (with built-in battery) to the wire that was disconnected. Ground the other test lead on the crankcase.

2. Install a dial gauge, with a spark plug hole adapter, into the spark plug hole. (Dial gauges made specially for setting the ignition timing on motorcycles are available from almost any dealer that handles two-stroke motorcycles.)

3. Rotate the flywheel in its normal direction of rotation and stop it when the piston reaches top dead center (TDC). Zero the dial of the gauge on the needle, taking care not to disturb the piston or the gauge.

4. Rotate the flywheel backward about ½ in. and then forward, very slowly, until the continuity light shows that the points have just opened. The dial gauge should be very near the specification given in the chart for your model. The specification given is the distance before top dead center (BTDC) of the piston when the breaker points should open.

5. If the light flickered during more than 0.02 mm of gauge travel, the points are dirty or pitted and should be cleaned or replaced. The points gap (maximum) should be between 0.35–0.45 mm. If the ignition timing is off by a small amount, it is possible to correct it simply by altering the points gap (while keeping it within specification).

6. If the timing is off by too great an amount, adjust it by loosening the mounting screws (after removing the flywheel) and rotating the magneto plate in the desired direction. Reinstall the flywheel loosely and recheck the timing. Repeat the operation, if necessary, until the timing is spot-on.

Ignition Timing

| Model | Distance BTDC | |
	Inches	Millimeters
Texas	0.118	3.00
Impala, Impala Sport	0.118	3.00
Comando 175	0.118	3.00
Kenya	0.118	3.00
250 Trial	0.118	3.00
Impala Cross 175	0.138	3.50
Impala Cross 250	0.216	5.50
Enduro	0.138	3.50
Sport 250	0.157	4.00
Cota 247		
To Serial No. 21M2999	0.157	4.00
Cota 247		
From Serial No. 21M3000	0.098	2.50
LaCross	0.236	6.00
Scorpion 250	0.157	4.00
Cappra 250	0.151	4.00
Cappra 250 GP	0.152	4.00
Cappra 250-Five	0.157	4.00
Cappra 250 MX	0.118	3.00
Cappra 360 GP/DS	0.157	4.00
Cappra 125 MX		
To Serial No. 18M0052	0.157	4.00
Cota 123	0.118	3.00
Cota 25	0.098	2.50

Electronic Ignition

1. Install a dial gauge, as for the other models, in the spark plug hole. Turn the engine until the piston is at TDC and then zero the gauge.

2. Rotate the engine backward until the piston is at the correct timing position. The proper timing specification for all models with electronic ignition is 0.118 in. (3.0 mm) BTDC.

3. Insert a thin phillips head screwdriver blade through the small timing hole provided in the flywheel (at about 8 o'clock) and into the hole in the stator plate. If the holes are aligned, the timing is correct.

4. If the holes are not aligned, slowly turn the flywheel until they do, noting the distance it was necessary to turn the flywheel.

5. Take off the flywheel (left-hand thread), loosen the stator plate screws slightly, and turn the stator plate the same amount it was necessary to turn the fly-

wheel for the holes to align, but in the opposite direction. Install the flywheel loosely and recheck timing. If necessary, repeat this operation until the timing is correct.

Fuel Systems

For adjustment, tuning, and repair procedures, refer to the Bultaco "Fuel Systems" section. Montesa uses the same makes and types of carburetors.

Electrical Systems

Montesa uses both an electronic ignition system and a conventional magneto ignition system. For an operational description of both types, refer to the "Ossa" section.

COMPONENT TESTS

Tests can be made with an ohmmeter or a multimeter. For an introduction to testing procedures, refer to the "Bultaco" section.

Magneto Ignition Models

IGNITION COIL

1. Measure the resistance between the primary terminals of the coil. The meter should read about 1 ohm.
2. Measure the resistance between one of the primary terminals and the center (high tension) terminal, where the spark plug cable plugs in. The meter should read 5,000–11,000 ohms.
3. Measure the resistance between the coil housing and any terminal. For an accurate reading, the paint should be scraped off the housing where the test lead is connected. If the meter does not read infinity, the insulation resistance has broken down.
4. If any of the above tests is not within specification, the coil should be replaced.

CONDENSER

1. Connect the body of the condenser to the negative terminal of a 12 volt battery and connect the condenser wire to the positive battery terminal. After allowing the condenser to charge for a few seconds, disconnect the battery and touch the condenser wire to the condenser body. If it sparks, the condenser is probably OK. If there is any doubt, replace it.

MAGNETO COILS

1. Remove the flywheel and check that the coils are not being rubbed by the flywheel.
2. Disconnect the wires to the magneto. Place a piece of paper between the breaker points. Measure the resistance between each magneto wire and ground. You should obtain the following results:
   a) Light equipped models—black wire, 0.6 ohms; pink wire, 0.6 ohms; green wire, 0.3 ohms; yellow wire, 0.3 ohms.
   b) Racing models—resistance of all coils should be about 0.5 ohms.

Electronic Ignition Models

COIL

1. Connect the negative ohmmeter lead to ground and connect the positive lead to the blue and black wires, in turn. The meter should read 200–800 ohms. Reverse the ohmmeter leads and retest. You should get an infinite reading in this case.
2. Connect the ohmmeter between the blue and black wires. It should read 10 ohms.
3. Connect the ohmmeter between the spark plug cable and the coil mounting bracket. The meter should read about 10,000 ohms.
4. Connect the ohmmeter between the coil mounting bracket and the blue terminal. As the connection is made, the meter needle should jump down the scale, then move to infinity. Repeat this test, using the black terminal.
5. If any of the above tests are failed, the coil should be replaced.

RECTIFIER

1. Using a continuity light with a self-contained battery, connect the leads to the rectifier one way, then reverse the test leads. The continuity light should light when connected one way, and *not* light when connected the other way. If it lights both ways, or not at all, replace the rectifier.

Wiring Diagrams

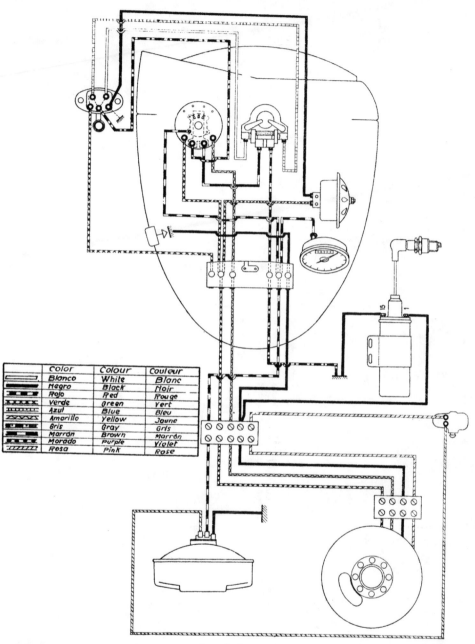

Color	Colour	Couleur
Blanco	White	Blanc
Negro	Black	Noir
Rojo	Red	Rouge
Verde	Green	Vert
Azul	Blue	Bleu
Amarillo	Yellow	Jaune
Gris	Gray	Gris
Marrón	Brown	Marrón
Morado	Purple	Violet
Rosa	Pink	Rose

Impala Sport

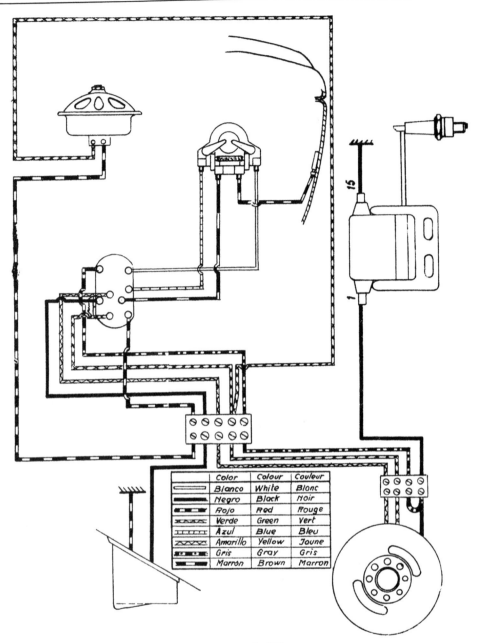

	Color	Colour	Couleur
	Blanco	White	Blanc
	Negro	Black	Noir
	Rojo	Red	Rouge
	Verde	Green	Vert
	Azul	Blue	Bleu
	Amarillo	Yellow	Jaune
	Gris	Gray	Gris
	Marrón	Brown	Marron

Commando 175

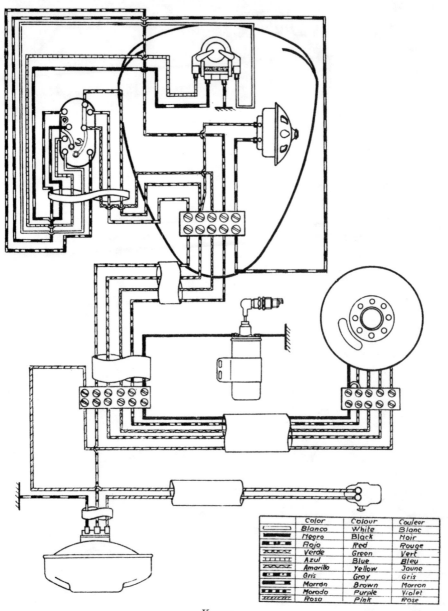

	Color	Colour	Couleur
	Blanco	White	Blanc
	Negro	Black	Noir
	Rojo	Red	Rouge
	Verde	Green	Vert
	Azul	Blue	Bleu
	Amarillo	Yellow	Jaune
	Gris	Gray	Gris
	Marrón	Brown	Morron
	Morado	Purple	Violet
	Rosa	Pink	Rose

Kenya

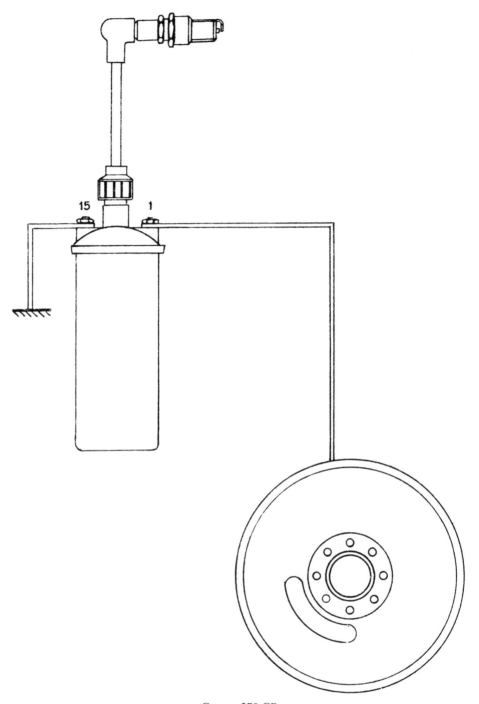

Cappra 250-GP

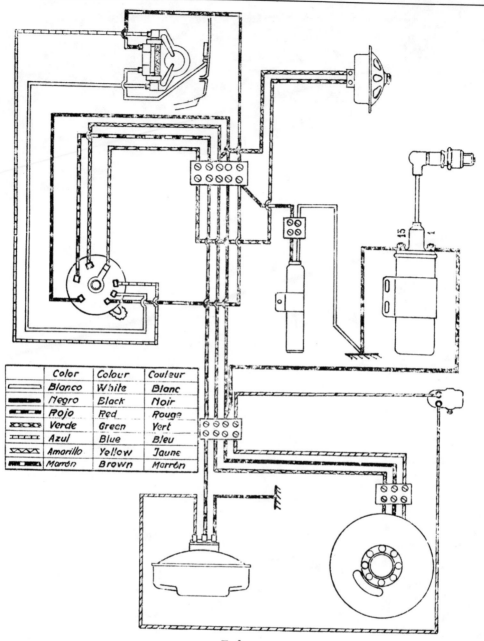

Color	Colour	Couleur
Blanco	White	Blanc
Negro	Black	Noir
Rojo	Red	Rouge
Verde	Green	Vert
Azul	Blue	Bleu
Amarillo	Yellow	Jaune
Marrón	Brown	Marrón

Enduro

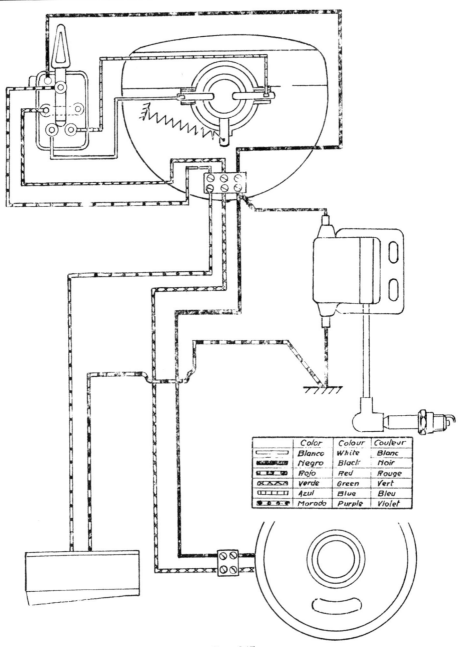

Color	Colour	Couleur
Blanco	White	Blanc
Negro	Black	Noir
Rojo	Red	Rouge
Verde	Green	Vert
Azul	Blue	Bleu
Morado	Purple	Violet

Cota 247

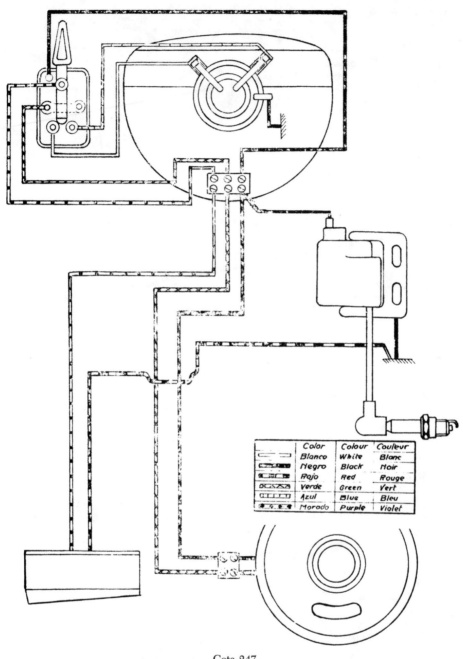

Color	Colour	Couleur
Blanco	White	Blanc
Negro	Black	Noir
Rojo	Red	Rouge
Verde	Green	Vert
Azul	Blue	Bleu
Morado	Purple	Violet

Cota 247

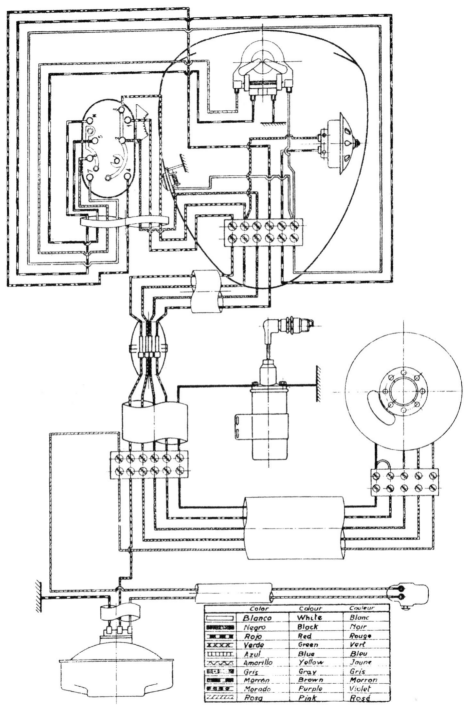

Color		Colour	Couleur
	Blanco	White	Blanc
	Negro	Black	Noir
	Rojo	Red	Rouge
	Verde	Green	Vert
	Azul	Blue	Bleu
	Amarillo	Yellow	Jaune
	Gris	Gray	Gris
	Morrón	Brown	Morron
	Morado	Purple	Violet
	Rosa	Pink	Rosé

Scorpion 250

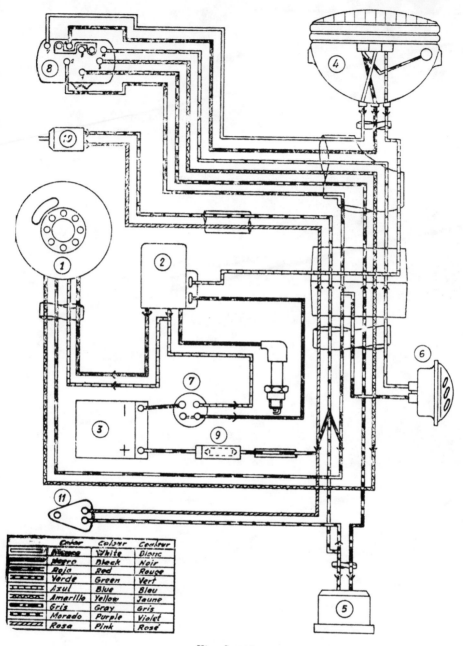

Color	Colour	Couleur
Blanco	White	Blanc
Negro	Black	Noir
Roja	Red	Rouge
Verde	Green	Vert
Azul	Blue	Bleu
Amarillo	Yellow	Jaune
Gris	Gray	Gris
Morado	Purple	Violet
Rosa	Pink	Rosé

King Scorpion

Chassis

FRONT FORKS

All Models

DISASSEMBLY

1. Disconnect the front brake cable at the brake drum.

2. Disconnect the brake anchor on the fork slider.

3. Remove the axle nut, and pull out the axle supporting the front wheel. Remove the wheel and brake drum. Remove the front fender.

4. Drain the oil from each of the fork legs. Early models may have the drain plug located directly above the axle. Other models are equipped with a drain plug at the rear

Removing the brake anchor bolt

Removing the axle nut

Removing the fork oil drain plug

of the fork slider. Pump each slider up and down several times to assure that all the oil is expelled.

5. Remove the allen bolt from the bottom of each slider.

6. Lift up the dust seal at the top of each slider, and remove the circlip there.

7. Pull the slider off the fork leg. A

Removing the fork slider circlip

rubber bush and a plain steel washer are located at the very bottom of the damper. Usually the washer will remain in the slider when it is removed.

8. Remove the fork cap nut. It may be necessary to remove the handlebars to enable the nut to be removed.

9. A check valve is fitted in the fork cap nut. If the valve sticks, oil will be forced out around the top of the cap nut. If this happens, take out the screw from the top of the cap nut, remove the small spring beneath the screw with the aid of a magnetic

Removing the fork slider allen bolt

Removing the fork slider

Damper tube rubber bush and washer

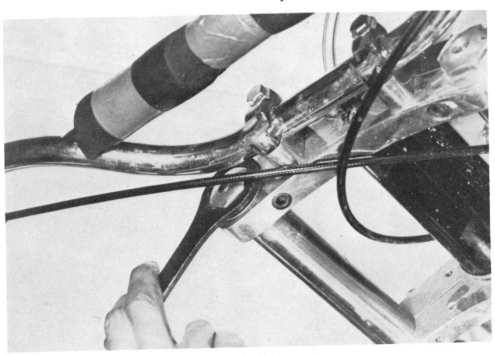

Removing the fork cap nut

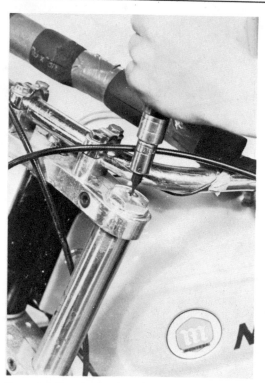

Removing the check valve screw

philips screwdriver, and remove the ball. Clean the assembly, then lightly reseat the ball in the cap nut with a hammer and drift. Reinstall the spring and plug.

10. Remove the large spring from the fork tube.

11. The damper assembly may be removed by first removing the circlip at the bottom of the fork tube.

12. If it is necessary to remove the fork tube itself, loosen the upper and lower triple clamp nuts; replace the fork cap nut, screwing it in several turns, and strike it sharply with a mallet to break the fork tube free from the triple clamps.

INSPECTION

1. Check all rubber seals, O-rings, etc. for torn or damaged condition.

2. The holes in the damper must be free of foreign matter.

3. Fork tubes must be perfectly straight.

4. Fork slider oil seals are replaced after prying the old seal out with a suitable instrument.

ASSEMBLY

1. When reinstalling the fork tube in the triple clamp, it is important that the tube be driven home until the top of the tube is perfectly flush with the top surface of the upper triple clamp.

2. The remainder of the assembly procedure is the reverse of disassembly.

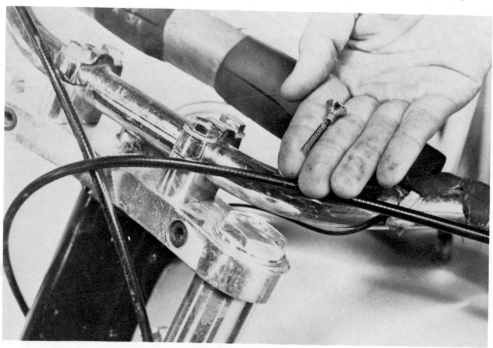

Check valve screw and spring

Removing the fork spring

Loosening the upper triple clamp nut

3. Be sure that the rubber bush is positioned at the bottom of the damper, and that the plain steel washer is at the bottom of the fork slider before refitting the slider.

4. Refill each fork leg with the correct amount and grade of oil. Fork leg capacity for the Cota 123 is 150 cc (5 oz.) for each leg. For all other models, the correct amount is 175 cc (6.5 oz.).

STEERING ASSEMBLY

Montesa steering assembly is similar to that of the Ossa machines. Refer to the Ossa "Chassis" section.

BRAKE SERVICE

Refer to the Bultaco section. Procedures are the same for the Montesa.

Removing the fork tube from the triple clamp

Loosening the lower triple clamp nut

REAR SUSPENSION AND SWING ARM SERVICE

Refer to the Bultaco section. Procedures are the same for the Montesa.

5 · Ossa

Engine and Transmission

ENGINE REMOVAL

1. Before removing the engine, clean the motorcycle thoroughly.

2. Loosen the clamp and remove the air filter from the carburetor.

3. Loosen the two nuts and bolts (or one nut) at the muffler mount.

4. Using a pin wrench, unscrew the exhaust pipe collar from the cylinder head flange.

5. Remove the muffler mount bolts (or nut) and take off the exhaust system.

6. Off-road models: Remove the six rear fender nuts and bolts. Remove the taillight lens (if applicable). Loosen the screw clamping the wire that goes out through the rear of the taillight assembly and remove the wire from the rear fender. Remove the rear fender.

7. Off-road models: Remove the four bolts and two nuts from the saddle mount portion of the gas tank.

8. Wildfire: Remove the spring hanger from the rear of the gas tank using a hook.

9. Remove the gas tank from the frame.

10. Take off the two screws from the plastic side panel on each side, then unscrew the nut and bolt from the panels and remove them.

11. Pioneer: Loosen the terminal screw

tnat mounts the wiring to the taillight assembly in the electrical junction block near the top of the rear downtube.

12. Take out the two screws at the top of the carburetor and remove the top and slide from the body of the carburetor.

13. Loosen the two carburetor mounting nuts so that you can pull the carburetor back enough to be able to remove the nuts, then remove the carburetor.

14. With the Ossa magneto flywheel holding tool, rotate the clutch arm clockwise and remove the cable from the clutch arm.

15. Take out the four screws and remove the magneto case from the engine. Be careful not to lose the clutch cam plunger from the case.

16. Remove the master link from the drive chain and remove the chain.

17. Cut the tape that mounts the electrical wiring to the rear downtube. Remove the wiring from the clamps on the rear tube.

18. Loosen all the terminal screws on the side of the electrical junction block that goes to the engine. Remove the wires from that side of the junction block.

19. Disconnect the two wires from the high tension coil. Unscrew the two bolts and remove the coil from the frame.

20. Remove the nuts from the top and bottom rear engine mount bolts.

21. Remove the nuts from the right and

Removing the engine from the frame

left front engine mount bolts; then tap out the two rear mount bolts using a drift. Remove the two front bolts; lift up the front of the engine so that the bolts come out easily.

ENGINE SERVICE

Removing the Piston

1. Mount the engine on the bench and remove the spark plug.

2. Looking down on the cylinder head and viewing the front of the cylinder as being 12 o'clock, loosen the four head nuts ¼ turn each in the following sequence: 10 o'clock, 4 o'clock, 2 o'clock, and 8 o'clock. Loosen the nuts another ¼ turn in the same sequence and then unscrew them completely.

CAUTION: *Failure to follow this procedure will probably result in a warped head.*

3. Lift off the cylinder head and its gasket.

Head nut loosening sequence

4. Remove the cylinder, taking care not to tear the cylinder base gasket or to allow the piston and rod to fall against the crankcase flange.

5. Stuff a towel in around the crankcase opening. Using a pair of needle nose pliers, remove the two wrist pin snap-rings. If you bend the clip during removal, do not re-use it on assembly.

6. Using a soft drift that is slightly smaller than the diameter of the wrist pin, press the pin out while supporting the piston to prevent any side-loading of the connecting rod. If the pin is tight, heat the crown of the piston with an electric iron or with rags soaked in hot water; *do not force the wrist pin out.*

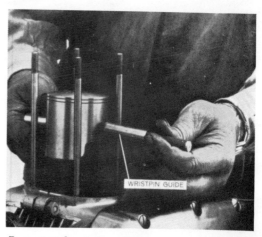

WRISTPIN GUIDE

Removing the piston wrist pin

7. Remove the piston from the rod and remove the needle bearing from the pin guide (or rod).

8. Remove the cylinder base gasket.

Disassembling the Magneto Side Engine Case

1. Fit the Ossa flywheel holding tool to the two holes in the flywheel. (You can get by without the tool by inserting a steel bar into each of the two flywheel holes and placing a pry-bar between them to hold the flywheel in position.) Unscrew and remove the flywheel retaining nut.

2. Back out the center bolt of the Ossa flywheel puller. Screw the puller into the flywheel (with the holder still in position). Tighten the puller in the flywheel, then tighten the center bolt of the puller until the flywheel is freed from the end of the

Removing the magneto flywheel nut

crankshaft. Remove the flywheel and its washer.

3. Scribe a line across the edge of the magneto backing plate and one of its mounting bosses (to be used as a reference when reassembling the engine).

Scribe a line across the magneto backing plate and mounting boss to facilitate reassembly

4. Take out the three screws and remove the magneto backing plate; fit it to the flywheel to prevent damage to either part.

5. Remove the woodruff key from the end of the crankshaft and place it on the side of the flywheel to prevent losing it.

Disassembling the Primary Side Engine Case

1. Unscrew the bolt completely from the shift lever and remove the shift lever from the selector shaft.

2. Remove the bolt from the kickstart lever and remove the lever from its shaft.

3. Place a pan beneath the engine and remove the drainplug. Tip the engine forward so that most of the gearbox and primary drive lubricant will drain.

4. Unscrew the ten screws that mount the primary case to the crankcase; leave the screws in the case.

5. Remove one of the screws which secure the inspection cover; loosen the other screw and swing the inspection cover aside. Insert a large screwdriver and lever it up against the outer clutch plate to break loose the primary case. If necessary, tap upward on the right edge of the primary case with a rubber mallet to free it. Hold the selector shaft in position in the cases as you remove the primary case.

6. Remove the case and the case gasket. Take care not to lose the two locating dowels in the case.

7. Remove the spring washer and the flat washer from the selector shaft.

8. Remove the five cotter pins from their studs at the outer clutch plate.

9. Unscrew the clutch spring nuts and remove the springs and spring cups.

10. Withdraw all the clutch plates except the inner one. Loosen the inner plate using two thin screwdrivers and then remove it.

11. Use the clutch tool (as shown) or a suitable substitute to prevent the clutch hub from turning. Brace it against the cush drive hub and unscrew the clutch hub nut.

12. With the holding tool still in position, loosen the allen nut in the cush drive hub (using a pipe on the allen wrench for additional leverage).

13. Remove the clutch nut, then remove the cush drive allen nut, the flange, spring, and the coupling.

14. Take off the inner clutch hub and remove the hub spacer from the mainshaft.

15. Remove the outer clutch hub, the engine sprocket, and the primary chain as an assembly. Remove the bushing and spacer from the mainshaft.

16. To remove the cush drive shaft, which is a press fit on the end of the crank-

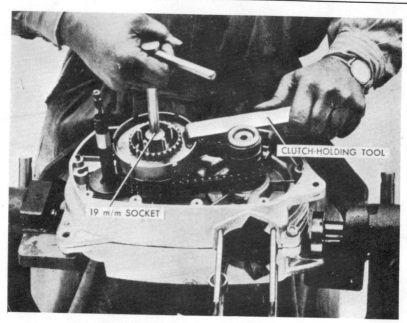

Removing the clutch hub nut

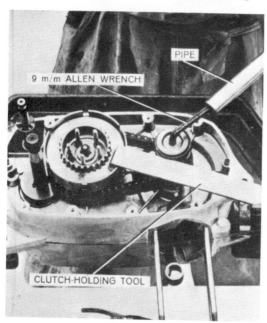

Removing the cush drive allen nut

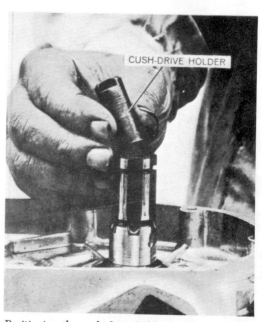

Positioning the cush drive holder on the crankshaft

shaft, you will need several Ossa tools. First, screw the cush drive holder into the crankshaft threads, then fit the spanner tool to the cush drive shaft. Install the two collars on the end of the cush drive holder and back out the center bolt in the puller. Mount the puller to the collars on the holder. Hold the spanner and tighten the center bolt of the puller to free the cush drive shaft from the crankshaft.

17. Remove the snap-ring from the kickstart shaft using snap-ring pliers.

18. Disengage the looped end of the kickstart return spring from its mount in the engine case using a large screwdriver. Be careful not to let the spring fly off the shaft. Free the other end of the spring from the kickstart shaft.

19. Remove the spring and large washer from the kickstart shaft.

Spanner tool in position

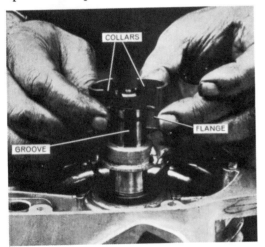

Fitting the collars to the end of the cush drive holder

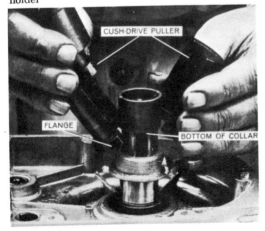

Installing the cush drive puller

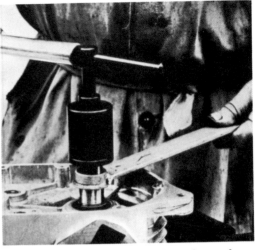

Removing the cush drive shaft from the crankcase

Splitting the Crankcases

1. Loosen the eleven engine case screws on the right side of the engine ¼ turn each. Remove the screws, working from the middle of the engine outward.

2. Unscrew and remove the engine case nut and bolt at the front of the engine. Do not let the cases fall apart.

3. Loosen the large screw with the nylon washer (the shift drum detent) at the bottom rear of the engine.

4. With the primary side engine case facing up, tap upward on it to separate it from the magneto side case. Lift off the primary side engine case, which will retain the crankshaft assembly. Check the mounting bosses on the primary side case for the mainshaft, layshaft, shift drum, and the selector shaft. Look for washers which might have stuck to the bosses in the case. If any washers have stuck to the bosses, remove them and put them on their shafts.

NOTE: *The washers control the end-play of the different shafts; it is very important not to mix the washers as you disassemble the gearbox.*

5. Lift the washers off the main bearing in the magneto side case and tag them.

Removing the Transmission Components

1. If the gearbox is not in need of repair, it is not necessary to remove the components. If you are going to remove them, first remove the engine case gasket and discard it.

2. Rotate the kickstart shaft clockwise until the cam on the engaging ratchet is

Crankcase screws to be removed

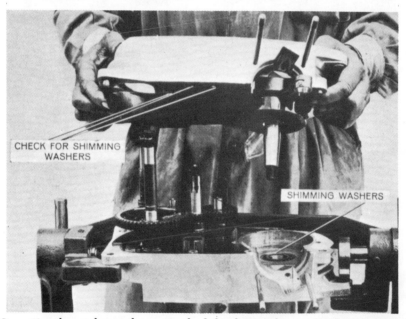

Separating the crankcases; be sure to check for shim washers in the places indicated

free of the gears and the large screw in the case. Lift out the shaft and its washers.

3. Lift out the selector shaft with its washers.

4. Pull up the shift fork shaft until the forks can be disengaged from the cam grooves in the shift drum. Lift out the drum with its washers.

5. Remove the large screw with the nylon washer from the outside of the engine case. (This is the detent plunger.)

6. Lift out the shift forks on their shaft.

7. Lift out the layshaft along with its washers.

8. Lift the mainshaft, with its bushing and washers, out of the countershaft.

9. Remove the plastic breather tube.

REMOVING THE COUNTERSHAFT ASSEMBLY

1. Lift the two needle bearings out of the countershaft from the inside of the case.

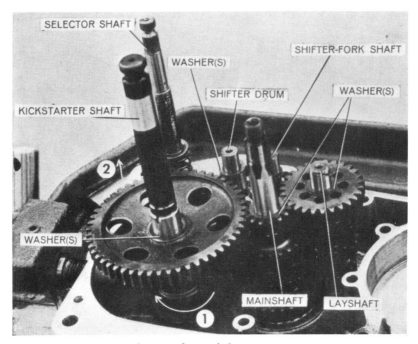

Kickstart and gear shift components

2. Bend back the locktab on the countershaft nut on the outside of the case.

3. Wrap a length of old chain around the countershaft sprocket and clamp the ends of the chain in a vise. The countershaft nut has a LEFT-HAND thread; unscrew and remove it.

4. Remove the countershaft washer and sprocket. Tap the countershaft with a mallet from the outside of the case to remove it.

5. Pry the oil seal off the countershaft with a screwdriver.

Removing the countershaft

Heating the crankcase prior to crankshaft removal

Servicing the Crankshaft Assembly

REMOVING THE CRANKSHAFT

1. Heat the primary side engine case, from the flywheel side, on a hot-plate or with a torch. If you use a hot-plate, heat the case for about ten minutes. If you use a torch, keep it moving around the crank-shaft boss, and heat it for only about 45 seconds. Do not heat the case from the other side or you may damage the seal.

2. Using a cloth for heat insulation, pull the crankshaft assembly out of the case. The primary side main bearing will remain on the shaft.

3. To remove the primary side main bearing, clamp the crankshaft in a vise, protecting it with blocks of wood, and care-

Removing the crankshaft assembly

fully pry the bearing off with suitable pry bars. (This bearing is marked with the inscription "C3" on its face; the magneto side main bearing is not marked.)

4. If any washers were fitted between the bearing and flywheel, tag and save them.

5. Pry the crankshaft seals out with a screwdriver.

Repairing the Crankshaft Assembly

It is recommended that the crankshaft assembly be sent to an Ossa dealer for disassembly, repair, and reassembly. Special jigs are needed for pressing the flywheels apart and back together; if these jigs are not used, the connecting rod and flywheels may be ruined. In addition, it is impossible to align the flywheels in the normal manner, with a hammer, after reassembly.

Installing the Crankshaft Assembly

1. To install a new crankshaft seal, first warm the crankcase around the crankshaft boss. Then install the seal, open side facing in, and drive it into position.

2. To install a new main bearing in the magneto side engine case, first warm the case around the crankshaft boss (from the inside, to prevent damaging the seal). Turn the case over and tap it gently against the bench, at which point the old bearing should fall out. Drop a new bearing (which

has no marking on its narrow face) into its mount before the case cools.

3. To install a new primary side main bearing on the crankshaft, first install the washers on the primary side of the shaft. Drive the new bearing (marked C3 on its narrow face) into position using a suitably sized pipe that bears against the inner race.

CAUTION: *Take special care not to intermix the primary side and magneto side crankshaft washers; piston side-load is determined by the number and thickness of the washers on each end of the crankshaft.*

4. To install the crankshaft, heat the primary side case around the crankshaft boss, taking care not to damage the seal. Fit the washers to the primary side of the crankshaft and press the crankshaft assembly into the case by hand. Be very careful not to damage the seal lip. Use the crankshaft seal guide (illustrated) if possible.

Assembling the Transmission

1. If you had removed the countershaft from the magneto side engine case, reinstall it now. From the inside of the case, press or tap the countershaft into its ball bearing. Install the countershaft spacer, the sprocket, washer, and nut from the outside of the case. Wrap a length of old drive chain around the sprocket and clamp its ends in

Installing the crankshaft assembly

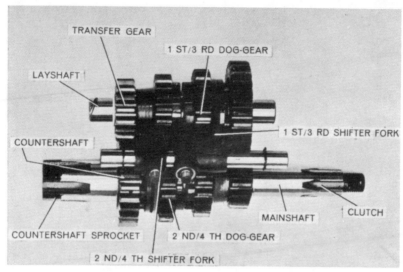

TRANSFER GEAR

1 ST/3 RD DOG-GEAR

LAYSHAFT

1 ST/3 RD SHIFTER FORK

COUNTERSHAFT

MAINSHAFT   CLUTCH

COUNTERSHAFT SPROCKET   2 ND/4 TH DOG-GEAR

2 ND/4 TH SHIFTER FORK

Transmission gear cluster

a vise. Tighten the countershaft nut securely.

NOTE: *The countershaft nut has a left-hand thread.*

Bend up the locktab against two flats of the nut.

CAUTION: *Do not intermix the washers that were installed on the gearbox shafts; these washers must be installed in their original positions to maintain correct endplay.*

2. Install the detent plunger, with its nylon washer, in the engine case. Do not tighten it.

3. Examine the illustration showing the dimples in the shift drum into which the detent can fit. Install the shift drum, with its washers, into its boss so that the detent is in the Neutral dimple. If the drum is in Neutral, you should be able to draw an imaginary line through the middle of the peg farthest to the left, the shift drum shaft, and the selector shaft mounting boss, as shown.

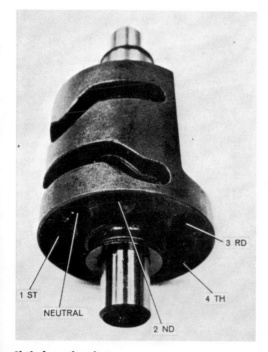

3 RD

1 ST

NEUTRAL

4 TH

2 ND

Shift drum dimples

LAST PEG

SELECTOR-SHAFT
MOUNTING BOSS

Shift drum installed, in Neutral

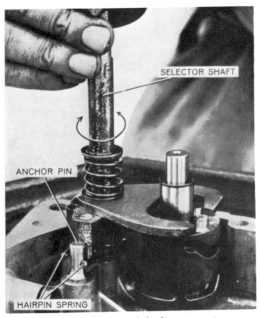

Checking the installation of the hairpin spring

4. Fit the selector shaft, with its washer, to the mounting boss. Clip the legs of the hairpin spring to the anchor pin. Gently turn the shaft; if it moves freely, then both legs of the spring are not parallel. Remove the shaft and bend one of the legs to make both legs parallel when the spring is fitted to the anchor pin. Install the shaft and check to make sure that it does not have any free-play.

5. The first peg on the shift drum will lie between the fingers of the selector. The peg should be midway between the two fingers. Rotate the shift drum to the 3rd gear position; there should be equal clearance between two of the pegs and the fingers. If there is not, remove the selector shaft and bend both legs of the spring in the opposite direction from which you wish to rotate the selector fingers. Make sure that the legs of the spring are still parallel, so that the selector shaft has no free-play. Remove the selector shaft, shift drum, and detent from the engine case.

6. Place the two needle bearings into the countershaft. Fit the mainshaft bushing on top of the needle bearings with the chamfered side of the bushing facing up.

7. Insert the mainshaft with its washers, spiral grooved end first, into the countershaft.

8. Install the layshaft, with washers, into its mounting boss in the case. Mesh the layshaft and mainshaft gears.

9. Insert the shift fork assembly into its boss in the engine case. The fork with the longer body should be uppermost on the shaft. Work the forks into their grooves in the mainshaft gears. It will be necessary to lift the mainshaft and layshaft to insert the forks.

10. Fit the shift drum, with its washers, to its boss in the engine case. Move it to

Shift drum properly positioned between the fingers of the selector

Installing the countershaft needle bearings

Installing the mainshaft

Installing the shift drum

the Neutral position; move the two dog gears up or down until they are in Neutral. Lift the mainshaft, layshaft, and fork assembly, and engage the follower pegs of the forks in the cam grooves in the drum.

11. Install the selector shaft assembly into its mounting boss.

12. Mount the kickstart shaft assembly into its boss so that the ramp will clear the large screw in the engine case. Rotate the shaft counterclockwise against its stop.

13. Fit the slotted breather tube to the boss at the top of the case. Make sure that that slot faces up or the oil will escape when the engine is running.

14. Mount the detent assembly, with the large nylon washer, from the outside of the case. Screw the threaded part of the assembly halfway into the case.

Assembling the Engine Cases

1. Coat both sides of a new center case gasket with grease and fit it to the magneto side case. Do not use gasket cement.

2. Oil the gearbox components with SAE 80 HP gearbox oil.

3. Replace the magneto side crankshaft shim washers on the main bearing in the magneto side case. Install the primary side engine case (with the crankshaft assembly) over the magneto side case. Hold the kick-

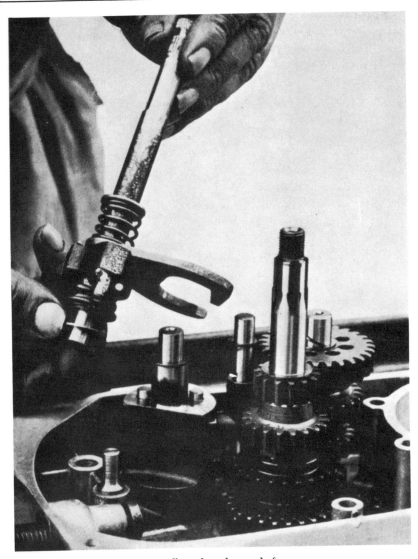

Installing the selector shaft

start shaft so that it is centered in its hole in the primary side engine case and tap the case at both ends with a rawhide mallet to mate it with the magneto side case.

4. Using a drift, seat the three locating dowels in the front and rear case bosses. Do not turn the engine over yet, as the cases can still easily be separated.

5. Insert the front case bolt into its bosses and install the washers and nut. Run the nut down finger-tight and then tighten it ½ turn with a wrench.

6. Turn the engine over so that the magneto side case faces up and mount the eleven case screws. The two screws at the rear of the engine are shorter than the

rest, and the flat-head screw goes at the bottom of the case.

7. Using a socket-mounted screwdriver bit on a torque wrench, torque each screw, beginning in the center of the case and working out, to 12 ft lbs. Torque the front engine case bolt to 12 ft lbs. Tighten the detent screw.

Assembling the Primary Side Components

1. Turn the engine over so that the primary case faces up and place one of the washers on the kickstart shaft.

2. Fit the kickstart spring on its shaft with the looped end of the spring facing

Installing the kickstart shaft

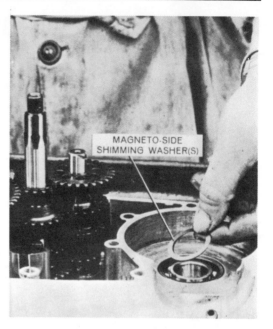

MAGNETO-SIDE SHIMMING WASHER(S)

Installing the breather tube

1 ½ TURNS

Fitting the kickstart return spring

left. Work the end of the spring into its mounting hole in the shaft.

3. Fit a drift into the looped end of the spring and tighten the spring 1½ turns. The drift should now be positioned above the spring retaining boss; work the looped end of the spring off the drift and into its retaining boss. Press the spring down flat against the washer beneath it.

4. Place the other large washer on the kickstart shaft.

5. Install the snap-ring in its groove on the kickstart shaft just above the top washer.

6. Fit the kickstart lever onto the shaft and test to make sure that the kickstart shaft operates correctly. Remove the lever.

7. Place the flat spacer on the ball bearing assembly on the mainshaft.

8. Place the clutch bushing on the main-

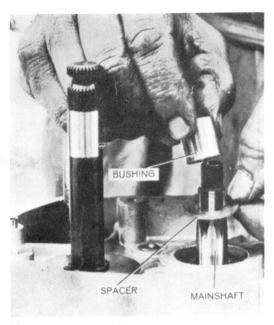

Installing the mainshaft spacer and bushing

shaft and bottom the bushing against the flat spacer.

9. Thoroughly clean all oil and grease from the primary side crankshaft and the inside of the cush drive shaft. Put the cush drive shaft on the crankshaft and tap it with a rubber mallet.

10. Fit the primary drive chain to the engine sprocket and the outer clutch hub, with the master link clip facing the clutch hub. Fit the primary drive assembly, as a unit, onto the mainshaft and cush drive shaft.

11. Install the short spacer on the mainshaft and bottom it against the clutch needle bearing. Put the inner clutch hub on the mainshaft. Align the splines of the inner hub with the splines of the mainshaft and work the hub down against the short spacer tube.

12. Install the lockwasher and nut on the mainshaft and tighten finger-tight.

13. Install the cush drive coupling on the shaft and fit the spring and spring stop, with the flanged end of the stop facing up.

14. Screw the allen nut into the threads of the crankshaft.

15. Fit your clutch holding tool to the hub and tighten the allen nut securely, using a length of pipe on the allen wrench for extra leverage.

16. With the holding tool still in position, torque the clutch nut to 60 ft lbs.

17. Spin the inner clutch hub to make sure that it can rotate while the outer hub remains still.

18. Install the inner clutch plate, which has plain faces and is thicker than the other plates, into the hub. Oil the plate.

19. Fit an idling plate, with cork inserts, and oil it.

Installing the primary drive train

Installing the clutch hub and spacer

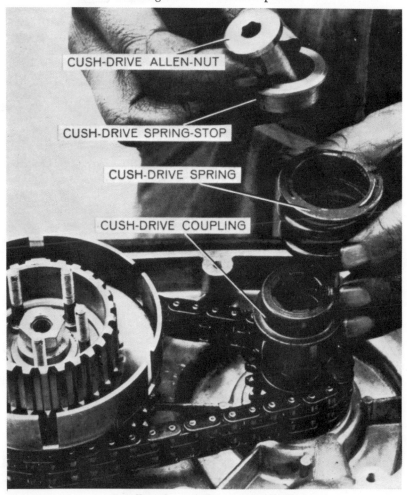

CUSH-DRIVE ALLEN-NUT

CUSH-DRIVE SPRING-STOP

CUSH-DRIVE SPRING

CUSH-DRIVE COUPLING

Installing the cush drive components

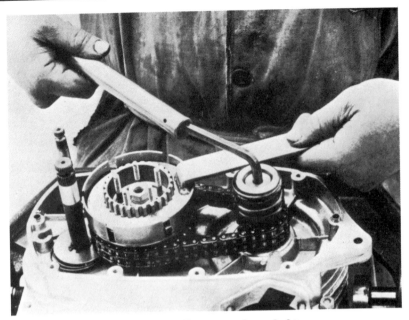

Tightening the allen nut on the cush drive

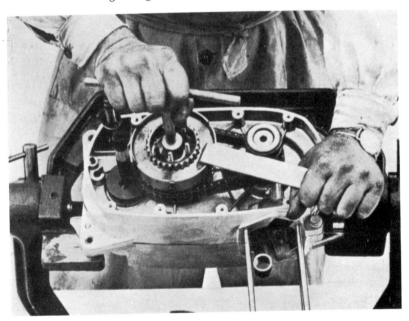

Tightening the clutch hub nut

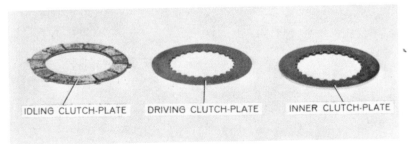

IDLING CLUTCH-PLATE   DRIVING CLUTCH-PLATE   INNER CLUTCH-PLATE

Three types of clutch plates

OUTER CLUTCH-PLATE

IDLING CLUTCH-PLATE

DRIVING CLUTCH-PLATE

INNER CLUTCH-PLATE

Clutch components assembled

20. Check all the driving plates on a flat surface such as a plate of glass to make sure they are flat. Replace any plates that are warped. Install a drive plate in the clutch.

21. Install an idling plate, then a drive plate, and continue to alternate the two types. The last plate installed will be a drive plate.

22. Fit the outer clutch plate and install the spring cups, springs, and nuts to the five studs. Tighten each nut until the bottom of its groove is level with the bottom of the cotter pin hole drilled in the stud.

23. Rotate the clutch and check to see if the outer plate wobbles. If so, mark the highest point on the outer plate and tighten the nut(s) nearest the high point. Back off the other nuts slightly and recheck. When the plate runs true, install the cotter pins.

24. Place the flat washer and spring washer on the selector shaft.

25. Grease both sides of a new primary case gasket and fit the gasket to the primary case.

26. Insert the two locating dowels into their mounts in the case and install the case carefully on the engine case. Tap the case with a rubber mallet to seat it.

27. Install and tighten the 10 primary case screws. Fit the short screws in the holes shown in the illustration.

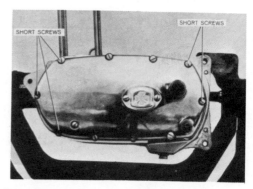

SHORT SCREWS   SHORT SCREWS

Primary case screws

28. Trim any protruding portion of the primary case gasket with a knife.

29. Install the shift lever on the selector shaft and work it to check the action of the shaft. Remove the lever.

Piston Clearance Information

1. Wash the cylinder in hot, soapy water and rinse it thoroughly. Dry it and allow the piston and cylinder to stand for two hours at room temperature.

2. Measure the cylinder bore from front to rear an inch or two down from the top.

3. Measure the outside diameter of the piston near the bottom of the skirt, at right angles to the wrist pin hole.

4. Subtract the diameter of the piston from the diameter of the cylinder to find the clearance.

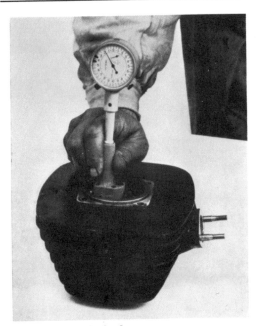

Measuring the cylinder bore taper

5. In the 230 cc street and trail models, the clearance should not be less than 0.02-0.03 mm (0.0008-0.0012 in.), or more than 0.06 mm (0.0024 in.). In the 230 cc scrambler, the piston clearance should not be less than 0.05-0.06 mm (0.002-0.0024 in.) or more than 0.10-0.12 mm (0.004-0.0047 in.).

6. Another way to measure the clearance is to place the piston inside the cylinder, upside down, so that the skirt is one or two inches below the top of the liner. Insert a feeler gauge between the skirt and the cylinder to determine the amount of clearance.

7. If the piston is worn beyond the tolerance, replace it.

8. If the cylinder is worn so much that the clearance is still too great with a new piston, you will have to install an oversize piston. Pistons are available in 0.2 and 0.4 mm oversizes. It will be necessary to bore and hone the cylinder to obtain the correct clearance. After honing, allow the cylinder to cool before measuring it again.

Installing a New Cylinder Liner

1. Put the new liner in a refrigerator and allow it to become as cold as possible.

2. Place the cylinder in an oven and support it in such a way that the old liner is free to fall out after reaching a temperature of 450-550° F. Do not heat the cylinder to a temperature greater than 750° F.

3. Insert the new liner into the cylinder before the cylinder has a chance to cool. Align the ports in the liner with those in the cylinder.

4. Support the cylinder, in its normal position, so that the bottom of the liner is not touching the bench. Place a weight on the liner flange to keep it in position as the cylinder cools.

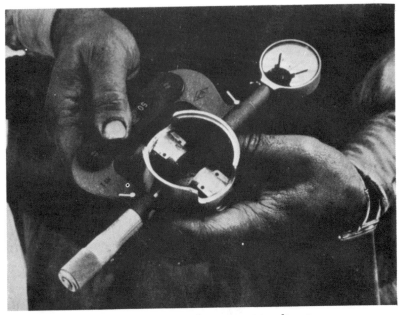

Using a micrometer to determine piston diameter

Measuring piston-to-cylinder wall clearance with a feeler gauge

Assembling the Top End

1. Remove any protruding portion of the case gasket at the cylinder bosses with a knife. Squirt some oil into the two holes drilled into the cylinder bosses.

2. Position the connecting rod at top dead center (TDC). Stuff a cloth into the crankcase opening to prevent the snap-rings from possibly falling into the cases.

3. Start the wrist pin into the piston.

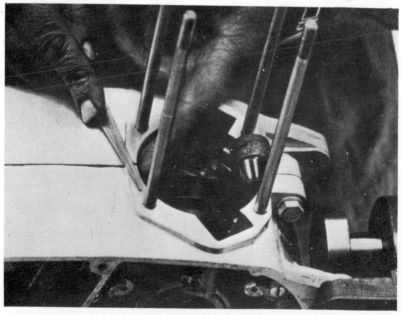

Trim any crankcase gasket material from the cylinder base flange

Install the wrist pin needle bearing in the rod and position the piston on the rod with the short skirt facing the rear of the engine.

4. Using a soft drift that is slightly smaller than the diameter of the wrist pin, PRESS the pin into the piston while supporting it so that there is no side-load on the connecting rod. If the pin will not go in, heat the piston with an electric iron or with rags soaked in hot water. *Do not force the wrist pin into the piston.*

5. Install the wrist pin snap-rings into their grooves using needle nose pliers. If a snap-ring can be rotated easily in its groove, remove and spread it, then reinstall it.

6. Grease the cylinder base gasket on both sides and install it over the studs.

7. Clean the ring grooves and the rings, then install the rings so that the peg in the grooves is between the ring ends. Make sure that the rings do not bind in their grooves.

8. Install a ring compressor over the rings, taking care not to allow either ring to ride up over its peg. Install the cylinder onto the studs and carefully work it down over the piston until the rings are inside the liner. Remove the compressor and seat the cylinder against the cases.

9. Check to see that the mating surfaces of the head and cylinder are smooth and clean. Install the head gasket and head on the cylinder. The higher ends of the cooling fins face the front of the engine.

10. Install the head washers and nuts; run the nuts down finger-tight. Tighten the head nuts in 3 ft lb. increments, until you reach 12 ft lbs., in the following sequence: 10 o'clock, 4 o'clock, 8 o'clock, and 2 o'clock. CAUTION: *Use a small, accurate torque wrench, or you will run the risk of warping the head or seizing the piston.*

Tightening the cylinder head nuts

11. Install the spark plug and stuff rags in the intake and exhaust flanges.

Location of piston rings. Note peg locations

Assembling the Magneto Side Components

1. Peen one of the curved edges of the crankshaft woodruff key so that it will fit tightly, then install it in the keyway.

2. Remove the backing plate from the flywheel and position it on the case, aligning the marks you made during disassembly. Install and tighten the three mounting screws.

3. Install the rubber grommet in the slot in the bottom of the case and run the electrical wires through the grommet.

4. Align the slot in the flywheel with the crankshaft key and press it onto the end of the crank with your hands.

IGNITION TIMING

1. Turn the flywheel until the small hole in its face is at 11 o'clock. Insert a pin into the hole and work the flywheel back and forth until the pin drops into the hole in the backing plate. This is the position at which the spark plug will fire.

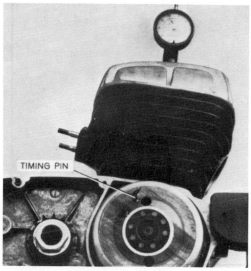

Timing pin in position

2. Remove the spark plug and fit an ignition timing dial indicator into the hole. Zero the gauge scale on the needle.

3. Remove the timing pin from the flywheel and rotate the flywheel clockwise, counting the number of complete revolutions of the gauge needle. The point at which the needle stops moving is TDC. Stop the flywheel at TDC and add to the number of revolutions the decimal frac-

Rotating the magneto flywheel with dial gauge in position

tion that the dial gauge now reads. For example, if the needle made three complete revolutions and stopped at "15", the timing is set at 3.15 mm before top dead center (BTDC). The correct timing specification for all models is 3.25–3.50 mm BTDC.

4. If the timing is not within specification, remove the flywheel and loosen the three magneto backing plate screws just enough to allow the plate to be rotated. If your reading was less than 3.25 mm BTDC, rotate the plate counterclockwise a small amount. If the reading you got was greater than 3.50 mm BTDC, rotate the plate clockwise a small amount. Tighten the screws, install the flywheel, and recheck the timing.

5. After the timing is set, remove the dial indicator and reinstall the spark plug. Fit the flywheel washer and nut, and run the nut down finger-tight.

6. Remove the small oil seal from the end of the countershaft with a screwdriver. Coat one of the pushrods with a heavy layer of grease and insert it into the countershaft. Seat it with the other pushrod.

Remove the second pushrod, install the bearing into the countershaft, and insert the pushrod so that the bearing is positioned between the two rods. Install the oil seal on the end of the second pushrod and press it into position in the countershaft.

ENGINE INSTALLATION

1. Install and tighten the drain plug with its washer.

2. Pour 1,000 cc of SAE 80 racing transmission oil into the inspection hole in the primary case, using a funnel. (You can add 1,000 cc of oil only after splitting the cases.)

3. Fit the engine into the frame, inserting it with the front mounting lugs positioned above their brackets and the rear lugs positioned beneath their brackets. Work the rear of the engine up so that the rear lugs are aligned in their brackets, then position the front lugs in their brackets.

4. Install the four engine mounting bolts and torque them to 14 ft lbs.

5. Mount the high tension coil on the top frame tube with the two bolts.

6. Fit the electrical harness into the clamps on the rear frame downtube. The two wires with spade clips go to the high tension coil, they are color coded with the coil terminals.

7. The remaining wires go to the electrical junction block near the top of the rear downtube. The wires are color coded with the terminals on the block. After connecting the wires, tape them to the rear downtube in two places with a high quality electrical tape.

8. Install the drive chain over the sprockets and fit the master link. The closed end of the master link clip must always be installed facing the direction of forward chain rotation. Lubricate and adjust the chain.

9. While a helper holds the rear brake on, torque the flywheel magneto nut to 60 ft lbs.

10. Coat the clutch arm plunger inside the magneto case with grease to keep it in position. Check to see that the two locating dowels are in position, then install the magneto case (which has no gasket) onto the engine case. The two longer mounting screws are installed at the front of the case; the two shorter screws at the rear.

11. Move the clutch arm on top of the magneto case; it should have at least ⅓ in. movement. If it does not, remove the inspection cover from the primary case and loosen the locknut on the adjusting screw that protrudes from the outer clutch plate. Turn the screw counterclockwise to increase play in the clutch arm, then tighten the locknut.

12. Using pliers or a box-end wrench for leverage, rotate the clutch arm clockwise and fit the clutch cable end into the arm.

13. Install the carburetor on the intake manifold and tighten the two nuts until they are compressing the O-ring. Plug the carburetor mouth with a cloth.

14. Install the gas tank and seat on the frame.

15. Install the rear fender and connect the wire to the taillight. Install the taillight lens.

16. Install the plastic side panel on each side of the bike.

17. Fit the carburetor slide down into the carburetor barrel with the slide cutaway facing to the rear. Install the carburetor top and secure it with the two screws. Work the throttle a few times to be sure that the slide does not bind.

18. Install the air filter on the carburetor.

19. Fit a new gasket in the exhaust pipe flange in the cylinder head. Position the exhaust system on the motorcycle and screw the exhaust pipe collar onto the flange finger-tight.

20. Install the muffler mounting nuts and bolts finger-tight, then fully tighten the pipe collar. Finally, tighten the muffler bolts.

Fuel Systems

The Ossa uses an IRZ model DG carburetor. Refer to the Bultaco section for details on carburetor tuning and overhaul.

Electrical Systems

OPERATION

Ossa motorcycles are equipped with a rather straightforward magneto ignition system. Instead of using a mechanical contact breaker points system, however, Ossa uses an electrically triggered signal generator on the magneto backing plate.

The magneto is basically a very simple type of alternator. As the magnets in the magneto flywheel pass the low voltage coil on the magneto backing plate, an alternating current is induced in the low voltage coil. The low voltage current passes through a half-wave rectifier, which converts it to DC (direct current). The current then charges the condenser, which is mounted on the frame above the engine. The condenser is connected to the high voltage coil via a silicon-controlled rectifier. At the moment of ignition, a magnet in the flywheel passes by the signal generator on the backing plate and a small current is generated. This current triggers the silicon rectifier, which then allows the condenser to discharge through the primary side of the high voltage coil. This induces a high voltage in the secondary windings of the coil and the spark plug fires.

On all models equipped with lights, additional coils are fitted on the magneto backing plate to provide current for the lighting system.

TESTING THE IGNITION SYSTEM COMPONENTS

These specific tests should be made only after you have determined the general area where the problem is originating. Refer to Chapter 6, "Troubleshooting".

Testing the high voltage coil

The High Voltage Coil

1. Remove the gas tank.
2. Disconnect the black and blue wires from the coil. Using an ohmmeter set on R x 1, connect the test leads to the two clips on the coil and check the reading. Reverse the test leads on the coil clips and take another reading. You should get 25–35 ohms in both tests.
3. Set the ohmmeter on R x 100 or R x 1,000. Connect the test leads to the clip inside the spark plug cable and to ground. You should get a reading of about 7,000 ohms.

Checking the high voltage coil

4. If you did not obtain the specified readings in either step 3 or 4, the high voltage coil is not working properly and must be replaced. Make sure that the mounting lug is grounded properly on the frame.

The Magneto Backing Plate Components

1. Remove the plastic side panels and disconnect all wires from the engine to the electrical junction box. Remove the flywheel.
2. Check the resistance across the low voltage coil (which is larger in diameter than the other coils). You should get a reading of 160–185 ohms.
3. Connect the ohmmeter to the small diode on the backing plate near the low voltage coil. (This is the half-wave rectifier.) You should get a reading of 800–1,200 ohms with the meter connected one way, and an infinity reading with the leads

Testing the magneto components

reversed. (The diode should only pass current in one direction.)

4. If the above tests give the specified results, check the two yellow wires at the signal generator. You should get a reading of 18 ohms across this small coil. If any of the tests at the magneto backing plate give the wrong results, replace the backing plate assembly.

Chassis

CHANGING THE FRONT FORK OIL

1. Loosen the two fork tube clamp bolts on the fork crown.

2. Unscrew and remove the plug at the top of one of the fork tubes.

3. Loosen the drain plug in the same slider leg just above the axle mount. Unscrew the plug, but do not remove it, as it also connects the slider leg to the damper in the fork tube.

4. Allow the oil to drain out of the leg,

then gently work the forks up and down to expel the rest of the oil.

5. Tighten the drain plug and pour 250 cc (Pioneer, Stiletto, and Plonker) or 125 cc (Wildfire) of SAE 20 or 30W fork oil into the top of the leg.

6. Prop the bike up so that the front wheel is off the ground. Install and tighten the top plug, then tighten the fork tube clamp bolts.

7. Drain and refill the other fork leg in the same manner.

CAUTION: *Take extreme caution if you find it necessary, for any reason, to remove both fork plugs from the top of the tubes at the same time, while the front wheel is still in position. If you don't hold the second plug firmly while removing it, it may catapult off.*

FRONT END SERVICE

Disassembling the Forks

1. Prop up the bike so that the front wheel is off the ground. Loosen the speed-

Testing the magneto components

Front fork components

FORK PLUG
FORK CROWN
FORK-TUBE PINCH-BOLT
STEERING UNIT
STEERING UNIT
PINCH-BOLT
FORK TUBE
STEERING HEAD
ANCHOR PLATE
DRAIN PLUG
AXLE-CLAMP NUT
SLIDER LEG

Removing the fork top plug and spring

The fork drain plug

ometer drive cap nut and disconnect the cable from the drive.

2. Push the cap nut up the speedometer cable and remove the small snap-ring from the cable. Pull the cable out of the guide on the fork tube.

3. Turn the knurled nut so that the outer brake cable moves into the handlebar

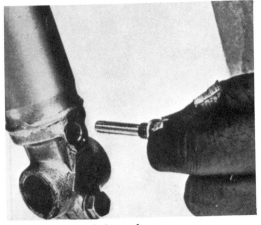

Removing the fork drain plug

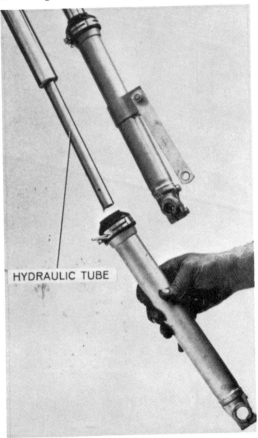

HYDRAULIC TUBE

Removing the fork slider exposing the hydraulic damper tube

lever mount. Move the front brake arm on the front wheel clockwise and remove the brake cable from the outer cable stop on the front wheel. Disconnect the brake cable from the arm.

4. Unscrew the bolt that mounts the brake anchor plate to the left slider leg.

5. Unscrew and remove the front axle nut and its washer.

6. Loosen the axle clamp bolt in each slider leg. Remove the front axle to the right, supporting the front wheel as the axle is withdrawn. A thin spacer will fall out from between the left leg and the wheel, and the speedometer drive and dust cover will fall from between the right leg and the wheel. Remove the wheel.

7. Unscrew and remove the drain plug just above the axle mount. Pull the slider leg down off the damper tube and remove the slider leg.

8. To remove the oil seal, first loosen the dust cover clamp screw and pull the clamp and cover off the slider leg. Remove the snap-ring from the mouth of the slider

Removing the fork slider circlip

leg and pry out the seal, taking care not to scrape the inside of the leg.

9. To remove the damper tube from the fork leg, first loosen the fork tube clamp bolt on the fork crown. Unscrew the fork plug at the top of the tube and lift out the fork spring.

Unscrewing the bottom plug

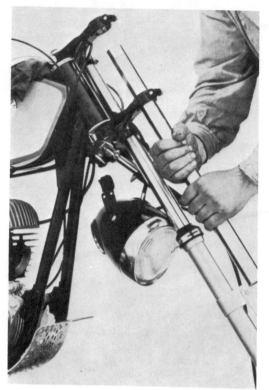

Removing a fork tube

10. Using a pair of needle nose pliers in the slots, unscrew the plug at the bottom of the fork tube. Pull the damper tube down out of the fork tube. Remove the plug and spring from the damper tube.

11. Disassemble the other fork leg in the same manner.

Disassembling the Steering Head

1. Unscrew the two nuts and bolts that mount the headlight brackets to the fork tubes.

2. Loosen the pinchbolt on the fork crown which secures one of the fork tubes. Loosen the other pinchbolt on the steering unit that clamps the same fork tube. Steady the headlight bracket and pull the fork tube down and out of the steering head assembly. Rotate the tube as you withdraw it.

3. Remove the other fork tube in the same manner.

4. Unscrew the four fender mounting bolts from the bottom of the steering head and remove the fender.

5. Unscrew the four U-bolt nuts and remove the handlebar assembly.

6. If a steering damper is fitted on top of the steering crown, remove it. If not, remove the rubber stopper from the top of the steering assembly tube.

7. Unscrew and remove the top fork crown nut.

8. Loosen the pinchbolt on the crown that secures the steering tube and remove the fork crown.

9. Unscrew the flat steering tube nut with a pin wrench, as shown. Lift off the top bearing dust cover.

10. Pull the steering assembly out of the steering head. The inner race of the lower bearing will stay on the steering tube and the upper bearing will remain in the steering head. Lift the upper bearing out of the head.

Assembling the Steering Head

1. Clean the steering head bearings carefully and then grease them.

2. Mount the inner race and dust cover of the lower bearing on the bottom of the steering tube, then insert the steering tube into the steering head from below.

3. Install the inner race of the upper

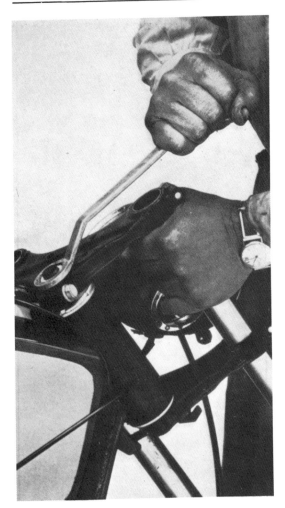

Removing the fork crown nut

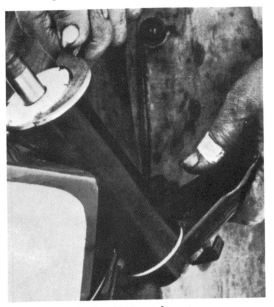

Unscrewing the flat steering tube nut

Upper and lower steering bearings are tapered roller units

Installing the steering head dust covers

bearing, with the small end facing down, in the top of the steering head. Install the upper bearing dust cover with the felt facing down.

4. Install the flat steering tube nut and tighten it until the bottom of the steering unit becomes difficult to rotate. Loosen the nut until you can feel the smallest amount of play when the bottom of the steering unit is pulled back and forth. At this point, when the steering unit is centered, it will prob-

ably not fall to one side or the other of its own weight, when released.

5. Install the fork crown onto the steering head, chamfered side first. Screw the top fork crown nut down finger-tight.

6. Insert the top of a fork tube into the steering brackets. Work the tube up until the top edge is level with the top of the fork crown. Tighten the fork tube pinchbolt on the bottom bracket. Install the other fork tube in the same manner.

7. Loosen the fork top crown nut slightly and tighten the flat steering unit nut very slightly until there is no play when you try to move the fork tube back and forth (toward the frame). Tighten the fork crown nut. There should be no play in the steering, and the forks should fall to either side of their own weight when centered and released.

8. Securely tighten the steering tube pinchbolt on the fork crown (top bracket).

9. Install both fork plugs and then tighten the fork tube pinchbolts on the fork crown.

NOTE: *Whenever any of the fork pinchbolts have been loosened, tighten them in the above sequence to avoid straining the forks. Never tighten them with the fork plugs removed.*

10. Install the front fender with the four mounting bolts.

Fitting the fork crown

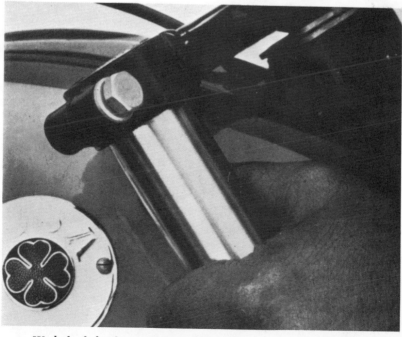

Work the fork tube up until it is flush with the top of the fork crown

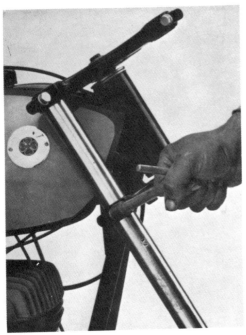

Tightening the lower triple clamp pinch bolt

Tightening the steering tube pinch bolt

Checking for steering head bearing play

11. Position the handlebar assembly on the fork crown and mount it with the U-bolts and nuts.

12. Install the headlight brackets on the fork legs.

Assembling the Front Forks

1. If the damper piston shows any wear, replace the damper assembly.

2. Install the buffer spring on the plain end of the damper tube (hydraulic tube).

3. Install the threaded plug onto the plain end of the damper tube with the slots facing away from the tube.

4. Insert the damper tube into the bottom of the fork tube, piston end first. Screw the plug into the bottom of the fork tube and tighten it securely with pliers. Insert the other damper tube into the other fork tube in the same manner.

5. Lubricate a new oil seal and drive it into the mouth of the slider leg until it bottoms on its flange. Use a length of pipe that is slightly smaller than the diameter of the seal as a drift. Install the snap-ring in its groove above the seal.

6. Fit the dust cover to the bottom of the fork tube and fit the clamp to the slider leg.

7. Rotate the damper tube so that the mounting holes in the bottom of the tube align with the hole in the slider leg (just above the axle clamp). Fit the slider leg onto the fork tube.

8. Install the fork drain plug into the slider leg and damper tube, with its steel and aluminum washers.

9. Pull the dust cover down so that the bottom is over the slider leg, then secure it with the clamp.

10. Mount the other slider leg in the same manner.

11. Loosen the fork tube pinchbolts on the fork crown and then remove the plugs from the top of the fork tubes. For the correct amount and grade of oil to use, refer to the preceding section on "Changing the Front Fork Oil."

12. After adding the fork oil, insert the fork springs and install and tighten the top plugs. Tighten the pinchbolts on the fork crown.

13. Position the wheel in front of the forks with the brake drum to the left. Install the backing plate on the front wheel and rotate it so that the anchor plate is aligned with the mounting hole in the left slider leg.

14. Thoroughly clean the front axle and coat it lightly with grease. Put the axle aside in a clean cloth so that it can't get dirty.

15. Install the felt pad and tab plate on the speedometer drive, and fit them to the right side of the front hub. Make sure that the tabs in the plate stay in the slots in the hub as the front wheel is installed.

16. Fit the wheel between the forks and insert the axle, from the right side, through the speedometer drive and wheel.

17. Fit the spacer (which is slightly thicker than the washer) between the backing plate and the left fork leg. Push the axle all the way through and fit the washer and nut. Do not fully tighten the nut.

18. Install the nut and bolt that secures the anchor plate to the slider leg and tighten finger-tight.

19. Tighten the front axle nut securely at this point.

20. Remove the prop and place the front wheel on the ground. Work the forks up and down a few times and then tighten the axle clamp bolts.

21. Tighten the anchor plate mounting bolt.

22. Press the brake arm up and fit the cable end into it. Adjust the front brake lever free-play with the knurled knob at the lever. If all the adjustment is taken up and there is still too much free-play, reposition the brake arm on its splined shaft.

23. Install the cap nut on the speedometer drive cable and fit the snap-ring in the cable. Tighten the cap nut on the drive unit with pliers.

BRAKE SERVICE

Refer to the Bultaco section. Procedures are the same for the Ossa.

REAR SUSPENSION AND SWING ARM SERVICE

Refer to the Bultaco section. Procedures are the same for the Ossa.

6. Troubleshooting

There are certain steps which, if followed, can transform the confusing task of troubleshooting into an exact science. Random efforts often prove frustrating, so a logical method should be adopted. Troubleshooting is nothing more than a systematic process of elimination, tracing back and checking various components until the fault is located. In most cases, this takes very little time and requires very few special tools.

Before you start, try to determine if this is a new problem, or one that's been coming on gradually. If you are an aware rider, you'll know whether or not performance has been diminishing, and consulting the troubleshooting guide in this section may provide an immediate solution. Also, whenever a problem shows up just after work has been done on the bike, check those areas that were involved first, regardless of the nature of the work.

When troubleshooting the engine, you will be concerned with three major areas: the ignition system, the fuel system, and cranking compression pressure. The engine needs spark, fuel, and compression to run, and it will be your job to determine which of these it lacks and why. Let's say that your engine won't start one morning, but was running fine the night before. The most obvious thing to check first, but which is often overlooked, is the fuel supply. Keep in mind that even if there is gas in the tank, a low supply can sometimes make starting difficult. Check to see that you have fuel at the carburetors by unscrewing one of the float bowl plugs. If so, you can be pretty sure that it is not a lack of fuel that is preventing the engine from starting.

As far as compression is concerned, there are only very few conditions that will cause a sudden loss of compression and such an occurrence will happen only while the engine is running. You should be able to tell if you have sufficient compression simply by the way the engine sounds and feels as it is cranked over. Or, if you have the spark plug out, cover the plug hole with your finger and kick the engine over. If the pressure forces your finger off the hole, there should be enough compression for the engine to start. Of course the most accurate way to check compression is by using a compression gauge.

So, you have found that the engine has relatively normal compression and is getting fuel. The final area of investigation is the electrical system. Check to see if you are getting spark to the cylinder by removing the plug lead, and inserting a metal object such as a nail into the plug connector. Using a piece of rubber as insulation, hold the nail about $\frac{1}{8}$ in. from the engine and crank it over with the ignition on. If you have spark at the lead, remove and check the spark plug. If not, trace the ignition system back with a test light (simply a bulb and battery with two wires attached, used to check electrical continuity). Start by checking for electricity at the points while they are open. If you have juice there, the problem lies in the coil, spark plug wire, or the wires between the coil and points. If you find that there is no supply of electricity to the coil, start looking for loose connectors in the wiring between the coil and ignition switch. Speaking of connectors, whenever you have a problem with the electrical system, they are the first things you should examine. These little devils have the habit of vibrating and pulling loose for no particular reason, and cause far more trouble and aggravation than any other part of the electrical system.

If you have a charging system problem, the most common faults to look for are loose connectors, a loose rectifier mounting nut, or a loose magneto flywheel. A large percentage of charging system troubles stem from these three minor faults.

All of the above can be considered troubleshooting the engine to get it running, not troubleshooting to cure running faults. Once you have found the general location of the trouble, it is usually quite simple to make pinpoint checks or to temporarily substitute new parts to determine exactly where the problem lies. The most important thing to remember is to try to remain rational and approach the troubleshooting procedure logically. If you do this, chances are you will find what you are looking for and save yourself some time, money, aggravation, and embarrassment (when the mechanic tells you that you pushed the bike four miles and paid him five dollars to replace a fuse).

Troubleshooting an engine that is running poorly is often a bit trickier than trying to determine why an engine won't start. You will still be involved with the compression, fuel system, and electrical system of your engine, but the problems will be more subtle and harder to detect. It pays here, if you are making adjustments or fine-tuning, to make *one adjustment at a time, thoroughly check the results, and record the findings.* Otherwise you will confuse yourself, ruin the results of one adjustment with another, and accomplish nothing.

Assuming that your engine has not expired with a big bang, any mechanical difficulties that you suspect will have taken some time to develop and are most often related to wear. Try to remember if a new sound shortly preceded the trouble, as sounds can often help trace the problems. (Don't become paranoid about "new" noises though, because you can imagine all kinds of terrible sounds if you really try.)

Remember, when you are trying to diagnose a running fault, to check all the parts related to the component you are examining. For example, suppose you are carefully scrutinizing a carburetor, expecting a revelation at any moment. In the meantime, don't forget to check the intake tube clamps, the air filter, and the fuel filter to make sure that the carburetor is not being sabotaged in one way or another by these associated components (too much air, or too little air or fuel). Or, if you are busy getting zapped by the high tension lead while checking for sufficient spark, don't forget to check to make sure that the plug connector is tightly attached to the wire, that the wire insulation is not worn or cracked, etc., etc. Look for the little things, and do it systematically and thoroughly. In many cases, a qualified mechanic may be able to help you with a specific problem without even having to look at the bike. He's seen it all before, so don't hesitate to ask. The worst it can get you is a service appointment for next week.

Engine Noises

As mentioned previously, engine noises are often the first indication of component malfunction or excessive wear. It is important, however, that you don't confuse *normal* noises with those indicating a problem. Nearly all motorcycles produced today are air-cooled, and use a great deal of aluminum alloy in their engines. Both of these factors contribute to the transmission of normal noises and should not be cause for alarm.

Two-stroke engine noises are the most susceptible to misinterpretation because of the varying levels. An engine that has been run under load in extreme heat, for example, can emit some very frightening sounds but run quietly the next morning.

This is not to say that you shouldn't be concerned when you hear these noises, but rather that you should learn the difference between the expensive thump of bad main bearings and the harmless piston slap of a cold off-road single.

Engine Troubleshooting
Difficult or No Starting

Possible Causes	Inspection and/or Remedy
1. Ignition System	
a. Weak or dead battery	Check for a bright blue spark by shorting the spark plug against the cylinder cooling fins and kicking the engine over. If there is no spark, or it is very weak, check battery output, then clean and tighten terminal connections.
b. Bridged, fouled, or dirty spark plug	Clean or replace. Make sure the plug is of the correct heat range.
c. Incorrect spark plug gap	Reset.
d. Burned, dirty, or incorrectly gapped ignition points	Clean or replace. Set correct gap.
e. Incorrect ignition timing	Reset.
f. Faulty condenser	Test condenser capacity and replace if necessary.
g. Faulty magneto	Test voltage output and isolate trouble source as described in "Electrical Systems."
h. Faulty wiring harness	Check for short circuits, poor grounds, etc., and repair as necessary.
2. Fuel System	
a. No fuel delivery	Check the fuel level and switch to reserve. Disconnect the delivery line at the carburetor and make sure there is free fuel flow. If not, look for a clogged gas tank vent, fuel petcock, or delivery line.
b. Stuck carburetor float	Dissassemble the float bowl and make sure that the float operates freely and that the float needle seat is free from obstruction.
c. Poor quality fuel	Inspect the spark plugs and if yellow-brown sulphur deposits are evident, flush and refill the fuel tank with fresh, good quality fuel.
3. Loss of Compression	Check cylinder compression.
a. Loose spark plug	Usually caused by overtorquing the plug and stripping the cylinder head threads. Either a HeliCoil insert or a new cylinder head will be required.
b. Loose cylinder head	Make sure the head is correctly fitted and torqued.
c. Broken head gasket	Replace.
d. Worn piston rings	Replace.
e. Excessive piston-to-cylinder wall clearance	Replace the piston and rings, rebore or replace the cylinder. (See "Engine and Transmission.")
f. Leaking crankcase seal	Replace. (See "Engine and Transmission.")
4. Fuel Mixture (Hard Starting)	Make sure that all adjustments are correct and the air cleaner isn't dirty.
a. Lean mixture	Check the intake manifold and inspect the throttle stop screw(s), starter jet(s), and pilot jet.
b. Rich mixture	Inspect the air screw, air jet, needle jet, and air cleaner element.

Hard Starting or Irregular Idle

1. Ignition System	
a. Weak battery output	Check battery voltage and make sure that all connections are tight and clean.
b. Dirty or incorrect spark plug	Check plug condition, heat range, and electrode gap.
c. Incorrect ignition timing	Reset.
d. Dirty or worn out points	Replace the points and check for any signs of oil leakage around the breaker cam. Wet points usually indicate a faulty oil seal.
e. Faulty condenser	If the points were badly burned or discolored, it's very likely that a bad condenser is the cause. Replace it and be safe.
f. Faulty magneto	Check the slip ring and pick-up for grease, dirt, etc., and clean as necessary.

Engine Troubleshooting (cont.)
Hard Starting or Irregular Idle

Possible Causes	*Inspection and/or Remedy*
2. Fuel System	
a. Incorrectly adjusted carburetor idle circuit	Check all parts associated with the idle circuit (see "Fuel Systems"). Clean and readjust as necessary.
b. Clogged carburetor fuel jets	If the bike has been stored or left sitting for some time, there is the possibility of sediment or oil residue obstructing fuel flow through the main and needle jets. Clean all the jets in solvent and blow them dry with compressed air.
3. Dirty Air Cleaner	Clean or replace.
4. Excessive Carbon Buildup	Decarbonize the engine as described in "Maintenance."

Misfire During Acceleration from Idle

1. Incorrect Idle Mixture	A misfire while accelerating from a standstill is often caused by too rich an idle mixture. Readjust the idle mixture and, if necessary, remove and clean the jets.
2. Water in Carburetor Float Bowl or Fuel Petcock	Drain and flush with fresh gasoline.
3. Faulty Spark Plug	Sandblast or replace the plug.

Misfire at a Given Throttle Opening Only

1. Faulty Carburetor	Disassemble and inspect all carburetor parts for nicks, scratches, etc. Pay particular attention to the needle jet and jet needle.

Intermittent Misfire

1. Ignition System	Check all items in the ignition/electrical system: points, plug, high-tension wire, grounds, and wiring harness connections.

Misfire Under Load

1. Faulty Spark Plug	Inspect the plug for signs of overheating. Install a cooler plug, if necessary.
2. Incorrect Ignition Timing	Make sure that the timing is right on because it becomes more critical as load increases.
3. Dirty Air Cleaner	Clean or replace.
4. Incorrect Fuel Mixture	Make sure that the fuel mixture is not too rich. Check main jet size.
5. Poor Quality Fuel	Check plug condition and, if necessary, drain and replace the fuel.

High-Speed Misfire

1. Ignition System	
a. Faulty spark plug	Check plug condition and heat range.
b. Incorrect spark plug gap	Reset.
c. Faulty condenser	Test and, if necessary, replace.
d. Faulty ignition coil	Inspect the leads for signs of corona discharge: soft rubber.
e. Faulty high-tension leads	Test and, if necessary, replace.

Engine Troubleshooting (cont.)
High-Speed Misfire

Possible Causes	Inspection and/or Remedy
2. Fuel System a. Incorrect fuel mixture	Inspect the main and needle jet for any nicks, etc. Also make sure the jet needle clip is properly positioned and the needle is not damaged.
b. Incorrect float level	Reset.
c. Air leak	Inspect the fuel induction passage and make sure there is no place for air to enter other than the carburetor throat.
3. Loss of Compression	Measure cylinder compression.
a. Broken head gasket	Replace.
b. Broken cylinder base gasket	Replace.
c. Leaking crankcase oil seal	Replace.
4. Dirty Air Cleaner	Clean or replace.
5. Carbon Buildup in Head and/or Exhaust Passage	Decarbonize.

Clutch and Transmission Troubleshooting
Clutch Slips or Drags

Possible Causes	Inspection and/or Remedy
1. Incorrect adjustment	Readjust as described in "Maintenance."
2. Incorrect grade or quantity of gearbox oil	Refill with the proper grade and amount.
3. Worn friction plates	Replace as described in "Engine and Transmission."
4. Worn steel plates	Replace as described in "Engine and Transmission."
5. Worn clutch springs	Replace as described in "Engine and Transmission."

Difficult Gear Changing

Possible Causes	Inspection and/or Remedy
1. Worn return spring or broken pin	Replace as described in "Engine and Transmission."
2. Faulty change lever or lever spring	Replace as described in "Engine and Transmission."
3. Faulty change drum lever or lever spring	Replace as described in "Engine and Transmission."
4. Worn change drum position plate	Adjust or replace.
5. Worn change drum or selector forks	Replace as described in "Engine and Transmission."

Chassis Troubleshooting
Heavy Steering

Possible Causes	Inspection and/or Remedy
1. Excessively tightened steering damper	Loosen adjustment.
2. Excessively tightened steering head	Loosen adjustment.

Chassis Troubleshooting (cont.)
Heavy Steering

Possible Causes	Inspection and/or Remedy
3. Damaged steering head bearings	Replace.
4. Defective steering oil damper	Replace.

Front or Read Wheel Wobble

1. Incorrectly adjusted drive chain	Readjust.
2. Loose or broken spokes	Tighten or replace, then true wheel.
3. Worn axle bearings	Replace.
4. Worn swing arm bushings	Replace.

Pull to One Side

1. Faulty right or left rear shock	Check shock operation and replace as necessary. Make sure the spring settings are the same for both units.
2. Incorrectly adjusted drive chain	Readjust as described in "Maintenance."
3. Incorrect front and rear wheel alignment	Check alignment on a flat surface, using two straight boards for reference. The problem may be incorrectly located axle spacers, worn swing arm bushings, a bent frame, or bent front forks.
4. Incorrectly balanced tires and wheels	Rebalance.
5. Defective steering head bearings	Replace.
6. Faulty steering oil damper	Replace.
7. Bent frame or front forks	Consult your dealer.

Weak Front Fork Action

1. Weak springs	Measure spring free-length and compare with specifications. Replace if necessary.
2. Leaking oil seal	Replace as described in "Chassis."
3. Insufficient amount of oil	Refill as described in "Maintenance."
4. Incorrect oil	Drain and refill with correct oil.

Stiff Front Fork Action

1. Excessive amount of oil	Drain as necessary.
2. Incorrect oil mixture	Drain and refill with correct mixture.

Chassis Troubleshooting (cont.)

Weak Rear Shock Absorbers

Possible Causes	*Inspection and/or Remedy*
1. Weak springs	Replace as necessary.
2. Oil leaking from damper unit	Replace shock absorber.

Stiff Rear Shock Absorbers

1. Faulty damper valve	Replace shock absorber.

Unadjustable Brakes

1. Worn brake linings	Replace.
2. Worn brake shoe cam	Replace.
3. Worn brake drum	Replace.

Noisy Brakes

1. Dirty or unevenly worn brake linings	Blow out the brakes with compressed air. If this does not cure the problem, disassemble the brakes and inspect the linings. Smooth the lining surface with fine sandpaper or emery cloth.
2. Scored brake drum	Replace the drum or have it turned by your dealer or a qualified machine shop.

No Brakes

1. Brake linings worn down to rivets	Replace the linings and have the brake drum turned or replaced.
2. Oil or water-soaked brake linings	Replace linings and wheel hub oil seals.

Magneto Ignition Troubleshooting

Probable Causes

Symptom	Bad Spark Plug—Replace	Coil Wire Burn-Back	Poor Grounding or Shorted Wiring	Primary Coil Shorted	Secondary Coil Shorted	Breaker Points Worn or Improperly Gapped	Condenser Shorted	Bad Main Bearings Causing Point Gap Wander	Tail-Stoplight System Open	Carburetion Problem	Engine Out of Time
PLUG CHECK Shows no Spark	X	X	X		X	X	X		X		
CYCLE CAN BE PUSH STARTED Has 100 lb Min. Compression		X	X			X			X		
ENGINE MISFIRES AT HIGH RPM	X	X	X		X	X		X		X	X
COIL OUTPUT OK But no Spark				X		X	X				
SECONDARY COIL OK But no Spark			X	X							
BREAKER POINT BADLY PITTED Engine Misfires						X	X	X			
ENGINE MISFIRES At all RPM'S						X	X	X		X	X
ENGINE LOADS UP										X	
ENGINE OVERHEATS	X									X	X

Bultaco Femsatronic Ignition Troubleshooting

Probable Causes

Symptom	Bad Spark Plug Replace	Coil Wire Has Open Circuit	Poor Grounding or Shorted Wiring	Start Windings Burned Out	Generator Coil Burned Out	Secondary Coil Burned Out	Kill Button System Grounded	Flywheel Dragging on Coils	Generator-Feeder Coil Shorted	Flywheel Magnets Weak	Secondary Coil Shorted	Kill Button Ingition Switch Malfunction
PLUG CHECK SHOWS NO SPARK	X	X	X	X	X	X	X	X	X	X		X
CYCLE WILL PUSH START (Engine has min. 100 lbs comp.)	X	X	X	X					X	X		
ENGINE RUNS WITH ERRATIC FIRING (Engine will kick start)	X	X	X						X	X	X	X
PEAK METER TEST SHOWS PROPER VOLTS		X	X	X							X	
PEAK METER TEST SHOWS IMPROPER VOLTS			X						X	X	X	
CYCLE HARD TO START— SPARK WEAK		X	X	X			X	X	X	X	X	

Bultaco Magneto MK-III and Femsatronic MK-IV
Accessory Troubleshooting

Probable Causes

Symptom	Battery Malfunction	Broken or Shorted Wiring	Bulbs Burned Out	Rectifier Malfunction	Dimmer Switch Malfunction	Generator Output Too High or Too Low	Bad Brake Light Switch Para	Bad Contacts in Bulb Socket	Horn Needs Replacement	Ignition Switch Malfunction	Current Stability Malfunction
NO LIGHTS FUNCTION Engine Off (Battery Equipped Models Only)	X	X	X							X	
NO LIGHTS FUNCTION Engine on or off		X	X	X		X				X	
NO HEADLIGHT Others OK		X	X		X			X			
NO TAILLIGHT Others OK		X	X					X			
HEADLIGHT WORKS ON ONE BEAM ONLY		X	X		X			X			
NO HIGH BEAM INDICATOR LIGHT		X	X								
BATTERY WILL NOT STAY CHARGED	X			X		X					
BATTERY GOES DRY VERY RAPIDLY						X					
NO HORN WITH CHARGED BATTERY		X							X		
NO BRAKE LIGHTS		X	X				X	X			
BRAKE LIGHTS WON'T GO OFF		X					X				
LIGHT BULBS BURN OUT FREQUENTLY						X					X

Appendix

Fractions to Decimals and Millimeters

Fractions	Decimals	mm	Fractions	Decimals	mm
1/64	0.015625	0.3969	21/64	0.328125	8.3344
1/32	0.03125	0.7937	11/32	0.34375	8.7312
3/64	0.046875	1.1906	23/64	0.359375	9.1281
1/16	0.0625	1.5875	3/8	0.375	9.5250
5/64	0.078125	1.9844	25/64	0.390625	9.9219
3/32	0.09375	2.3812	13/32	0.40625	10.3187
7/64	0.109375	2.7781	27/64	0.421875	10.7156
1/8	0.125	3.1750	7/16	0.4375	11.1125
9/64	0.140625	3.5719	29/64	0.453125	11.5094
5/32	0.15625	3.9687	15/32	0.46875	11.9062
11/64	0.171875	4.3656	31/64	0.484375	12.3031
3/16	0.1875	4.7625	1/2	0.5	12.7000
13/64	0.203125	5.1594	33/64	0.515625	13.0969
7/32	0.21875	5.5562	17/32	0.53125	13.4937
15/64	0.234375	5.9531	35/64	0.546675	13.8906
1/4	0.25	6.3500	9/16	0.5625	14.2875
17/64	0.265625	6.7469	37/64	0.578125	14.6844
9/32	0.28125	7.1437	19/32	0.59375	15.0812
19/64	0.296875	7.5406	39/64	0.609375	15.4781
5/16	0.3125	7.9375	5/8	0.625	15.8750

Fractions to Decimals and Millimeters

Fractions	Decimals	mm	Fractions	Decimals	mm
41/64	0.640625	16.2719	53/64	0.828125	21.0344
21/32	0.65685	16.6687	27/32	0.84375	21.4312
43/64	0.671875	17.0656	55/64	0.859375	21.8281
11/16	0.6875	17.4625	7/8	0.875	22.2250
45/64	0.703125	17.8594	57/64	0.890625	22.6219
23/32	0.71875	18.2562	29/32	0.90625	23.0187
47/64	0.734375	18.6531	59/64	0.921875	23.4156
3/4	0.75	19.0500	15/16	0.9375	23.8125
49/64	0.765625	19.4469	61/64	0.953125	24.2094
25/32	0.78125	19.8437	31/32	0.96875	24.6062
51/64	0.796875	20.2406	63/64	0.984375	25.0031
13/16	0.8125	20.6375	1		25.4000

Millimeters to Inches

mm	0	10	20	30	40	mm	50	60	70	80	90
0		0.39370	0.78740	1.18110	1.57480	0	1.96851	2.36221	2.75591	3.14961	3.54331
1	0.03937	0.43307	0.82677	1.22047	1.61417	1	2.00788	2.40158	2.79528	3.18891	3.58268
2	0.07874	0.47244	0.86614	1.25984	1.65354	2	2.04725	2.44095	2.83465	3.22835	3.62205
3	0.11811	0.51181	0.90551	1.29921	1.69291	3	2.08662	2.48032	2.87402	3.26772	3.66142
4	0.15748	0.55118	0.94488	1.33858	1.73228	4	2.12599	2.51969	2.91339	3.30709	3.70079
5	0.19685	0.59055	0.98425	1.37795	1.77165	5	2.16536	2.55906	2.95276	3.34646	3.74016
6	0.23622	0.62992	1.02362	1.41732	1.81103	6	2.20473	2.59843	2.99213	3.38583	3.77953
7	0.27559	0.66929	1.06299	1.45669	1.85040	7	2.24410	2.63780	3.03150	3.42520	3.81890
8	0.31496	0.70866	1.10236	1.49606	1.88977	8	2.28347	2.67717	3.07087	3.46457	3.85827
9	0.35433	0.74803	1.14173	1.53543	1.92914	9	2.32284	2.71654	3.11024	3.50394	3.89764

Millimeters to Inches—Fractions

1/1000		1/100		1/10	
mm	inches	mm	inches	mm	inches
0.001	0.000039	0.01	0.00039	0.1	0.00394
0.002	0.000079	0.02	0.00079	0.2	0.00787
0.003	0.000118	0.03	0.00118	0.3	0.01181
0.004	0.000157	0.04	0.00157	0.4	0.01575
0.005	0.000197	0.05	0.00197	0.5	0.01969
0.006	0.000236	0.06	0.00236	0.6	0.02362
0.007	0.000276	0.07	0.00276	0.7	0.02756
0.008	0.000315	0.08	0.00315	0.8	0.03150
0.009	0.000354	0.09	0.00354	0.9	0.03543

Inches to Millimeters

Inches	0	10	20	30	40
0		254.0	508.0	762.0	1016.0
1	25.4	279.4	533.4	787.4	1041.4
2	50.8	304.8	558.8	812.8	1066.8
3	76.2	330.2	584.2	838.2	1092.2
4	101.6	355.6	609.6	863.6	1117.6
5	127.0	381.0	635.0	889.0	1143.0
6	152.4	406.4	660.4	914.4	1168.4
7	177.8	431.8	685.8	939.8	1193.8
8	203.2	457.2	711.2	965.2	1219.2
9	228.6	482.6	736.6	990.6	1244.6

Decimals to Millimeters—Fractions

1/1000		1/100		1/10	
inches	mm	inches	mm	inches	mm
0.001	0.0254	0.01	0.254	0.1	2.54
0.002	0.0508	0.02	0.508	0.2	5.08
0.003	0.0762	0.03	0.726	0.3	7.62
0.004	0.1016	0.04	1.016	0.4	10.16
0.005	0.1270	0.05	1.270	0.5	12.70
0.006	0.1524	0.06	1.524	0.6	15.24
0.007	0.1778	0.07	1.778	0.7	17.79
0.008	0.2032	0.08	2.032	0.8	20.32
0.009	0.2286	0.09	2.286	0.9	22.86

Conversion Table

To change	Multiply
cc → cu in	cc X .0610 = cubic inches
cc → oz (Imp)	cc X .02816 = ounces (Imperial)
cc → oz (U.S.)	cc X .03381 = ounces (U.S.)
cu in → cc	cu in X 16.39 = cubic centimeters
ft-lb → in-lb	ft-lb X 12 = inch pounds
ft-lb → kg-M	ft-lb X .1383 = kilogram-meters
gal (Imp) → liter	Imp gal X 4.546 = liters
gal (U.S.) → liter	U.S. gal X 3.785 = liters
in → mm	in X 25.40 = millimeters
kg → lb	kg X 2.205 = pounds
kg-M → ft-lb	kg-M X 7.233 = foot-pounds
kg/sq cm → lb/sq in	kg/sq cm X 14.22 = pounds/square inch
km → mi	km X .6214 = miles
lb → kg	lb X .4536 = kilograms
lb/sq in → kg/sq cm	lb/sq in X .0703 = kilograms/square centimeter
liter → cc	liter X 1,000 = cc
liter → oz (U.S.)	liter X 33.81 = ounces (U.S.)
liter → qt (Imp)	liter X .8799 = quarts (Imperial)
liter → qt (U.S.)	liter X 1.0567 = quarts (U.S.)
mi → km	mi X 1.6093 = kilometers
mm → in	mm X .03937 = inches
qt (Imp) → liter	Imp qt X 1.1365 = liters
qt (U.S.) → liter	U.S. qt X .9463 = liters